Reweaving the Relational Mat

Religion and Violence

Series Editors
Lisa Isherwood and Rosemary Radford Ruether

This interdisciplinary and multicultural series brings to light the ever increasing problem of religion and violence. The series will highlight how religions have a significant part to play in the creation of cultures that allow and even encourage the creation of violent conflict, domestic abuse and policies and state control that perpetuate violence to citizens.

The series will highlight the problems that are experienced by women during violent conflict and under restrictive civil policies. But not wishing to simply dwell on the problems the authors in this series will also re-examine the traditions and look for alternative and more empowering readings of doctrine and tradition. One aim of the series is to be a powerful voice against creeping fundamentalisms and their corrosive influence on the lives of women and children.

Forthcoming in the series:
America, Amerikkka
Religion and Violence in the Making of US Imperial Identity
Rosemary Radford Ruether

Weep Not for Your Children – Essays on Religion and Violence
Lisa Isherwood and Rosemary Radford Ruether (eds.)

In Search of Solutions – The Problem of Religion and Conflict
Clinton Bennett

Meditations on Religion and Violence in the United States
T. Walter Herbert

Reweaving the Relational Mat

A Christian Response to Violence
Against Women from Oceania

Joan Alleluia Filemoni-Tofaeono
and Lydia Johnson

LONDON   OAKVILLE

Published by
Equinox Publishing Ltd., Unit 6, The Village, 101 Amies St., London SW11 2JW, UK
DBBC, 28 Main Street, Oakville, CT 06779, USA

www.equinoxpub.com

First published 2006

Cover artwork by Lori Tuiavi'i

British Library Cataloguing-in-Publication Data
A catalogue record for this book is available from the British Library.

ISBN-10   1 84553 210 4   (hardback)
             1 84553 211 2   (paperback)

ISBN-13   978 184553 210 9 (hardback)
             978 184553 211 6 (paperback)

Library of Congress Cataloging-in-Publication Data

Filemoni-Tofaeono, Joan Alleluia
Reweaving the relational mat : a Christian response to violence
against women from Oceania / Joan Alleluia Filemoni-Tofaeono and Lydia Johnson.
        p. cm. — (Religion and violence)
Includes bibliographical references and index.
ISBN 1-84553-210-4 (hb) — ISBN 1-84553-211-2 (pb)
1. Women — Crimes against — Religious aspects — Christianity. 2.
Violence — Religious aspects — Christianity. 3. Church work with women.
4. Sexism — Religious aspects — Christianity. 5. Patriarchy — Oceania. 6.
Patriarchy — Religious aspects — Christianity. 7. Women — Oceania. I.
Johnson, Lydia, D. Min. II. Title. III. Series.
BT704.F55 2006
261.8′327 — dc22
                          2006007949

Typeset by S.J.I. Services, New Delhi
Printed and bound in Great Britain by Lightning Source (UK) Ltd, Milton Keynes

To our mothers:
the late Pulotu Galeai Filemoni and Maxine Weaver Johnson

To our sisters:
Lina Rosa F. Faasalele, Faleu Pulotu F.Tausaga,
Osana Faatausala Filemoni, and Barbara Johnson McLean

To our daughters:
Luiama Talei Tofaeono, Kelly Weaver Johnson-Hill,
and Erin Grace Johnson-Hill

Acknowledgments

There are many people whose support and encouragement have made this book possible, not all of whom can be mentioned here. Together we would like to express our appreciation to Norma Beavers, Valerie Hall, and their colleagues at Equinox Publishing, who have been helpful, efficient and patient throughout the publishing process. We are extremely grateful for the vision of Rosemary Ruether and Lisa Isherwood in spearheading this significant series on Religion and Violence. We are also indebted to the World Council of Churches' Ecumenical Theological Education program, and especially to Wati Longchar and Nyambura Njoroge, for their publishing grant which makes possible the dissemination of our book to church women and theological libraries throughout Oceania. We are most thankful of all to the pioneering women who are joining with us to establish *Manahine Pasefika* (the Association of Oceanian Women Theologians), and to the wounded women who have shared their stories of suffering with us.

Joan is particularly thankful for the mentorship of Professors Dr. Letty Russell and Dr. Shannon Clarkson and her colleagues in the D.Min. program at St. Francisco Theological Seminary. She also wishes to thank her brother and sister-in-law Tafatoluomalua and Karite Filemoni and their children, Leuluaialofinailetai Pulotu, Filemoni Folasamanaia and Katalina Rosa Niutonia; and her brother and sister-in-law Filemoni Apelu and Mealefu Filemoni and their children, Dusty Filimoni, Jo-Lin Faaluaumete, Afeafeaupitoaluga Jordan and Faleu Joamah. Finally, her deepest thankfulness goes to her life partner and best friend, Ama'amalele Tofaeono.

Lydia would like to express her appreciation to the Board of Global Ministries of the United Church of Christ and Christian Church (Disciples of Christ) in the USA for their unwavering support of her vocation in Oceania, including their support for this project. Sincerest thanks also go to her lifelong friend Cissy Moore-Swartz, her sister Barbara, brother John and their families, and her mother, who sadly passed away before the completion of the book. Her profoundest gratitude goes to her daughters Kelly and Erin, for their constant encouragement, companionship, insight and love.

CONTENTS

Prologue

BEHIND THE DESIGN

The Why Behind this Study

Violence against women damages or destroys the lives of millions of women from every corner of the globe, including the Pacific Islands cultures of Oceania[1] which are a particular focus of this work. Numerous international research efforts have been conducted, academic studies published, and programs initiated to address the issue of violence against women, from both secular and religious perspectives. Meanwhile this scourge continues to spread like an incurable epidemic.

Why add yet another voice to the chorus of voices condemning the evil of violence against women? First, as Christian women living and working in Oceania we have witnessed first-hand how this problem, like many other women's issues, has not been adequately addressed by the churches in this part of the world.[2] This apathy demands a response and a challenge. In a larger sense, this work represents an attempt to address the problem of violence against women in a new way—not merely exposing its manifestations and effects, or engaging in yet another theological or sociological analysis, or proposing remedies. Most contributions to the literature on this issue have focused on one of these tasks. Ours is an attempt

---

1. The term 'Oceania' is used in this work to refer collectively to the island nations of the South Pacific, encompassing the three major ethnic and geographical groupings of Polynesian, Melanesian and Micronesian cultures. It does not necessarily include here the Pacific Islander diaspora in neighboring countries such as New Zealand and Australia, since the ecclesial and cultural ethos for these communities is somewhat different than in the island communities of Oceania proper.

2. The only concrete response by Oceanian Christians to date has come from small groups of Christian women representing women's Non Governmental Organizations (NGOs) and, most recently, the initiative of *Weavers*, the women's advocacy arm of the South Pacific Association of Theological Schools, which is described in Chapter Eight of this work.

at an *integrated* theological response to violence against women that incorporates all of the above tasks. As such it is a project in praxis-analysis.

The stories and other evidence presented in this work speak for themselves as a grim witness to the reality of violence against women in Oceania. The gravity of this reality means that an urgent challenge for Oceanian Christians today is to better understand the ways in which both culture and church have become inextricably interwoven in the fabric of violence against women. We hope to be able to take a first step toward articulating this challenge to the churches of Oceania.

As noted above, while we will analyze the problem of violence against women broadly, it is the Oceanian context which will be highlighted. We will situate the Oceanian churches in this problem by offering a constructive critique of the ways in which their theology, traditions and practices have contributed to a mindset that has tolerated violence against women. This critique includes an examination of flawed biblical interpretations, ecclesial and cultural traditions, and male clergy power. Our hope is that this analysis will also resonate with and suggest implications for Christians in other parts of the world, especially in other non-Western churches.

Theological reflection alone, however, is not sufficient. There can be no adequate Christian reflection without praxis. It is for that reason that this study incorporates 'real stories' of violence against women in Oceania and includes concrete recommendations for change which flow organically from our praxis-analysis. While the praxis component is centered in the theological education arena, it has implications for the larger mission of the churches. Without such a praxis orientation, the value of this study would be negligible.

Parameters and Methodology

The Overall Structure

Chapter One grounds our study in a discussion of both the broad parameters of and contributors to violence in general, as well as the sources and categories of violence against women. It makes the case that there is a direct correlation between the ideology of patriarchy and many forms of violence, especially violence against women.

Against this backdrop, Chapter Two elaborates the myriad manifestations of violence against women. This tracing of the contours of the various strands of violence against women lays the groundwork for a contextualization of the problem of violence against women in Oceania in Chapter Three. There we examine the complex web of social and cultural sources of violence against women in Oceanian communities, and provide evidence of the scope and severity of violence against women in the region.

In Chapter Four, we analyze the interplay of religion and violence, moving from a general discussion to our primary focus on the interrelationship between the captivity of Christianity to patriarchy and its theological justifications for discrimination and violence against women. We focus particularly on problematic theological and biblical interpretations in the Oceanian churches. Chapter Five continues our analysis of the patriarchal stranglehold over the church in a critique of Oceanian churches' traditions and practices. We highlight especially the problem with male clergy power as it is manifested in Oceanian churches, with their veneration of the clergy as Men of God whose authority cannot be questioned.

In Chapter Six, we open up the milieu of theological education in relation to the problem of violence against women. Here we incarnate our theological analysis in praxis by re-telling the stories of Oceanian women's abuse in the theological school environment. This praxiological foundation paves the way for our critique in Chapter Seven of the whole ethos of theological education in Oceania. This includes critiques of these institutions' polity, curriculum and leadership styles.

Finally, in Chapter Eight we move from our critique of the 'patriarchal relational mat,' which condones a 'power-over' way of relating to women (and can thus provide justification for treating women abusively), to a constructive act of theological re-envisioning. Making use of the Oceanian metaphor of weaving, we 'reweave the relational mat' so that it becomes a Christocentric 'egalitarian relational mat.'

Grounding our new relational paradigm in praxis, we then offer concrete proposals for transformation in Oceanian theological institutions and churches, including a new curriculum and a four-year action plan aimed at dismantling the patriarchal foundations of the theology and ecclesiology which have contributed to violence against women in Oceania. In a final Epilogue we pull together the various strands of our study, and issue specific challenges to the churches and theological institutions of Oceania.

The Methodology

All methodologies are influenced by contextual factors. Ours is intentionally influenced by Oceanian ways of conceptualizing and communicating ideas. Most significantly, we employ in this work the core Oceanian metaphor of *weaving* to explain the interwoven strands that contribute to violence against women and to suggest ways of 'reweaving the mat' of relationality between women and men. While weaving symbolism is not new to Oceanian women's theological method,[3] it is utilized here in a new and more holistic way than has previously been attempted.

A qualitative research methodology[4] has been chosen for portions of this work. It is demonstrated most concretely in research tools such as the design and analysis of a questionnaire used with theological students. This entailed developing an open-ended format that would enable respondents to comment freely on theological assumptions behind biblical interpretations and church teachings that have been used to sanction violence against women. A qualitative research method was further employed in the gathering and analysis of case studies used to concretize this research. In all

3.   Oceanian women's theological method has been described as a process of interweaving the strands of lived experience, cultural, biblical and church traditions in Lydia Johnson and Joan A. Filemoni-Tofaeono, (eds.), *Weavings: Women Doing Theology in Oceania* (Suva, Fiji: Institute of Pacific Studies / South Pacific Association of Theological Schools [SPATS], 2003). See especially, the Introduction by Lydia Johnson, ' "Weaving the Mat" of Pacific Women's Theology: A Case Study in Women's Theological Method', pp. 10–22.

4.   Qualitative research is research that, in Valerie Janesick's terms, is holistic, contextual, personal, and focused on understanding. It requires the researcher to sharpen observation skills and to develop sensitivity to ethical concerns in research. It is explicit about the researcher's own biases. This is 'interactive research' that is admittedly shaped by the researcher's own history: It assumes that there is no value-free research. For an elaboration of qualitative research methodology, see Valerie Janesick, 'The Dance of Qualitative Research Design: Metaphor, Methodology and Meaning', in Norman K. Denzin and Yvonna S. Lincoln (eds.), *Handbook of Qualitative Research* (Thousand Oaks, CA: SAGE Publications, 1994) pp. 209–19. See also, Jerome Kirk and Marc L. Miller, *Reliability and Validity in Qualitative Research* (Beverly Hills, CA: SAGE Publications, 1988).

cases the confidentiality of persons whose experiences were included in the case studies was guaranteed.

Our holistic approach seeks to integrate insights from the scholarly theological literature, other relevant social research, and the wisdom gleaned from the shared experiences of many women who have been victims of male violence in Oceanian ecclesial contexts. It reflects a commitment to a feminist approach to theologizing that interweaves the experiential and the analytic.

Indeed, one important aspect of feminist theological methodology is the acknowledgement and embrace of the personal experience and social location of those who are engaged in the theological reflection. One of the unique aspects of this study, moreover, is that it represents the interweaving of the perspectives of two women, one a native Oceanian (Samoan) and the other a transplanted Westerner (Caucasian by birth but immersed in Oceanian cultures for many years). Because the validity of experiential claims is so fundamental to feminist theological methodology, we will adopt first-person voices for the following summary of what we as joint authors bring to this study.

Where We Stand

Joan Alleluia Speaks[5]

As a secular counselor and social worker in my native American Samoa in my previous vocation, the majority of cases I dealt with had to do with broken family relationships, teen suicides or attempted suicides, and parent-children crises. Most of these cases involved violence. The contradiction of living in a society that highly respects women as their brothers' *feagaiga* (sacred covenant) and claims to be Christian, yet tolerates the use of harsh physical, verbal and emotional violence, especially against women and children, has long motivated me to address the problem of violence in Oceanian societies.

Growing up as a minister's daughter, living amongst both ordinary villagers and prestigious church leaders, I had an insider's view of the Samoan cultural and ecclesial worldview. Within this framework it was considered perfectly acceptable to use physical

5. Since naming is so important in Samoan culture, it is necessary to include here my Samoan Christian name, Alleluia.

force through heavy beating as a means of disciplining children, disciplining the flock, putting wives in their place, proving a point, using violence to counter violence (as in fistfights), and upholding order and authority in the community.

Being a part of this system, accepting my privileged ascribed role as the daughter of a prominent church leader, this violence did not affect me directly and was thus not an issue for me. I believed in the importance of discipline and so I overlooked the fact that such harsh forms of discipline, women-bashing, child-bashing and people-bashing were highly problematic. It was not until later, as I grew older and became more critical and analytical, that I realized that no one deserves to be treated violently and that there is always an alternative to violence.

I also became acutely aware of the passivity of the church on the issue of violence. I saw first-hand how some aspects of the church's theology and practices have ignited the burning flame of abuse against women. During my time as a lecturer at Pacific Theological College, I also discovered that most students could not even openly identify violence as a problem, especially violence against women. I often asked students to specify the most pressing social issues in Oceania in my Pastoral Care and Counseling classes. None of the theological students, not even the female students, identified violence against women as a serious social problem. Yet everyone knew it was wreaking terrible havoc on women's lives, routinely and pervasively—among many church members, and even in the theological school.

This brought home to me starkly the reality that the response to violence against women in Oceanian church circles is largely one of silence. This reality has fuelled my passion to break the silence on this hidden problem, as a Christian, a Pacific Islander, and a woman. This commitment became a focal point of my ministry as Coordinator of *Weavers*, the women's advocacy arm of the South Pacific Association of Theological Schools. Combating violence is also at the core of my personal pastoral care ministry with persons damaged by personal and interpersonal brokenness.

The critical analysis applied in this work may be rejected by some Oceanians on the grounds that it betrays the sacredness of the island cultures and disparages the very life-ways that define who one is as an islander. This has been the most heart-wrenching personal dilemma entailed in engaging in this work: admitting and exposing the flaws in my 'collective self,' the very system that gives meaning to my life. However, this pain cannot compare with the excruciating pain experienced by the women who are victim-survivors of violence. It is empathy with their pain that has motivated me to break the silence in Oceania about violence against women.

Lydia Speaks

I come to this endeavor as a transplanted Caucasian who was raised in a devoutly Christian home—like Joan Alleluia, the child of a minister, but reared in America rather than in Samoa. In the theological worldview of my family, violence was never acceptable, and it was instilled in me from an early age that, as a female, I was equal in every way with men. For that reason, I was taught that I should never accept any demeaning behavior or attitudes from males—whether directed toward myself or toward anyone else who found themselves in a position of vulnerability or exploitation.

Yet, as I grew older, I came to see that I lived in a world of contradictions. My birth culture proclaimed that all people were 'created equal' yet discriminated against some of those so-called equals—racial minorities, women, and others who happened to be 'different'. Indeed, my culture, which ostensibly placed such a high value on individual rights and freedoms, was in reality a violence-ridden society. It perpetrated violence on other nations, on some of its own citizens, and on God's creation, in a collective *hubris* gone mad. I was ashamed. I wanted to atone by living in other cultures, amongst peoples who are on the receiving end of this hubris and cultural hegemony.

As a consequence, I have served the world church in pastoral and theological education ministries for most of my adult life, in places as diverse as Jamaica and South Africa. But the place where I made the greatest leap toward engagement, immersion, enculturation and life-investment, has been the South Pacific, where I have lived and worked for fourteen years.

Perhaps because of my privileged upbringing (never directly suffering the ravages of sexism), I had not been forced to put my feminist principles to the test until I lived in Fiji, where I served on the faculty of Pacific Theological College. As its first female faculty member, I encountered not only institutional patriarchy, but the personal struggles of female students and student wives in the face of a system which limited their horizons and kept them in their subservient place. Part of that system included both subtle and not-so-subtle acts of violence against them simply because they were women — physical, sexual and psychological violence. The gift given to me — to enter into their world, to hear their stories of suffering, and to witness their courage — made their struggles my own. The commitment to keep their struggles as my own has become the defining vocational calling of my adult life.

I came to this present work as the result of my exposure to Joan Alleluia's doctoral research at San Francisco Theological Seminary, which led both of us to re-examine shared experiences from our years at Pacific Theological College. Her explorations and analysis led me to my own deeper reflection and to parallel research.

After the successful completion of her D.Min. dissertation a genuine collaboration evolved, which entailed soul-searching dialogue, mutual probing, and a search for common ground. In the process of collaborating on this work, I have been given another great gift: a shared vision and understanding around what is a life and death matter for the women of Oceania.

Chapter One

INTERWOVEN STRANDS: THE FABRIC OF VIOLENCE

One cannot hope to understand the causes and character of violence against women without first situating it within the larger framework of systemic violence — what we might call the *culture of violence.* This chapter therefore begins by grounding our study in an overview of general definitions and parameters of violence. This will provide an interpretive framework within which we can gain a clearer understanding of the specific phenomenon of violence against women.

The Larger Fabric of Violence

Violence can be depicted as a complex woven mat or fabric, whose strands of varying colors and materials interlock and overlap. These individual strands are distinctive and may be highlighted, as we will undertake to do, but in important ways the individual strands also depend upon each other. It is as they are interwoven that they strengthen the larger fabric of violence. In this first section we unravel the *causative strands* of violence, those systemic forces which contribute to a culture of violence. That will enable us to better understand how the collective fabric of patriarchy contributes to violence against women.

Defining violence is problematic, since every definition is influenced by the cultural values that shape the way particular groups of people choose to live in any given society. What is deemed to be violent in a pejorative sense in one society may be viewed as acceptable behavior in another. In some cultures, for example, it is permissible for a husband, or male family member, to kill a female relative accused of adultery, while in other cultures this would clearly not be the case. In order to have a platform from which to proceed, we will take as a starting point the definition promulgated by the World Health Organization, which understands violence as—

> the intentional use of … force or power, threatened or actual, against oneself, another person, or against a group or community, that either results in or has a high likelihood of resulting in injury, death, psychological harm, maldevelopment or deprivation.[1]

We acknowledge that there are situations in which persons, communities or nations resort to defensive acts of force that result in unintended harm to others. The deaths of civilians in war zones is a case in point. We do not take lightly the severity of the devastation that results from such violent acts. Our particular concern in this study, however, is not unintentional violence but the deliberate use of power (by men) for the purpose of asserting control over others (women). The WHO's focus on the *intentional use of power* to reinforce domination of others, whether in personal relationships or in groups, is at the heart of our concern.

While written and oral histories have provided ample evidence of the suffering of humanity from acts of violence in the past, the technology of mass communications has brought to the attention of the whole world the stark reality of the cruelty and sheer magnitude of violence today. Nelson Mandela, the former President of South Africa, has rightly stated that 'the twentieth century will be remembered as a century marked by violence … with its legacy of mass destruction, of violence inflicted on a scale never seen and never possible before in human history.'[2]

Why is this so? Why does violence pervade our collective consciousness on such a grandiose scale? It is because, in the words of Aldo Etchegoyan, 'we are living in a "civilization" based on power and, in a context like this, violence is built into the system, with all the consequences we know for the lives of people and the natural world.'[3] Put another way,

> A great deal of violence arises because those with power oppress those without power. Much of this violence occurs in circumstances of

1. World Health Organization, *Violence: A Public Health Priority*, Global Consultation on Violence and Health, Document WHO/EHA/SPI.POA.2 (Geneva: WHO, 1996).

2. Nelson Mandela, 'Foreword', in Etienne G. Krug *et al.*, *World Report on Violence and Health* (Geneva: WHO, 2002), p. ix.

3. Aldo M. Etchegoyan, 'Editorial on Violence', *Echoes: WCC Justice, Peace and Integrity of Creation Newsletter* 17 (2000), http://www.wcc-coe.org/wcc/what/jpc/echoes/echoes-18-00.html.

great injustice and social decay. Poverty, unemployment, displacement, exploitation and oppression … provide the context in which violence takes place. They breed the suspicion and frustration, the prejudice and the hostility which lead to violence.[4]

This characterization of our contemporary landscape compels us to explore some of the forms of abusive power that may lead to, condone, or rely on violence. We will focus particularly on three such causative strands in the fabric of violence: the global economic world order, militarism, and colonial conquest. It will become clear as this exposition unfolds how this larger fabric of violence provides the raw materials out of which violence against women is generated.

Economic Inequity and Violence

The abuse of power which is inherent in the so-called global economy is a potent form of violence. Global economic arrangements engender a network of power alignments that force poorer nations and peoples into a downward spiral of indebtedness and servitude to wealthier powers — whether these be nations, multi-national corporations, or financial entities such as the International Monetary Fund and the World Bank. As a consequence of this servitude, millions of people in these weaker nations must struggle daily to survive in situations of extreme deprivation.

This globally interwoven web of economic power arrangements is maintained through the ever-growing profits of state, multinational or private corporations, from production sucked out of the natural resources and labor of the exploited nations and peoples. It is a fact of contemporary life that 'the political power of the rich nations determines the life and decisions of the impoverished countries. *The (related) powers of racism and sexism go on generating violence against women, blacks and indigenous peoples.*'[5] (Italics added)

Virtually every human community on earth is now confronted with the challenge of living in a world in which economic power is vested in the hands of the few, who must exploit the many in order to retain and solidify their position of privilege. Some of the worst consequences include unregulated child labor, debt slavery, sweat shops, and the trafficking of women. The suffering of these powerless people, according to Mandela,

4. World Council of Churches, 'Overcoming Violence', Decade to Overcome Violence (DOV) document, http://www.wcc-coe.org/wcc/dov-e.html.
5. Etchegoyan, 'Editorial on Violence'.

> ... is a legacy that reproduces itself, as new generations learn from the violence of generations past, as victims learn from victimizers, and as the social conditions that nurture violence are allowed to continue. No country, no community is immune.[6]

In relation to the primary focus of this work, an important point to be made here is that the violence which results from global economic inequities affects women (and children) disproportionately. Such violence has been recognized as 'a serious cause of ill-health among women world-wide.'[7] Later we will analyze in greater depth the specific connection between globalization and violence against women, with particular reference to the situation in Oceania. It is sufficient to note here that the global capitalist economic juggernaut has created many new forms of disempowerment, exploitation, and vicious cycles of poverty which have impacted most severely on women and children.

Militarism and Violence

The most widely sanctioned and brutal form of violence worldwide is warfare, still enacted primarily by military forces but increasingly also by para-military and non-conventional forces. The current world climate of terrorism and fear of terrorism is a stark example of how the military option so readily becomes the option of choice, despite the loss of the lives of untold numbers of innocent victims. Yet critiquing military violence, especially in the post-September 11th world, has become a taboo in many quarters, as it is presented by the Big Powers as the only way to preserve peace and combat terrorism.[8]

What these Powers forget is that violence breeds fear and anger, which leads to revenge and retaliation. The resentment of the 'losers' erupts in new waves of violence and the never-ending cycle continues. The wars of the past century alone have left millions dead, homeless, uprooted and victimized. Many survivors struggle for a lifetime to deal with their wounded memories of state-sanctioned violence.

6. Mandela, 'Foreword', p. ix.

7. John M. Grange, 'Violence is a Major Health Issue', *Overcoming Violence Newsletter* 3 (WCC/DOV Newsletter) (3 January 2002): p. 7.

8. It should be noted that many millions of people around the world demonstrated against the invasion of Iraq by the United States of America and its allies. These demonstrations persisted throughout the build-up to war and are continuing today, if in smaller numbers. Women have been prominent in these protests.

Women are especially victimized by the spill-over consequences of war and armed conflict. A common form of victimization during such conflicts is the use of women to entice enemy soldiers with sexual favors in order to gain information which is then passed on to military authorities. Many women in war-torn areas are also forced into being prostitutes or 'comfort women' to entertain lonely soldiers who are deprived of sex through separation from their wives, partners and lovers.[9] Other women are more generally bought and sold as workers for the commercialized sex businesses which flourish in the upheaval of war.[10] Women are also given as payments for debts accumulated from wars and tribal conflicts.[11] Many are raped and sometimes killed in the presence of their own families, in order to humiliate and teach their husbands, fathers or brothers a lesson about power and powerlessness.

An additional indirect link between militarism and violence against women is the employment of female workers from poorer nations in the production of weapons for the superpowers. The menial earnings from the production of armaments are the only source of income for millions of women. The irony is that these workers can end up being slaughtered by the very sophisticated weapons they have produced as exploited laborers.

Colonialism and Violence

There is also a clear connection between violence and the imperialistic patterns of conquest through colonization. Western colonizers have in fact made a major contribution to the worldwide culture of violence. Western imperialism succeeded largely by means of an underlying ideology which relied on an ethic of superiority that could often only be implemented and maintained by means of force.

As the Western patriarchs conquered and colonized at any cost, the patriarchs of the colonized nations often became embroiled in internal conflict with each other over their diminishing spheres of power. The patriarchs on both sides manipulated each other to gain or cling to power, and in all cases women were the biggest losers in

9. An old Japanese military myth was used to justify soldiers having 'comfort women': it claimed that sex before or outside marriage was understood to provide protection in times of war.

10. For an in-depth discussion of sexual slavery and the trafficking of women, see L. Brown, *Sex Slaves: The Trafficking of Women in Asia* (London: Virago Press, 2001).

11. An example of this practice is discussed in detail in K. Dinan, *Owed Justice: Thai Women Trafficked into Debt Bondage in Japan* (New York: Human Rights Watch, 2000).

these power plays. Geraldine Moane's research on gender and colonization offers convincing evidence that the strategies used by the colonizing powers are in fact identical to those used by men to dominate women as 'lesser' beings and 'the weaker sex.'[12]

For example, just as male superiority is assumed by men who exploit women, the concept of ethno-cultural superiority was used by the colonizers as a justification for their domination. Western colonizers claimed their divine right to rule over colonized peoples on the basis that they were the superior race, the more intelligent species, their way of life the only viable way of life, their god the god above all other gods, and their language the universal language of communication.[13] Although the colonizers eventually left, this internalized self-denigration continued in the leftover governmental and educational systems in the societies which had been colonized.

Indeed, one of the most enduring legacies of colonialism has been the colonizers' justification of their demeaning treatment of indigenous populations around the world in the name of the imposition of 'civilization.' The assumption of the colonizers that their version of civilization was normative resulted in the demonizing of colonized peoples' ancient traditions and the deprecation of their languages, religions and customs.[14] Indigenous communities were brainwashed into believing that they were inferior beings in intellect, spirituality, life-ways and appearance. Those who challenged this view by clinging tenaciously to their own cultural values and demanding their right to their land and customs were punished, killed, forced to be obedient or sent into exile.[15]

12. See Geraldine Moane, *Gender and Colonialism: A Psychological Analysis of Oppression and Liberation* (New York: St. Martin's Press, 1966). Moane is an Irish political scientist and sociologist whose research has contributed immensely to the understanding of the connections between gendered and colonizing domination.

13. In many of the colonized countries the indigenous people were forbidden to speak in their own languages and practice their own life-ways in the presence of the colonial masters. Once students entered the gates of their school, for instance, they were not allowed to speak in their own mother tongue. The reason given was that this was a discipline to help the students speak better English. In reality, it was a perpetuation of the internalized oppression imposed on the colonized by the colonizers.

14. These stories are recorded in the ancient songs of Oceanians, songs about how they were uprooted and sent into exile through the use of violence.

15. The practice of colonial masters sending 'troublemakers', as they were called, into exile was commonplace in Oceania. Very few of these exiles or their descendants were ever able to return after the island groups became independent nations. The majority died in exile, or went missing and were never heard of again.

At the heart of this violent colonizing strategy was the differentiation of conquered peoples as *Other*. This meant that the race, language, culture, and religion of the colonizers were positioned at the center of human existence, while the colonized *Others* were moved to the periphery, relegated to a role of servitude to their masters.[16] Such dehumanizing violence has largely been forgotten by the colonizing nations, but it has been permanently tattooed into the memories and identities of its victims in formerly colonized cultures such as those of Oceania.

It is important to note that women were additionally *othered* in this system, a sub-caste within the conquered *Others*.[17] They were classified as weaker *others* in their relationships with both colonizing and colonized men.[18] As the most vulnerable and powerless of the *Others*, women were the most accessible objects of violent conquest, in the form of rape, humiliation, silencing, and enslavement of various kinds.[19] Many of these forms of violence which were endemic to colonization are still used against women today. The underlying motivation of domination and control remains the same, whether the victims are powerless peoples or powerless women.

The myriad manifestations of violence associated with colonization and imperialism were a dire form of oppression for the peoples of Oceania, and a significant factor contributing to the rise of violence against women in Oceania in the modern era. Colonization came with a hierarchy of oppressions that reinforced

16. A good example was the common usage of indigenous groups to perform cultural items to entertain the colonial masters while having their meals. This tradition continues today through the promotion of tourism, with no critical awareness of how it functions as a form of internalized oppression.

17. The multiple oppressions of women are well articulated in the works of many non-Western feminist theologians. See, for example, Kwok Pui-Lan, *Introducing Asian Feminist Theology*, Introductions in Feminist Theology Series (Cleveland, OH: The Pilgrim Press, 2003); Chung Hyun Kyung's powerful keynote address to the WCC 7th Assembly, 'Come Holy Spirit – Renew the Whole Creation', in Michael Kinnamon (ed.) *Signs of the Spirit: Official Report, WCC Seventh Assembly* (Geneva: WCC, 1991), pp. 37–47; and also her work, *Struggle to Be the Sun Again: Introducing Asian Women's Theology* (Maryknoll, NY: Orbis Books, 1990).

18. Moving stories of women's oppression in the colonial era are found, for instance, in Virginia Fabella and Mercy A. Oduyoye (eds.), *With Passion and Compassion: Third World Women Doing Theology* (Maryknoll, NY: Orbis Books, 1988).

19. Women were raped, tortured and killed to humiliate and teach the so-called 'colored' people about the power of the superior race.

or superceded the existing indigenous patriarchal system.[20] Oceanian women were commodified[21] as exotic playmates whose purpose was to satisfy the sexual desires of the British, French, German and other colonizing powers, not to mention the occupying foreign armies — especially American soldiers during the two world wars. Earlier, in the era of first contact, women were the sexual victims of the many foreign sailors, adventurers, entrepreneurs and other settlers who anchored at Oceanian docks.[22]

Our discussion, thus far, has disclosed how the interwoven strands of economic inequity, militarism and imperialistic conquest work together to create a totalizing system of violence, a system which affects women most adversely because they are the most powerless. Certainly a further formidable contributory strand in the worldwide fabric of violence, one which has had particularly devastating consequences in terms of violence against women, has been religious dogmatism. However, since that is the focus of our theological reflection in Chapter Four, we will defer the discussion of religion and violence at this point, simply noting here that it is another significant strand in the interwoven fabric of violence. Against the backdrop of our characterization of this larger interwoven fabric of violence, we can now proceed to an unraveling of the specific phenomenon known as violence against women.

Violence Against Women: Unraveling the Fabric of Patriarchal Power

All of the interwoven strands of violence highlighted in the preceding sections trace their origins to a patriarchal construction

20. The extent of socially sanctioned violence in Oceania in the pre-contact era is a complex issue. The point to be made is that the patriarchal cultural foundations which tolerated certain forms of violence (including oppressive practices against women) were only strengthened and made more pathological by the encounter of island societies with the larger patriarchal system of colonization.

21. Rita Nakashima Brock and Susan Brooks Thistlethwaite provide powerful and painful information on the commodification of women as sexual objects in their book, *Casting Stones: Prostitution and Liberation in Asia and the United States* (Minneapolis, MN: Fortress Press, 1996).

22. This was the era of the baby boom in the Pacific and the beginning of a generation of mixed-blood Pacific Islander children, many of whom later became leading politicians, after their fathers left the islands because of their illegitimate relationships. Many of them have died not knowing who their fathers were, and for some this had to be kept a secret, as their conception was the outcome of their mothers being forced into prostitution. This is an issue that is never talked about but is a tragic part of the story of many Oceanian women.

of power. In this section we focus attention specifically on the cause and effect relationship between patriarchal understandings of power and men's resort to attitudes and acts of violence against women.

In that light, we wish to define *violence against women* as any male behavior which results from a patriarchal view of women as objects rather than subjects. Following Pamela Cooper-White, we understand violence against women as 'the annihilation of connectivity, the dulling and erasure of human relationality through objectification.'[23] Violence against women is thus not restricted to overt forms of physical violence such as battering, sexual assault or rape, but includes a broad range of actions and attitudes, from harassment to psychological and physical abuse, existing along a broad continuum of objectifying behaviors toward women.[24]

Clearly it would be over-stating the case to make the claim that all expressions of violence against women flow from patriarchal abuse of power. We acknowledge that there are feminists who question the ironclad grip of patriarchy over women's lives,[25] and also that in some instances women commit acts of violence against men, and even against other women. Nonetheless, our position is that, in the overwhelming majority of cases, violence against women is a consequence of patriarchy's construction of power relations between men and women.

Bernard Loomer has defined power as 'the ability to make or establish a claim on life.'[26] Power is also a relational construct; it is exercised in all of the many relational webs in which we participate. Hence a fitting use of power would be 'the ability to engage in

23. Pamela Cooper-White, *The Cry of Tamar: Violence Against Women and the Church's Response* (Minneapolis: Fortress Press, 1995), p. 18.

24. For a fuller discussion of the continuum of behaviors that constitute violence against women, see Liz Kelly and Jill Radford, 'Sexual Violence Against Women and Girls: An Approach to an International Overview', in Rebecca E. Dobash and Russell P. Dobash (eds.), *Rethinking Violence Against Women* (Thousand Oaks, CA: SAGE Publications, 1998a), pp. 56–57.

25. For an alternative view that rejects the universality of patriarchy, see Peggy Reeves Sanday, *Female Power and Male Dominance: On the Origins of Sexual Inequality* (Cambridge: Cambridge University Press, 1981); and Peggy Reeves Sanday and Ruth Gallagher (eds.), *Beyond the Second Sex: New Directions in the Anthropology of Gender* (Philadelphia: University of Pennsylvania Press, 1990).

26. Bernard Loomer, 'Two Conceptions of Power', *Criterion* 15 (1976): p. 12. For a discussion of violence against women in the context of the abuse of patriarchal power, see James N. Poling, *The Abuse of Power: A Theological Problem* (Nashville, TN: Abingdon Press, 1991).

relationships in a mutual way'[27] that empowers both parties in the relationship. The ideal relationship between men and women would then be what Rita Nakashima Brock has described as *erotic power* — that is, the 'holistic expression of communion and freedom between (equal partners) in ways that are appropriate to their relationships.'[28] Violence against women is an abuse of power understood in this way as the legitimate claim of equal partners to life.

Power becomes abusive when it is motivated by the desire to control — to have *power over*. Loomer calls this *unilateral power*: the 'presumed ability to produce an effect on another with only minimal impact on the self.'[29] This is the kind of power upon which patriarchy rests. Peter Rutter's work on violence against women asserts that the exploitation or abuse of women happens because of men's 'wish that women remain deferential to masculine power.'[30] In other words, violence against women occurs because it allows men to 'keep women in their place' — a place of subordination and submission.

Such objectification of women is a dominant strand in the larger fabric of patriarchal social control. Put another way, individual cases of violence against women both further and are dependent upon a larger social mosaic of power inequalities (such as those outlined in the preceding sections). Patriarchy provides institutional and cultural sanction for violence against women. As Brock puts it, 'women in patriarchy find themselves on the downside of power hierarchies … (such that) women have fewer resources and choices to protect themselves from abuse.'[31]

In other words, there is a direct link between violence against women and a collective patriarchal history in which men 'have traditionally enjoyed the prerogative of sexual initiative'[32] and have objectified women as beings designed for their use, to serve their needs. In Cooper-White's words, 'exploitative power and objectification go hand in hand.'[33] Using our own weaving metaphor,

27. Poling, *The Abuse of Power*, p. 25.

28. Rita Nakashima Brock, *Journeys by Heart: A Christology of Erotic Power* (New York: Crossroad, 1988), p. 41.

29. Loomer, 'Two Conceptions of Power', p. 16.

30. Peter Rutter, *Sex in the Forbidden Zone: When Men in Power — Therapists, Doctors, Clergy, Teachers and Others — Betray Women's Trust* (Los Angeles: Jeremy Tarcher, 1989), p. 68.

31. Brock, *Journeys by Heart*, p. 31.

32. Jill Goodman, 'Sexual Demands on the Job', *The Civil Liberties Review* (1978): p. 57.

33. Cooper-White, *The Cry of Tamar*, p. 18.

patriarchy provides the raw materials out of which the strands of violence against women are woven together.

The correlation between patriarchy and violence against women can be seen clearly in the 'highly asymmetrical gender roles to which the members of each sex are assigned at birth in patriarchal cultures, and to which they are powerfully conditioned to conform through-out the rest of their lives.'[34] These clear demarcation lines between gender roles 'make it possible for men to ward off or undo feelings of shame, disgrace and dishonour by means of violence, whereas that is significantly less true for women.'[35] The gender role stereotyping inherent in patriarchy, in short, 'involves the expecta-tion, even the requirement, of (male) violence, under many well-specified conditions: in times of war; in response to insult; in response to extramarital sex on the part of a female in the family; while engag-ing in all-male combat sports; and so on.'[36]

It is therefore necessary to dispel the myth that acts of violence against women are simply unfortunate instances of individual men momentarily losing control. On the contrary, such acts are most often the end result of a mindset congruent with the rules of patriarchal power, in which the perpetrator views the woman not as a person 'equally precious as himself' but as an 'object to be manipulated.'[37] Such objectification could not be further from the Gospel mandate which calls us always and in every relationship to love the other as we would love ourselves.

In every patriarchal setting, then—workplace, school, home, church, seminary, community, nation—it is women's lower status *as women* that makes them vulnerable to the violence that is the natural handmaiden of patriarchy. Rather than being merely the private moral failing of random individuals, violence against women is the natural outworking of a 'systematic and pervasive oppression of women, designed to reinforce male dominance over individual women.'[38] It occurs within a wider context of shared presuppositions about the nature of male-female relations which rests on the premise

---

34. James Gilligan, *Preventing Violence* (New York: Thames and Hudson, 2001), p. 56.

35. Gilligan, *Preventing Violence*, p. 56.

36. Gilligan, *Preventing Violence*, p. 56.

37. Cooper-White, *The Cry of Tamar*, p. 18.

38. Linda LeMoncheck and Marie Hajdin, *Sexual Harassment: A Debate* (New York: Rowman and Littlefield Publishers, 1997), p. 25.

that male power can be used to achieve or maintain domination. It is for this reason that violence against women can only be addressed by taking into account the whole patriarchal web—the social construction of male domination—that tolerates or encourages it.[39]

Now that the underlying (patriarchal) causative strands of violence against women have been disclosed, in the following chapter we can further unravel the effects of the patriarchal fabric of violence against women by examining the overt and covert patterns of violence created by masculine abuse of power.

39. For insights into the social determinants of male aggression, see the work of C. Enloe, *The Morning After: Sexual Politics at the End of the Cold War* (Berkeley, CA: University of California Press, 1994); and Peggy Reeves Sanday, 'The Socio-Cultural Context of Rape: A Cross-Cultural Study', *Journal of Social Issues* 37/4 (1991): pp. 5–27.

Chapter Two

Patterns in the Fabric of Violence Against Women

Our discussion thus far has provided an overview of the various 'source materials' which, when woven together, create the fabric of patriarchal violence that supports attitudes and acts of violence against women. With these causative strands in mind, we can now turn our attention to the end result: the fabric of effects, the fabric whose strands constitute the myriad manifestations of violence against women. It is only as we can identify and trace these patterns of violence against women, highlighted against the backdrop of the larger fabric of patriarchal abuse of power, that we can begin to unravel, disassemble and destroy them. Only then can the reweaving begin.

The Scope of the Problem

The United Nations has included under the umbrella of acts of violence against women 'any act of gender-based violence that results in, or is likely to result in physical, sexual or psychological harm or suffering to women, including threats of such acts, coercion or arbitrary deprivation of liberty, whether occurring in public or private life.'[1] This broad spectrum of violent acts occurs both inside and outside the family, and may even be perpetuated or condoned by the State. In short, 'violence against women and girls knows no boundaries. It cuts indiscriminately across class, race, ethnic, geographic and economic divides.'[2]

---

1. United Nations, *Declaration on the Elimination of Violence Against Women*, Resolution No. A/RES/48/104 (New York: United Nations, 23 February 1994).

2. Nancy Spence, address, Pacific Regional Workshop on Strengthening Partnerships for Eliminating Violence Against Women, Pacific Forum Secretariat, Suva, Fiji, 17–19 February 2003.

Acts of violence against women are detrimental to the health and human rights of many millions of women and girls across the globe. Available statistics suggest that 'at least one in five of the world's female population has been physically or sexually abused by a man or men at some time in their life.'[3] Women are not only at risk of being violated once they are in relationships with men; they are in fact subject to violence from the moment of their conception up to the last years of their lives, as we will shortly see.

Violence against women is also found in every society in the world, and it is on the increase in many societies today. Yet, because of entrenched patriarchal attitudes, little is done to protect women from violence in many contexts. Consider the following research findings quoted below:

- Of 193 nations in the world, just over a quarter — 44 — have laws against domestic violence, and only 17 see marital rape as a crime.
- Violence against women is carried out by people of all faiths, including Christians. For instance, in predominantly Christian Papua New Guinea, 60% of women suffer violence from men, in Muslim Pakistan 80%, and in Buddhist Thailand 50%.
- Cultural attitudes which discriminate against women often make violence appear justifiable. For example, in Samoa the assumption that wives should be obedient leads to widespread wife-beating. In several countries the custom of dowry or bride-price reinforces the view that women are the property of men without individual rights.[4]

Cultural socialization regarding the nature of womanhood strongly impacts the way girls and women are depicted and treated. These cultural stereotypes feed into the collective mindset that tolerates the use of force to confine women into restrictive spheres. The following quoted points are just a few of an almost limitless list of illustrations of this gender stereotyping:

3. World Health Organization, *Violence Against Women: Definition and Scope of the Problem* (Geneva: WHO, 1997), p. 1.

4. Council for World Mission, *Women and Violence*, FACTS Action Sheet 4 (London: CWM, 2002b). This information has been gathered by CWM from the United Nations Development Programme, US Advisory Council on Violence Against Women, Panos Institute, and World Vision.

- In India, girls are referred to as *paraya dhan* — 'somebody else's wealth.'
- In Taiwan, 98% of characters in primary school textbooks are male. Images of women are as obedient, beautiful or preparing food for the family.
- Despite legislation, in Zimbabwe customs exist which force a widow to marry her brother-in-law and offer young girls as compensation in inter-family disputes.[5]

Such findings confirm the sad reality that there exists a vast patriarchal mosaic of social norms and customs worldwide which legitimize a wide array of both overt and subtle forms of violence against women. We proceed now to highlight the more overt strands of this mosaic.

Unraveling the Strands of Physical and Sexual Abuse

As noted earlier, violence against women occurs not simply in the context of adult relationships, but from the moment of conception. With that in mind, it will be instructive to begin our overview of the major categories of violence against women by tracing the trajectory of violence against females across the life cycle. This is summarized in Figure 1.

It is sobering indeed to consider that the denigration of females begins so early in life and continues so late. In all of the above forms of violence, one can see the hand of patriarchy at work, making women expendable, derivative, and objectified as 'less' than males. If males had themselves experienced anything remotely like any of these forms of abuse, they would undoubtedly begin to view women's suffering in an entirely different light.

In the following sections we will provide an overview of the major categories of violence against adult women. These include physical and sexual violence, occurring both inside and outside the home. The category of harassment will be addressed in a separate section.

5.   Council for World Mission, *Women, Culture and Equality*, FACTS Action Sheet 6 (London: CWM, 2002c). CWM sources in this publication are taken from *The Economist*, the World Student Christian Federation, *Mapusaga o Aiga*, (Samoa), *The Mail and Guardian* (South Africa), and the journal *Womankind*.

Figure 1: Violence Against Women Through the Life Cycle

Phase	*Type of Violence*
Pre-Birth	Sex-selective abortion; effects of battering during pregnancy on birth outcomes
Infancy	Female infanticide; physical, sexual and psychological abuse
Girlhood	Child marriage; female genital mutilation; physical, sexual and psychological abuse; incest; child prostitution and pornography
Adolescence and adulthood	Dating and courtship violence (e.g., acid throwing and date rape); economically coerced sex (e.g. school girls having sex with 'sugar daddies' in return for school fees); incest; sexual abuse in the workplace; rape; sexual harassment; forced prostitution and pornography; trafficking in women; partner violence; marital rape; dowry abuse and murders; partner homicide; psychological abuse; abuse of women with disabilities; forced pregnancy
Elderly	Forced 'suicide' or homicide of widows for economic reasons; sexual, physical and psychological abuse.[6]

Intimate Partner Violence (Domestic Violence)

Intimate partner violence or domestic violence refers to any behavior within an intimate relationship that causes physical, psychological or sexual harm to someone in the relationship.[7] The WHO elaborates by defining intimate partner violence as any 'acts of physical aggression, psychological abuse, forced intercourse and other forms of sexual coercion, and various controlling behaviors such as isolating a person from family and friends or restricting access to information and assistance.'[8] The evidence confirms the horrifying reality that a large majority of female victims suffer violence from the very people with whom they are most intimately involved: their partners or male relatives.[9] This is as much the case in Oceanian societies as in other parts of the world.

6. WHO, *Violence Against Women: Definition and Scope*, p. 2.

7. Lori Heise and Claudia Garcia-Moreno, 'Violence by Intimate Partners', in Etienne G. Krug *et al.*, *World Report on Violence and Health* (Geneva: World Health Organization, 2002), p. 89.

8. Council for World Mission, *Intimate Partner Violence*, FACTS Action Sheet [unnumbered] (London: CWM, 2002a), p. 1.

9. CWM, 2002b, *Women and Violence*, p. 1. This information is also found in CWM 2002a, *Intimate Partner Violence*, p. 1.

One of the most commonplace forms of domestic violence is *physical assault*. One international survey found that 'between 10% and 69% of women reported being physically assaulted by an intimate male partner at some point in their lives.'[10] Physical violence in intimate relationships is frequently 'accompanied by psychological abuse, and in one-third to over one-half of cases by sexual abuse.'[11]

The available statistics on physical assault of women in various countries are horrific in the extreme. Here are just a few such examples:

> In Costa Rica, one of every two women can expect to be a victim [of assault] … In Canada, one in four women can expect to be assaulted at some point in their lives, half of these before the age of 17. In the U.S., a woman is beaten every 15 seconds. Three-quarters of the women interviewed in a … study in Sri Lanka said they had been beaten by their husbands. … In South Africa, one adult woman out of every six is assaulted regularly by her mate. In Papua New Guinea, 60 percent of the persons murdered [in a recent year] were women, the majority by their spouses during or after a domestic argument.[12]

In many traditional societies, wife beating is 'largely regarded as a consequence of a man's right to inflict physical punishment on his wife.'[13] This 'right' stems from men's belief that their wives are not only their possessions but completely dependent upon them and in need of their control. Consequently, 'if a man feels that his wife has failed in her role or overstepped her limits …, then violence may be his response.'[14] Such violence is so routinized that even its

10. Heise and Garcia-Moreno, 'Violence by Intimate Partners', p. 89. See especially, selected population-based studies (1982–1999), p. 190, Table 4.1, for more information on physical assault on women by an intimate male partner.

11. Heise and Garcia-Moreno, 'Violence by Intimate Partners'. This study also draws on the following sources: M.P. Koss, *et al.*, *No Safe Haven: Male Violence Against Women at Home, at Work, and in the Community* (Washington, DC: American Psychological Association, 1994); and J. Leibrich and J. Pauline Ransom, *Hitting Home: Men Speak about Domestic Abuse of Women Partners* (Wellington, NZ: New Zealand Department of Justice/AGB McNair, 1995).

12. These examples are extracted from *The Tribune* 46 (International Women's Tribune Centre newsletter June 1991): n.p, cited in Aruna Gnanadason, *No Longer a Secret: The Church and Violence Against Women*, rev. edn (Geneva: WCC Publications, 1997), pp. 2–3, 9–10.

13. Heise and Garcia-Moreno, 'Violence by Intimate Partners', p. 94. For a study of wife-beating in an Oceanian context, see C.S. Bradley, 'Attitudes and Practices Relating to Marital Violence Among the Tolai of East New Britain', in PNG Law Commission (ed.), *Domestic Violence in Papua New Guinea* (Goroko, PNG: PNG Law Reform Commission, 1985), pp. 32–71.

14. Heise and Garcia-Moreno, 'Violence by Intimate Partners', p. 95.

victims are often socialized to accept it. Studies have shown that, 'in many developing countries, women often agree with the idea that men have the right to discipline their wives, if necessary by force.'[15]

In some cultures, women can also be physically assaulted by their brothers or other male family members if they are perceived to have engaged in an unsanctioned relationship with a male, to have lost their virginity, or to have committed adultery. Cultural presuppositions about 'male honour and female chastity put women at risk; ... a man's honour is often linked to the perceived sexual 'purity' of the women in his family.'[16]

In comparing the injuries of women and men from violence by intimate partners, studies have shown that women are far more likely to be injured from such acts of violence than men.[17] The few women who do respond violently themselves almost always do so out of self-defense.[18] Yet there is a growing movement in some developed countries for men to portray themselves as victims of their wives' or partners' abuse. This receives considerable media attention, but serves mainly to deflect attention from the fact that the vast majority of domestic abuse victims are women.

The finding above that all too many female victims of assault are conditioned to accept their battering as normative is part of a disturbing pattern which can also be seen in many cases of sexual abuse and harassment. We will analyze this phenomenon further in our discussion of harassment. Suffice it to say here that the problem is not simply that women tend to be physically weaker than men. This is typically the case, but that alone would not necessarily prevent women from trying to defend themselves, or from leaving the men who assault them in their own homes. Many other factors are also at work, such as women's inability to leave domestic abusers because they are financially dependent upon them. The most important source of women's passivity in the face of assault, however, is the social conditioning inherent in patriarchy which can lead women to feel that they merit the 'punishment' meted out to them by men.

15. Heise and Garcia-Moreno, 'Violence by Intimate Partners' p. 94. See, also, Table 4.2, p. 94, for more detailed information.

16. Heise and Garcia-Moreno, 'Violence by Intimate Partners', p. 93.

17. See, for instance, Canadian Center for Justice Statistics, *Family Violence in Canada: A Statistical Profile* (Ottawa: Statistics Canada, 2000).

18. M.P. Johnson, and K.J. Ferraro, 'Research on Domestic Violence in the 1990s: Making Distinctions', *Journal of Marriage and the Family* 62 (2000): pp. 948–63.

We turn our attention next to the other major manifestation of domestic abuse, *sexual violence*. A World Health Organization study defines sexual violence as 'any sexual act, attempt to obtain a sexual act, unwanted sexual comments or advances, or acts to traffic a person's sexuality, using coercion, threats of harm or physical force, by any person regardless of relationship to the victim, in any setting, including but not limited to home and work.'[19] Sexual violence, according to this report, includes:

> physically forced or otherwise coerced sex, attempts at coerced sex, assault with a sexual organ, sexual harassment including sexual humiliation, forced marriage or cohabitation, forced prostitution and trafficking in women, forced abortion, denial of the right to use contraception or protect oneself from disease, and acts of violence against women's sexuality such as female genital mutilation and virginity inspections.[20]

Once again, the information provided by international studies on sexual assault is shocking. We include here only a small sampling of these findings. Referring specifically to domestic sexual abuse, we discover that, for example,

> In the U.S. ..., a [domestic] rape occurs every six minutes. ... In Peru, one of every four girl children will be the victim of sexual abuse before she reaches her sixteenth birthday, and a third of all adult women report that they have been forced to have sex against their will. In cases of sexual abuse of [girl] children in Canada, most assailants are ... family members.[21]

One of the most traumatic and prevalent forms of domestic sexual assault is rape. Although many rapes are committed by strangers outside the home, a large proportion are also committed within the home, by a spouse, partner or someone else well-known to the woman. Domestic rape involves even fewer negative repercussions for the perpetrator than rape by a stranger, because in so many societies the prevailing view continues to be that men have the right to demand sex from their wives or partners. But rape is rape, no matter who commits it, and its effects on women are devastating.

19. Rachel Jewkes, Purna Sen and Claudia Garcia-Moreno, 'Sexual Violence', in Etienne G. Krug *et al.* (eds.), *World Report on Violence and Health*, p. 149.
20. Jewkes *et al.*, 'Sexual Violence', p. 1.
21. *The Tribune*, cited in Gnanadason, *No Longer a Secret*, pp. 3, 10.

> Rape, which is the most aggressive demonstration of unjust power relationships … is symbolic of the degradation of womankind, and is a violation of the most sensitive part of the human psyche. Susan Brownmiller defines it as a "conscious process of intimidation by which … men keep women in a state of fear." … The shocking sentiment implicit even today … is that a woman "asks for it," or … that a rapist is an individual giving in to his natural virility.[22]

The WHO has identified risk factors for rape and other forms of sexual violence (see Figure 2), both for perpetrators and victims.[23] What is instructive about the risk factors outlined in Figure 2 is the incontrovertible evidence that sexual abuse is the result of the entire complex, interwoven fabric of patriarchy. It is a holistic problem. Men's personal attitudes of masculine superiority and dominance are reinforced by familial and societal patriarchal values. Each strand of the fabric upholds the other strands, until the vicious cycle of sexual abuse is so impregnable it cannot be broken. Core social norms such as 'male superiority' and 'male sexual entitlement' overlap neatly with 'weak social sanctions' against men who are sexually violent. These, in turn, buttress female victims' conclusions that they must have deserved their domestic sexual abuse in the first place, or that they have no option but to accept it because nothing can be done about it.

Violence Outside the Home

Violence against women is also widespread in settings outside the home — and, in many countries today, it is on the increase. This strand of violence encompasses all the usual forms of physical and sexual assault. Research conducted in developed countries has shown that 'the likelihood of a woman being raped or having to fight off an attempted rape at some point in her life is high.'[24] In developing countries, research suggests that 'rape is an ever-present threat and reality for millions of women.'[25]

> According to UN reports, India leads the world in 'custodial' rape (rape committed by men in positions of power such as police officers, prison

22. Cited in *Madhu Bhusan*, unpublished document issued by Vimochana, a feminist group in Bangalore, India, n.d.

23. Jewkes *et al.*, 'Sexual Violence', p. 1.

24. Jewkes *et al.*, 'Sexual Violence', p. 1.

25. World Health Organization, *Violence Against Women: Rape and Sexual Assault* (Geneva: WHO, 1997), p. 3, http://www.who.int/violence_injury_prevention/violence/itnerpersonal.html.

Figure 2: Risk Factors for Sexual Violence

Factors Increasing Women's Vulnerability	*Factors Increasing Men's Risk of Committing Rape*
Individual Level	
• being young • using alcohol or drugs • having mental health problems, particularly with post-traumatic stress disorder • having previously been raped or sexually abused	• men using alcohol or drugs • men holding attitudes and beliefs supportive of sexual violence, including coercive sexual fantasies and blaming women for arousing them • a pattern of behaviour that is impulsive, antisocial, and hostile toward women • having been sexually abused as a child
Family and Close Environment Level	
• having many sexual partners • involvement in sex work • being in an intimate relationship, especially one characterized by physical and emotional violence	• growing up in a family environment characterized by physical violence, little emotional support, and few economic resources • associating with sexually aggressive peers
Community Level	
• being educated and economically empowered, at least where sexual violence perpetrated by an intimate partner is concerned • poverty	• poverty – mediated through a crisis of masculine identity • weak sanctions against men who are sexually violent
Societal Level	
• community and social expectations that women are responsible for protecting their modesty and controlling their sexuality • community and societal norms of male superiority and male sexual entitlement • societies where laws and policies related to gender equality and sexual violence are weak	• community and social expectations that women are responsible for protecting their modesty and controlling their sexuality • community and societal norms of male superiority and male sexual entitlement • societies with weak laws/policies

and hospital staff, doctors). ... In the Philippines, one out of every two women arrested by the military is forced to undress; ... 14 percent are threatened with rape or death. ... In July 1991, 271 teenage girls were attacked by male classmates at a boarding school in Kenya because they refused to join a strike against the school authorities. ... 71 were raped. The comment by the school's deputy principal was revealing: "The boys never meant any harm against the girls; they just wanted to rape." '[26]

While the same personal, familial and social factors are at work whether women are abused inside or outside the domestic sphere, violence against women by strangers is associated with distinctive traumas. As debilitating and horrific as domestic violence is, its victims are at least familiar with their abusers and can at times develop coping mechanisms which may help them in their struggle for physical or emotional survival. When the perpetrator is a stranger, women face other formidable obstacles.

All too often such victims find that they have little or no recourse to societal protection or justice. In many countries, even when men who rape or assault women are apprehended and brought to trial, they are acquitted or given brief prison sentences. As with domestic rape, it is commonplace for their lawyers to argue that the sex was consensual, or that the woman enticed them or aggravated them. With rape outside the home, the victim's past sexual history is often paraded before the court, as a way of portraying her as a seductress who asked for what she got.

Women who are raped or assaulted by strangers must also contend with a larger complex of fears because their perpetrators are not known to them. When these women are raped they have no way of knowing what the perpetrators may have passed on to them. In the contemporary era of the pandemics of HIV/AIDS and other sexually transmitted diseases, rape by a stranger may become a death sentence.

When such women become pregnant as a result of rape, they must also live with the knowledge that they do not know what problems they may be passing on to their child. Additionally, they must live with the trauma of bearing a child which is the result of a violent sexual assault rather than a committed relationship. The tragic ordeal of the huge numbers of Muslim Bosnian women raped by Serbian soldiers during the armed conflict in Bosnia-Herzigovina

26. *The Tribune*, cited in Gnanadason, *No Longer a Secret*, pp. 3, 14.

in the 1990s is all too typical. Many of these women did not want to keep the babies born as a result of their rapes, and many sank into deep depressions which have debilitated them to this day.[27]

The plight of these Bosnian women is echoed again and again in the experiences of women who are raped during wars and other social upheavals, a phenomenon we highlighted in Chapter One in our discussion of the correlation between militarism and violence against women, and to which we will return in our discussion of violence against women in Oceania. Rape and state-sanctioned violence go hand in hand.

Amnesty International is in the forefront of attempting to bring to the world's attention the appalling plight of the many thousands of women around the world who are raped or otherwise sexually assaulted in situations of conflict or imprisonment by repressive regimes. Commenting specifically on the high incidence of rapes of women in police or military custody, one of their reports states:

> Through their failure to institute adequate investigations, prosecutions and procedural safeguards, governments around the world bear full responsibility for the persistence of widespread rape and sexual abuse [of women] in custody. … Many governments clearly regard rape and sexual assault as less serious offences than other human rights violations. This is a particularly frightening prospect when the perpetrators of these rapes are the same policemen and military personnel charged with the protection of the public.[28]

The grim realities described above are just some of the consequences of acts of violence against women which take place outside the home or by strangers. These women's feelings of violation, fear, shame and hopelessness in the face of what has happened to them can wreak havoc on all of their other relationships, particularly their primary intimate relationships with husbands or partners.

Our discussion, thus far, has been an attempt to provide an accurate overview of the scope and manifestations of the most overt forms of violence against women. Because harassment constitutes

27. The plight of these Muslim Bosnian rape victims has been depicted poignantly in 'The Rape of Bosnia', editorial, *International Herald Tribune*, 8 December 1992, p. 2. This article mentions an interview with a Serbian soldier who stated that raping Muslim women was 'good for raising a fighter's morale.'

28. Amnesty International, 'Rape and Sexual Abuse: Torture and Ill-Treatment of Women in Detention', *ACT 77* (November 1991): n.p.

such a serious—yet often unexamined—form of violence against women, it is given more extensive treatment.

Unraveling the Strand of Harassment

We seek to focus particular attention on that aspect of violence against women known as harassment[29] because it is the most widespread, prevalent form of violence against women, yet the least addressed. It is unrecognized or ignored, a silent scourge affecting women and girls in a multitude of subtle and not-so-subtle forms. It is a complex phenomenon which requires careful analysis.

The Parameters of Harassment

One of the difficulties involved in accurately defining what we will, for the present, refer to as sexual harassment, is that it can be disguised or subjected to a myriad of interpretations by its perpetrators. Sexual harassment is generally not viewed as seriously as other forms of violence against women precisely because of its subtlety, covertness and veneer of social acceptability. Yet, as Pamela Cooper-White has aptly pointed out,

> Although it is often considered one of the "milder" forms of violence against women, because it does not generally result in visible bruises or wounds, sexual harassment must be considered a serious form of violence. In it are found all the themes of power and betrayal of trust that characterize all violence against women.[30]

In reality, sexual harassment has been found to have equally 'devastating consequences'[31] as the more overt forms of violence against women.

Despite the complexities surrounding sexual harassment, there have been serious attempts in recent years to arrive at workable definitions that will both clarify a murky topic and enable it to be

---

29. *Harassment* in this work will be limited to that perpetrated by men against women. We acknowledge that there are instances of harassment by women of men. However, these constitute a tiny minority of harassment cases, and when such harassment does occur it is almost always in the rare instance where a woman is in a position of authority over the man she harasses. Since many efforts to include female harassment of males are an attempt to dilute or sidestep the much more serious and widespread incidence of male harassment against women, this essay examines harassment only in terms of its predominant manifestation—as males harassing females.

30. Cooper-White, *The Cry of Tamar*, p. 66.

31. Cooper-White, *The Cry of Tamar*, p. 66.

taken more seriously. The term *sexual harassment* first came into common usage in the early 1970s, and has been defined in the most general terms as 'any form of uninvited sexual attention' that either explicitly or implicitly has a negative impact on a woman's work or educational experience, sense of safety and belonging in a community, and emotional or physical well-being.[32] In its explicitly sexual guise, it is any behavior that 'sustains male dominance and women's subordination by privileging the sexual desires of men over the needs of women.'[33]

In the broadest sense, then, sexual harassment is yet another avowal of male control. Lin Farley has defined it as 'unsolicited … male behaviour that asserts a woman's sex role'[34] over any other role. Put a slightly different way, it is 'deliberate and/or repeated sexual or sex-based behaviour that is not welcome or not asked for.'[35] The sexual harassment policy of the Presbyterian Church in the USA defines sexual harassment as 'any unwanted (male behaviour) … perceived by the recipient as demeaning, intimidating or coercive.'[36]

A more finely nuanced definition, which takes into account the broader social framework of sexual harassment, asserts that it is any act that 'constitutes a sexual imposition or intrusion upon the harassed, which is facilitated by organisational hierarchies or informed by cultural stereotypes, or both, in ways that delegitimise, manipulate or threaten the harassed or pressure sexual access to her.'[37] In other words, it is any behaviour by males that denies the female recipient equal relational status and freedom as a gendered being. Key words in the above definition that describe this reality are 'imposition,' 'intrusion' and 'manipulate.'

32. U.S. Equal Employment Opportunity Commission, *Sexual Harassment (1998)*, http://www.access.gpo.gov/nara/cfrwaisidx29cfrl604.html, cited in Phoebe Morgan, 'Sexual Harassment: Violence Against Women at Work', in Renzetti, Edelson and Bergen (eds.), *Sourcebook on Violence Against Women* (Thousand Oaks, CA: SAGE Publications, 2001), p. 210.

33. Morgan, 'Sexual Harassment', in Renzetti, Edelson and Bergen (eds.), p. 212.

34. Lin Farley, *Sexual Shakedown: The Sexual Harassment of Women on the Job* (New York: McGraw-Hill Publishers, 1978), p. 14.

35. Susan L. Webb, *The Global Impact of Sexual Harassment* (New York: MasterMedia Ltd., 1994), p. 15.

36. Presbyterian Church USA, 'Policy Statement on Sexual Harassment in the Workplace', cited in Gnanadason, *No Longer a Secret*, p. 11.

37. LeMoncheck, and Hajdin, *Sexual Harassment: A Debate*, p. 59.

Given the breadth and depth of intentions, actions and contexts which characterize sexual harassment, the repertoire of defining behaviors is indeed extensive. Examples can be 'visual, verbal or physical' and can occur in a 'wide range of relationships and locations.'[38] What follows are just some of the behaviors that have been identified as constituting sexual harassment.

There is, first, what is known as *street harassment*, which occurs in public settings where the harasser generally does not know the victim. Street harassment can include anything 'from whistles, catcalls of a sexual nature, kissing noises, comments ranging from "hello baby" to vulgar suggestions' — all of which 'objectify women and assert coercive power over them.'[39]

Researchers who have studied *workplace harassment* have delineated harassing behaviors which include 'staring at, commenting upon, or touching a woman's body,'[40] non-reciprocated propositions, sexual joking or innuendoes, or suggestive remarks (one study includes here 'ambiguous or embarrassing comments'[41]), and any other acts, words or gestures that make women feel uncomfortable and objectified because of their sex. The New Zealand Human Rights Commission, borrowing from a tertiary institution harassment policy, incorporates in its definition any unwanted physical contact (however subtle), including invasion of personal space, or inappropriate questions or comments about one's personal life.[42]

We would want to widen the contexts of harassment far beyond the workplace, because of the clear evidence that it occurs in every conceivable arena. In addition to street harassment and workplace harassment, there is harassment in schools, neighbourhoods, tourist areas, among peers and friends, in churches and church institutions. In other words, wherever women are, sexual harassment occurs.

---

38. Liz Kelly and Jill Radford, ' "Nothing Really Happened": The Invalidation of Women's Experiences of Sexual Violence', in Marianne Hester, Liz Kelly and Jill Radford (eds.), *Women, Violence and Male Power* (Buckingham, UK: Open University Press, 1997), p. 58.

39. Webb, *Global Impact of Sexual Harassment*, p. 39.

40. Farley, *Sex and Shakedown*, p. 15.

41. Gnanadason, *No Longer a Secret*, p. 12.

42. See, Auckland Technical Institute, 'Policy Statement on Sexual Harassment', 1987, cited in Audrey Colbert, *Dealing with Sexual Harassment: A New Zealand Handbook* (Wellington, NZ: GP Books, 1989), p. 12.

The Prevalence of Harassment

Sexual harassment is, moreover, a global problem, but one whose pervasiveness is only now beginning to come to light. Accurate statistics are hard to come by, as cultural norms in many societies make it almost impossible for women to report harassing behaviors (a dilemma which we will explore further). In the growing body of international studies, estimates suggest that 40–60% of working women have experienced some form of sexual harassment in the workplace alone.[43]

Those most likely to be targeted for workplace harassment tend to be 'younger women, divorced or separated women,' or those otherwise perceived as being particularly vulnerable.[44] It should also be noted, however, that the most recent evidence also suggests that even women who are in a position of some authority may be targeted precisely as a way of 'putting them down' because they are threatening to their male peers.[45]

Because this work has a particular concern for the role of Oceanian theological education in relation to violence against women, it is relevant to include here insights from recent research that has examined *sexual harassment in educational institutions*. The statistics are shocking. Seventy-six per cent of females in one international study and 85% in another study reported experiencing sexual harassment in an educational setting.[46] Sexual harassment in the educational arena has been defined as any 'objectionable emphasis on the sexual identity of a student' or, in the case of harassment by academics, 'the use of one's authority to emphasize the sexual identity of a student' (or colleague).[47] Such harassment by academics runs the gamut from 'generalised sexist remarks or behavior' to

43. Webb, *Global Impact of Sexual Harassment*, p. 52.

44. Webb, *Global Impact of Sexual Harassment*, p. 52.

45. For example, Phoebe Morgan has found in her research that 'women who challenge the superiority of men by acquiring social, economic or organizational power over them are visible targets for sexualized hostility.' See Morgan, 'Sexual Harassment', p. 215. Another study found that 'the more power a woman acquires, the more she is perceived to be a threat to (males) in power and the greater her risk of being harassed will be.' See, S. DeCoster, S.B. Estes and C.W. Mueller, 'Routine Activities and Sexual Harassment in the Workplace', *Work and Occupations* 26:1 (1999): p. 39.

46. Webb, *Global Impact of Sexual Harassment*, p. 300.

47. National Advisory Council on Women's Education Programs (NACWEP), *A Report on the Sexual Harassment of Students* (Washington, DC: US Department of Education, 1980), p. 2.

'inappropriate and offensive' (but usually sanction-free) sex-linked behaviors.[48] These can range from unwelcome sexual jokes, comments, gestures, looks, and propositions, to being touched inappropriately or pressured into sexual encounters.

Beyond 'Sexual' Harassment

The term *sexual harassment* is now being relegated to the back burner by some researchers precisely because, as one commentator has aptly stated, 'it can so easily be construed as not violent, not criminal, not even wrong.'[49] Sexual harassment is perceived as existing in a 'grey area' of at times quite cleverly calculated male behaviors that 'could be' interpreted as something other than explicitly sexual harassment. As numerous researchers have shown, such 'grey area behaviors' are very often 'socially acceptable in a given culture.'[50]

Many men, using this defence of social acceptability, thus frequently argue either that their remarks, looks or touches were 'not really sexual,' or that 'it's not sexual harassment unless the woman says no.' (There are many reasons why women are predisposed not to be able to say 'no' to men, to which we will return.) This ease with which the term 'sexual' harassment can be diluted or misconstrued points up the need to propose a broader, more accurate term that reconfigures the parameters of the complex phenomenon generally described as sexual harassment.

The fact is that some forms of harassment against women are not overtly sexual in nature. Nonetheless, their harassment happens to them *only* because they are women, and because as such they are devalued. Hence, in an effort to provide an overarching category which situates the harassment of women more accurately within its broader context—the power imbalance between the sexes that is endemic to patriarchy—we propose the use of the term *gender harassment*.

Gender harassment can be defined as any male behavior that objectifies and ultimately has the effect of demeaning women *simply because they are women*. At times this happens when men feel threatened by women's potential strength. We will encounter this phenomenon in one of our case studies in Chapter Six, in which female Oceanian theological students are 'put down' by their male

48. NACWEP, *A Report on the Sexual Harassment of Students*, p. 3.
49. Kelly and Radford, 'Nothing Really Happened', p. 21.
50. Webb, *Global Impact of Sexual Harassment*, p. 17.

counterparts in the classroom. The male attitudes in that case echo the responses of male students in one study who, when asked why they had made harassing comments in classroom settings, routinely responded with comments such as 'they were asking for it,' or 'they think they're smart'.[51] In other words, the harassment took place as a means for men to assert or recover their sense of power over women.

We wish, then, to join the growing body of researchers who prefer the broader term of gender harassment both as a way of incorporating forms of harassment that are 'not overtly sexual in content but still degrade women,'[52] and also in order to locate the roots of harassment where they properly belong: not in the sphere of sex, but in the sphere of patriarchy and its abuse of power. In that light, it will be helpful to examine in greater depth the routinization of harassment in patriarchal contexts.

The Normalization of Harassment

If patriarchy is the norm in most of the world's cultures, we can begin to understand why gender harassment is so difficult to combat. It has become, in a word, *normalized*. It is accepted as part and parcel of the way things are—simply because 'boys will be boys' (even though many of them are otherwise mature men). All available international research has shown that the dominant cultural worldview of most societies still accepts male domination of women through harassment as 'just the way things are.'[53]

What this normalization means is that, although there are generally some social sanctions against the most overtly violent forms of male domination, such as rape and sexual assault, gender harassment is widely tolerated. Men practice it at least partially because of the 'perceived acceptability of discrimination against

51. Colbert, *Dealing with Sexual Harassment*, p. 56.

52. Of interest in this regard is recent work on the differentiation between gender harassment, sexual harassment and sexual coercion, in L. Fitzgerald and M. Hesson-McInnis, 'The Dimensions of Sexual Harassment: A Structural Analysis', *Journal of Vocational Behaviour* 35 (1989): pp. 309–26.

53. In the few known societies in which violence against women did not tradition-ally exist—such as the Ashanti culture in West Africa, or certain tribal cultures in the Philippines—women traditionally shared power equally with men and 'participated fully in religious leadership.' See Marie Fortune, 'Religious Issues and Violence Against Women', in Renzetti, Edelson and Bergen (eds.), *Sourcebook on Violence Against Women*, p. 373.

women.'[54] They know that they can engage in such harassment with impunity. They know that they are members of a male power structure which characterizes gender harassment as inconsequential and harmless to women and resists any notion that it is threatening or intrusive. They know they can escape accountability by claiming 'it was a joke,' or 'I didn't know she didn't feel the same way,' or 'she misinterpreted my intentions,' or simply 'nothing happened.'[55]

Because gender harassment is normalized, women who are its victims are effectively silenced. They know that their complaints are likely not to be taken seriously, or that they will be blamed and punished for 'rocking the boat.' In one survey, it was found that only 2%–3% of women took any formal steps against their harassers — and this even in a Western context in which women are ostensibly encouraged to speak their minds.[56] Moreover, nearly half of this tiny minority reported that taking formal action either had no effect or made things worse.[57] This outcome is confirmed by our knowledge of what has happened (or, more accurately, has *not* happened) in the few instances where women have attempted to seek redress in the harassment cases of which we are aware in Oceanian theological institutions.

The end result of the normalization of gender harassment is that it becomes shrouded in avoidance. Women are 'socialised to keep their victimization silent.'[58] It is interesting that this tends to be the case even when the victim is a peer of the harasser and technically 'equal' to him. She knows or soon discovers that her complaints are likely to be disbelieved, ignored or discounted — because, even if the institution in which the harassment took place has an anti-harassment policy, it is still 'under the auspices' of the given patriarchal power structure.[59] Hence the woman knows intuitively that giving voice to her harassment is, in fact, likely to worsen her

54. Diana Russell, *Sexual Exploitation: Rape, Child Sexual Abuse, and Workplace Harassment* (Beverly Hills, CA: SAGE Publications, 1984), p. 277.

55. Elizabeth A. Stanko, 'Reading Danger: Sexual Harassment, Anticipation and Self-Protection', in *Women, Violence and Male Power*, p. 50.

56. U.S. Merit Systems Protection Board, *Sexual Harassment in the Workplace: Is it a Problem?* (Washington, DC: U.S. Government Printing Office, 1981), p. 14.

57. U.S. Merit Systems Protection Board, *Sexual Harassment in the Workplace*, p. 14.

58. Morgan, 'Sexual Harassment', p. 212.

59. LeMoncheck and Hajdin, *Sexual Harassment: A Debate*, p. 12.

situation, for 'naming reality' will 'challenge the prevailing view that sexual harassment is natural and normal.'[60]

A key by-product of the normalization of gender harassment is therefore that redress for its victims becomes extremely problematic, since it involves 'questioning who decides "what counts" as victimization and who defines its meaning and seriousness.'[61] Since one cannot question the power structure without negative consequences, gender harassment actually becomes fortified or protected by women's coping response of *minimizing*—known in research circles as the 'nothing-really-happened' response.[62] There is huge pressure brought to bear on women to accept the advice of others not to 'over-react' to 'normal' behavior that was 'not intended to cause discomfort.'[63] As with all forms of violence and exploitation, women's ability to resist or challenge harassment depends on the degree to which they are valued as females in their culture. The more patriarchal the culture, the less women's capacity to resist.

Some women have gradually begun to resist the institutionalized forms of patriarchy that subsidize gender harassment in their societies, such as judicial systems that refuse to penalise men for harassment because holding harassers accountable is seen as 'interfering' with culturally sanctioned ways of doing things.[64] Such resistance, however, is a hugely daunting challenge in the patriarchal context of Oceania, and most efforts by Oceanian women to date have focused on addressing the more overt forms of male violence, such as wife-battering, sexual assault and rape.[65] Seeking legal redress for gender harassment is so daunting precisely because, when patriarchal cultural values are challenged in the justice system, such resistance becomes 'treacherous ground to travel.'[66] Women

60. Kelly and Radford, 'Nothing Really Happened', p. 19.
61. Kelly and Radford, 'Sexual Violence Against Women and Girls', p. 71.
62. Kelly and Radford, 'Sexual Violence Against Women and Girls', p. 74.
63. Gnanadason, *No Longer a Secret*, p. 21.
64. See, the work by S. Razack on the problem of cultural sanctions for gender abuse and harassment, 'What is to be Gained by Looking White People in the Eye? Culture, Race and Gender in Cases of Sexual Violence', *Signs: Journal of Women in Culture and Society* 19:4 (1994): pp. 24–48.
65. In the Oceanian context, significant work in the areas of counseling and advocacy has been done by organizations such as the Fiji Women's Crisis Centre, Fiji Women's Rights Movement, and FemLink Pacific.
66. Razack, 'What is to be Gained', p. 28.

who resist are made to feel that they are being disloyal to their culture.

Women's Vulnerability to Harassment

Why is it that women are so vulnerable to harassment? Why is it that so many women, even otherwise self-confident women, are said to 'allow' harassment to happen to them? Women who are victims of the more explicitly sexual forms of gender harassment are sometimes accused by feminists of naiveté. They are asked questions such as: 'Why did you miss the danger signs?' 'Why did you let yourself in for this?' 'Why did you go to his office alone?' — and so on.

In part, women's naiveté is a function of the cleverness of men's harassing behavior referred to earlier: It can often be difficult for women to distinguish 'safe' from 'unsafe' male behaviour, as harassing behavior may begin in a 'safe zone' and move with great subtlety into an 'unsafe zone.' This is particularly the case with respect to harassment by clergy and other men in positions of respect and authority. Thus, in the first instance, women can be vulnerable to harassment precisely because they have been indoctrinated to respect men, and because the beginnings of harassment can at times appear to be innocent.

But this is by no means the whole story. Many women are not naive. They may not have sufficient awareness to say 'this is harassment,' but they know that what is happening makes them feel uncomfortable, or worse. They know that something is wrong, yet they have been conditioned into silence or acquiescence. They are vulnerable to harassment because they intuitively know the negative consequences for themselves of resisting it. In one study, even in a relatively open, egalitarian Western context only 24% of harassment victims told anyone at all, and less than 12% attempted any formal action.[67] Their reluctance to report harassment was well-founded: Less than 1% of all sexual harassment claims are ever heard in court, and only one-third of those find in favor of the victim.[68]

---

67. U.S. Merit Systems Protection Board, *Sexual Harassment in the Federal Government Workplace* (Washington, DC: U.S. Government Printing Office, 1992), p. 57.

68. See, D. Terpestra and D. Baker, 'Outcomes of Sexual Harassment Charges', *Academy of Management Journal* 31:1 (1988): pp. 181–90.

Women's Coping Mechanisms

In the face of harassment they feel powerless to resist head-on, women develop a variety of coping mechanisms. Perhaps the most common such mechanism is to 'cultivate an immune system' that makes it appear that they are indifferent to their harassment—as we saw above, to 'pretend that nothing happened.'[69] Victims may engage in self-censuring behaviors by, for example, 'imposing restrictions of time, space and movement upon themselves.'[70] This can include a variety of forms of avoidance,[71] such as female students changing courses to avoid being near a certain teacher, or the pattern of the Pacific Theological College student wife in our case study in Chapter Six who goes to great lengths to avoid crossing the path of a harassing male student on campus.

Avoidance is a common reaction in all patriarchal cultures, where women are conditioned not to question male hegemonic power because they know that 'women who challenge male dominance are at much greater risk than those who comply.'[72] As we have already noted, they are, above all, at risk of being labeled as traitors to their culture, a risk perceived to be greater than that of resisting harassment.

Disempowered by this immune system that has been forced upon them, women are left with a variety of inadequate 'explanations' for the harassment they have experienced, and for why they can do nothing to resist it. Among the most common are statements such as the following—all of which we have heard from harassment victims at Pacific Theological College: *I was not sure about his intentions* (in cases of the 'grey area' behaviors noted above); *It must have somehow been my fault* (the self-doubt and self-blame so endemic to women's gendered experience in a patriarchal ethos); *I really care about him and I just can't call his reputation into question* (men's needs always take precedence); *I know my own credibility will be called into question if I tell anyone* (not only because the harassment is normalized but because it usually takes place in such a way that the woman's

69. Gnanadason, *No Longer a Secret*, p. 11.

70. Gnanadason, *No Longer a Secret*, p. 12.

71. For a discussion of female victims' avoidance and escape mechanisms, see J. Gruber, 'How Women Handle Sexual Harassment', *Social Science Research* 74:1 (1989): pp. 3–7; and B. Gutek, A. Groff and A. Tsui, 'Reactions to Perceived Sex Discrimination', *Human Relations* 49:6 (1996): pp. 791–814.

72. Morgan, 'Sexual Harassment', p. 215.

evidence cannot be corroborated—it's 'my word against his'—and the powers-that-be are predisposed to believe *his* word). [73]

This female self-censuring coping mechanism in the face of harassment is exacerbated by the fact that, in the power imbalance inherent in patriarchy, it is women who are always held responsible for 'negotiating and maintaining relationships;' hence, in the case of sexual forms of harassment, women can even be inculcated with a sense of guilt for not appreciating men's supposed 'flattery.'[74] If they do not willingly assume this burden for upholding the normative relational power (im)balance, attempts will be made by male authority figures to impose it on them. This is precisely what we will see in our case study in Chapter Six in which the male authority figure in a theological college responds to a woman's plea for help (regarding a voyeur) by saying, 'maybe he just enjoys seeing you with no clothes on'—as though the woman should actually feel flattered! As so often happens, the woman was doubly harassed: first by the man who was stalking her on campus, and again by the man to whom she went for help.

The consequence of the many forms of self-censure which fortify women's 'harassment immune system' is that women become voiceless victims. *Webster's Dictionary* defines a victim as 'one who is acted on ... adversely affected by a force or agent ... is sacrificed and suffers a loss.'[75] As Marie Fortune reminds us, traditionally, in religious usage, a victim has been someone who is sacrificed to a deity. Women who suffer the effects of harassment in silence have thus been described as 'victims sacrificed to the worship of patriarchy.'[76] The end result is clear: '*to be a victim is to be made powerless.*'[77] Female victims of harassment internalize the paradox of, on the one hand, their *responsibility* (to maintain the status quo of the relational power imbalance) and, on the other hand, their *powerlessness* (to change this status-quo).

Further Effects of Harassment

The litany of negative effects of gender harassment on women is long indeed. A number of excellent studies in recent years have

73. For an elaboration of these and other 'nothing-really-happened' explanations by women victims, see Cooper-White, *The Cry of Tamar*, pp. 72–3.

74. LeMoncheck and Hajdin, *Sexual Harassment: A Debate*, p. 8.

75. *Webster's Dictionary* (New York: Simon and Schuster, 1979), p. 532.

76. Fortune, 'Religious Issues and Violence Against Women', p. 374.

77. Fortune, 'Religious Issues and Violence Against Women', p. 374.

investigated these consequences, and it is interesting to discover that, although the coping mechanisms and access to redress may differ from culture to culture, the psychological effects are remarkably similar across cultures—whether the victims are well-educated women from highly industrialized Western societies or rural village women from a Two-Thirds World context. Thus, although the overt reaction of a white European feminist may differ from that of a Pacific Islander woman, the internalized feelings of such disparate women have been shown to be virtually identical. There is no space here to enumerate the whole range of disastrous consequences of gender harassment for women's lives, but we will attempt to summarize key features.

We begin with the experience of those few women who do manage to 'name' and challenge the harassment they experience. The primary consequence for them is that of *isolation*. They are stigmatized as trouble-makers, and labelled as 'hysterical, irrational or humourless.'[78] They are made to feel discredited. They can only avoid this estrangement and labeling if they sacrifice their own sense of integrity by keeping silent.

Then there is the genuine sense of *fear* which many victims of gender harassment often experience. Male harassers create fear by 'demonstrating that any man may choose to invade a woman's personal space, physically or psychologically.'[79] The fear entailed in harassment is not always a matter of 'what did happen' but a sense of dread about 'what might happen.' Harassment carries with it an implicit sense of threat and uncertainty, a feeling that some sort of sexual coercion *could* possibly happen in the future ('what might he do next?').[80] This vague sense of anxiety is present even in cases of seemingly innocuous 'street harassment,' as will be evident in our case study in Chapter Six of young girls' experiences of being harassed while walking along the seawall in Fiji.

The self-censuring coping mechanisms described in the previous section in themselves create all sorts of *psychological stresses* and strains for women who are victims of harassment. To participate in avoidance, secrecy and silencing—to be powerless—is to be forced to deny one's very self. One study of the effects of gender harassment across a broad spectrum of cultures has detailed a

78. Stanko, 'Reading Danger', p. 54.
79. Webb, *Global Impact of Sexual Harassment*, p. 39.
80. Kelly and Radford, 'Nothing Really Happened', p. 22.

number of common psychological side-effects of this self-violation: embarrassment, nervousness, decreased ability to concentrate, withdrawal, anxiety, unexpressed anger, unjustified guilt, erosion of feelings of satisfaction, and physical stress symptoms such as insomnia, headaches, fatigue and stomach ailments.[81] In one study, fully 63% of harassment victims associated *physical illness* with their harassment.[82] Other studies have highlighted the overwhelming sense of *humiliation* which victims of harassment experience — humiliation that can produce not only physical symptoms but emotional distress, depression, helplessness, and social isolation.[83]

Still other research has unearthed the fact that 'the greater the power disparity (between harasser and harassed), the more distressing the experience is likely to be' for the victim.[84] Female victims feel the most extreme sense of violation when the harasser is someone entrusted with their care, or someone in a position of authority whom they respect.[85] Nowhere is this experienced more acutely than when the harasser is a pastor or priest, a dilemma to which we will return in Chapter Five. The core experience in this type of harassment can be epitomized as one of loss — loss of trust in men and in themselves. The latter can be associated with the loss of self-esteem, dignity, or reputation.

*   *   *

In this chapter we have traced the contours of the various strands of violence against women, both overt and covert. We have seen how all forms of violence against women can be traced back to the male abuse of power associated with patriarchy. We have seen the dire consequences of every manifestation of violence against women

81. Colbert, *Dealing with Sexual Harassment*, p. 39.

82. The relationship between gender harassment and stress-related illnesses has been examined in P. Crull, 'The Stress Effects of Sexual Harassment on the Job,' *American Journal of Orthopsychiatry* 52 (1981): pp. 539–44.

83. These long-term psychological effects have been documented in studies such as M.P. Koss, 'Changed Lives', in Michele Paludi (ed.), *Ivory Power* (New York: SUNY Press, 1993), pp. 73–92; and E. Van Roosmalen and S. McDonald, 'Sexual Harassment in Academia: A Hazard to Women's Health', *Women and Health* 28: 2 (1998): pp. 33–55.

84. Morgan, 'Sexual Harassment', p. 216. See, also, D. Benson and G. Thompson, 'Sexual Harassment on a University Campus: The Confluence of Authority Relations, Sexual Interest, and Gender Stratifications', *Social Problems* 29: 3 (1992): pp. 236–51.

85. This phenomenon has been analyzed in depth by Rutter, in *Sex in the Forbidden Zone*.

for women: their increased vulnerability, victimization, silencing, physical and psychological damaging. Against the backdrop of this general overview of the many manifestations of violence against women, we now turn our attention to the social and cultural context of violence against women in one particular region of the world: the Pacific Islands nations of Oceania. We would guess that what we find there mirrors in many ways the situation in other parts of the developing world.

Chapter Three

CONTEXTUALIZING THE FABRIC OF PATRIARCHAL VIOLENCE:
VIOLENCE AGAINST WOMEN IN OCEANIA

In this chapter we situate the problem of violence against women
in a particular social location by examining the intertwining strands
that contribute to its distinctive character in Oceania. Like the
causative strands described in Chapter One which, when woven
together, sustain an interconnected global culture of violence, there
are a number of discrete yet interrelated sociological and cultural
realities in Oceania that create the conditions in which violence
against women manifests itself in this part of the world.

By way of introduction, it should be noted that Oceanian societies
are small, fragile island nations which are vulnerable to the
machinations of larger, more powerful external forces and, at the
same time, loyal to deeply ingrained indigenous cultural values.
Underlying Oceanian patriarchal values have commingled with the
overlay of patriarchal values introduced through the onslaught of
Western colonization. The interplay of these value systems has
created a hybrid culture of patriarchy that has drastically impacted
upon the lives of the inhabitants of the island nations in Oceania.

As the tides of social change swept over the shores of Oceania in
the colonial and post-colonial eras, what was considered a necessary
hardening of gender role divisions (in order to maintain the
cohesiveness of indigenous communities) contributed to a further
marginalization of women over time. This rigid role stratification
has resulted in a social ethos that supports the exploitation of
Oceanian women and explains the crawling pace of progress for
these women.[1]

---

1. This view has also been articulated by Keiti Ann Kanongata'a, in 'A Pacific
Women's Theology of Birthing and Liberation', *Pacific Journal of Theology* II: 7 (1992):
p. 6.

The rapid social changes in recent decades, in the rush to embrace modernization and 'development,' have in many ways worsened the situation of women across the region. University of the South Pacific researcher, Clare Slatter, contends that women's increasing inequality in island societies that are racing to gain a foothold in the world economy 'is one of the main factors contributing to violence against women.'[2]

The following sections will examine several current social and cultural realities which have a bearing on this widespread and worsening scenario of violence against women across the region. Because the patterns of globalization are replicated across cultures, we suspect that the social realities we describe in Oceania may well be mirrored fairly closely in other non-Western 'developing' countries.

The Impact of Socio-Economic Forces on Oceanian Women

The End Results of Globalization

The most pervasive worldwide economic development in recent decades has been the ideology of capitalist 'free market' principles known as *globalization*. In the most positive sense, globalization could suggest a view of 'the world as One humankind and One ecosystem in its interdependence ... [envisioning] a life in dignity for all (human and non-human beings) and with fair participation of everyone.'[3] Unfortunately, this idealistic vision has been far outweighed by the harsh reality that globalization has 'reduced the world in all its diversity to a monotonous single model of economy, culture and political system, dominated through a few decision-makers and giving highest priority to economic values only.'[4]

2.   Clare Slatter, 'Violence Against Women: The Social, Political and Economic Factors', paper presented, Consultation on Violence Against Women, Bergengren House, Suva, Fiji, 1992.

3.   Christoph Stückelberger, 'Globalization: Ethical Perspectives', unpublished article in the authors' possession, April, 2003, p. 2. Stückelberger is a professor at the University of Basel, Switzerland. For a similar view, see 'Is Free Trade Really Beneficial?' (13 March 2003), on-line at http://www.aworld connected.org.

4.   Stückelberger, 'Globalization: Ethical Perspectives', p. 3. He suggests the alternative term 'Oikolization – global sustainable development in five dimensions (cultural, religious, ecological, economic and social)' as the ethical response to Globalization, and points out that 'Oikolization seeks to establish a balance between a globalized form of ethics and a contextualized form of ethics.'

There are of course many nuanced definitions of globalization.[5] But for the majority of the world's peoples, especially those in the non-Western world, it is merely a new mask superimposed over an already existing Western capitalist economic hegemony. Behind the contemporary mask is the old face of the patriarchal ideologies of colonialism and imperialism that now promise a globally interconnected community for all who can afford to live in the global village. It is a system that breeds materialism and consumerism and benefits a tiny privileged elite, leaving the majority to suffer through the exploitation of both natural resources and human resources (through cheap labor).

Oceanian societies have found themselves caught up in this ideology of global market integration which benefits wealthy developed nations at the expense of small, poor nations with weak economies such as those in Oceania. Being at a further disadvantage due to their geographic isolation and small size, they easily fall prey to the powers that control global markets and profits — not only the powerful nation states but multinational corporations and financial bodies such as the World Trade Organization, World Bank and International Monetary Fund, which 'pull the strings' of globalization.

In the Oceanian context, Clare Slatter has examined the question, 'What has globalization meant for the Pacific, and why does it concern us as women?'[6] Slatter's research demonstrates that the free-market philosophy which undergirds globalization has dictated that the only way Oceanian societies can compete in the global marketplace is by keeping wages low, removing or diluting wage regulations that protect workers, and cutting back on social services. She summarizes the effects on Oceanian societies in this way:

> The economic growth policies are opening up new avenues for private wealth accumulation by enterprising individuals (who are economically and/or politically well-placed to take advantage of them) and, at the same time, eroding the living standards of ordinary people ... who form the majority of our populations. Consequently, *poverty is visibly*

5.   For further definitions of globalization, see, for instance, David Andrews, 'What is Globalization, and What is an Ethical Response?', *Witness* (Fall, 2002): pp. 15–21; and Carmen Lora, 'Globalization and its Effects in Latin America, Especially on Women' (2002), on-line at http://www.mtsusidelines.com/ news/2002/1 0/02.

6.   Clare Slatter, 'Women and Political/Economic Issues', in *Women's Theology: Pacific Perspectives* (Suva, Fiji: SPATS, 1996), p. 62.

> *increasing in island countries and ... especially in female-headed households,*
> *which are steadily on the rise.*[7] (Italics added)

There are many faces of this increasing poverty. In return for desperately needed loans, international enforcers of globalization such as the IMF and the World Bank require developing countries to adhere to Structural Adjustment Programs (SAPS) centered around privitization of state assets, opening of local markets to foreign ownership (guaranteeing low wages), and so on. These countries pass along their spiraling indebtedness to their citizens through further draconian measures.

In Oceania, for example, 'the introduction of Value Added Taxes ... in Fiji and Samoa and the withdrawal of state-subsidised housing have inflicted particular hardship on the poor.'[8] Rising costs in education as a result of reduced government allocations have caused a major decline in the numbers of children attending school. And, as Slatter points out, since 'the choices forced by poverty entail gender bias,'[9] more girls than boys have dropped out of school because it is assumed that, since boys will become the breadwinners, their education is more important than girls'.

Slatter has more to say about the growing feminization of poverty in Oceania. She cites statistics indicating that 56% of all female-headed households in Fiji live in poverty, and that 80% of families needing urgent housing assistance in Fiji are headed by women, 'mostly deserted wives and the unemployed.'[10] The grim statistics continue (and since the latest reliable statistics are from the mid- to late 1990s, discounting the dire economic effects of a coup and civil unrest in the early 2000s, the actual statistics today are likely to be much worse):

> A majority of the 10,900 workers in the garment industry[11] who earn
> the minimum weekly wage of F$38 a week are poor women, mostly

7.   Slatter, 'Women and Political', p. 63.

8.   Slatter, 'Women and Political', p. 64. For a larger discussion of the nature of poverty in the Fijian context, see Kevin Barr, *Poverty in Fiji* (Suva, Fiji: Fiji Forum for Justice, Peace and the Integrity of Creation, 1990).

9.   Slatter, 'Women and Political', p. 64.

10. Slatter, 'Women and Political', p. 64.

11. The garment industry in Fiji is largely owned and controlled by foreign business interests, which were given huge tax breaks to invest in Fiji following the military coups and subsequent economic collapse in the late 1980s; this industry remains severely under-regulated today. For an analysis of how women are exploited and abused in the garment industry, see Ilisapeci Meo, 'The Role of the Church in Combating the

> with dependents, who have few alternative employment options. The rise in teenage prostitution, female suicide, and infanticide are additional indicators of the feminization of poverty. *The increasing incidence of female-directed violence suggests that women bear the brunt of the pressures of economic crises.*[12] (Italics added)

Amelia Kinahoi Siamomua has also addressed the feminization of poverty in Oceania, and the ensuing need to 're-allocate resources to ensure women's survival.'[13] Speaking at the Pacific Regional Workshop on Strengthening Partnerships for Eliminating Violence Against Women in Fiji in 2003, she concluded, 'In order for violence to cease being a daily reality for women in our region ..., we must work towards more equal power relations between women and men.'[14]

A related economic factor is women's almost complete financial dependence on men in Oceanian societies.[15] While this stems from the cultural ethos (which we will discuss later in this chapter), we mention it here because of its bearing on violence against women in that abusive husbands or partners know that their women cannot leave them since they have no independent means of economic survival. This leaves women 'trapped,' and as Winston Halapua has observed, 'from such traps women and children have very grim hopes of emerging unscathed.'[16]

The rise in poverty and unemployment in recent years has only exacerbated this problem, as not only women but greater numbers of men find themselves unemployed or marginally employed. Their frustration at their own loss of power is often taken out on their spouses or partners. Because these abused women have no way to survive on their own they have no option but to remain at home, on the receiving end of ever-increasing violence.

Exploitation of Women Garment Workers in Fiji', M.Th. thesis, Pacific Theological College, 1993.

12. Meo, 'The Role of the Church', p. 34.

13. Amelia Kinahoi Siamomua, address, Pacific Regional Workshop on Strengthening Partnerships for Eliminating Violence Against Women, Pacific Forum Secretariat, Suva, Fiji, 17–19 February 2003.

14. Siamomua, Pacific Regional Workshop.

15. See the discussion of this issue by Lisa Meo, 'Asserting Women's Dignity in a Patriarchal World', in Johnson and Filemoni-Tofaeono (eds.), *Weavings*, p. 153.

16. Winston Halapua, 'Militarism and the Moral Decay in Fiji', *Fijian Studies* 1/1 (2003): p. 112.

Iosefa Maiava, Deputy Secretary of the Pacific Islands Forum Secretariat, frames the relationship between economics and violence against women in utilitarian terms:

> … from a developmental perspective, violence against women … is a waste of resources. This is because violence reduces women's opportunities to earn for their families, and limits their mobility and their participation in community life and development activities. It imposes restrictions on women's economic and political participation.[17]

Hence, even a pragmatic economic philosophy ought to acknowledge that the 'rules of the game' of globalization and free-market capitalism, which have had the end result of placing increasing numbers of Oceanian women at risk, come at the expense of social stability and well-being. As just one example, the Reserve Bank of Fiji has conservatively estimated that violence against women costs government and business approximately F$300 million annually.[18]

It is clear, then, that the economic inequities which go hand in hand with post-modern globalization have contributed to rising poverty in Oceania, and that this has been especially disastrous for women. As women's status has become ever more precarious in society, they have become increasingly vulnerable to abuse. Poverty breeds violence, and as more Oceanian men experience economic uncertainty themselves, they tend to take out their frustrations on women in violent ways. The following section examines other social forces in Oceania which are contributing to a rise in acts of violence against women.

The End Results of Social Stress

A number of researchers have documented the increased incidence and severity of all forms of violence against women in situations of acute social stress. Recent studies have highlighted the extent to which violence against women is exacerbated by social upheaval and by societies' recourse to violence as a means of 'solving' social problems.[19] Given the growing social unrest and reliance on force

17. Iosefa Maiava, paper presented, Pacific Regional Workshop on Strengthening Partnerships for Eliminating Violence Against Women, Pacific Forum Secretariat, Suva, Fiji, 17–19 February, 2003.

18. Cited in Edwina Kotoisuva, 'Domestic Violence: A View from the Fiji Women's Crisis Centre', *Pacific Journal of Theology* II: 30 (2003): p. 43.

19. See especially, Monica McWilliams, 'Violence Against Women in Societies Under Stress', in Dobash and Dobash (eds.), *Rethinking Violence Against Women.*

in the face of social conflicts in Oceania — most notably in Fiji, the Solomon Islands, Papua New Guinea and, more recently, Tonga — it is imperative that we address the impact of societal stress and breakdown on the incidence of violence against women in the region.

In international studies on this issue, *societies under stress* have been defined as those undergoing rapid modernization, facing civil disorder or internal tensions, or confronted with political upheaval.[20] It has been found that, when the use of force becomes normative in society, or when key social players 'take the law into their own hands,' violence against women increases as part of a 'pervasive and interactive system for legitimizing violence.'[21]

The most common association of societal violence and violence against women is the widespread incidence of rape and sexual assault in times of war or armed conflict, where male power is 'buttressed' through the abuse of women's bodies seen as a symbol of 'victorious conquest.'[22] This phenomenon was noted in our general discussion of the relationship between violence against women and militarism in Chapter One. Conversely, men also buttress their sense of power through acts of violence against women when this power is threatened in times of economic or political instability — for example, as we saw in the previous section, when men find themselves unemployed, or otherwise on the losing end of economic power.

Both of these realities are confirmed in the rising incidence of domestic and other forms of violence against women in Fiji since the 1987 and 2000 coups, during the civil war on the island of Bougainville in the 1990s, and in the Solomon Islands since interethnic warfare has erupted in recent years. Winston Halapua's research has shown how the militaristic ethos in Fiji has contributed to social stress in numerous ways, including 'weakening the economic strength of the nation, thereby creating stress within the family unit ..., (and) leading to a breakdown in law and order.'[23]

The dramatic rise in cases of domestic violence since the 2000 coup in Fiji is one of the end results. Referring to the economic fall-out of the coup, Susan Boyd has also observed that 'it is the women

<hr>

20. McWilliams, 'Violence Against Women', p. 112.

21. McWilliams, 'Violence Against Women', p. 113.

22. This phenomenon has been analyzed in H. McCollum, Liz Kelly and Jill Radford, 'Wars Against Women', *Trouble and Strife* 28 (1994): pp. 12–18.

23. Halapua, 'Militarism and the Moral Decay in Fiji', p. 111.

who, in times of economic crisis, are the first to be laid off work, for they occupy the lower paid jobs and, because of their duties at home … they are often those in part-time or casual employment who are the first to be let go.'[24] The ensuing loss of family income and stability, and the shame which that entails, particularly for men, has clearly contributed to accelerated levels of domestic violence in Fiji, as in other Oceanian societies under stress.

The increased incidence of harassment of women and girls by groups of young Fijian men since the 2000 coup is likewise alarming. But most shocking has been the skyrocketing of cases of rape and sexual assault, based on the case loads of organizations such as the Fiji Women's Crisis Centre. The Centre has confirmed a direct correlation between the flow-on effects of social unrest and negative impacts on women, seen in 'a multitude of factors: job losses, pay cuts, fear and insecurity … family tensions … and emotional trauma.'[25]

In the broader socio-political atmosphere in several parts of Oceania, where it has become permissible to take the law into one's own hands, it is no wonder that increasing numbers of young Oceanian men feel they have license to sexually or otherwise exploit women. The reality is that, in societies under stress, prevailing patriarchal attitudes about women sanction the acceleration of levels of violence against women.

The de-stabilizing effects of conflict situations also means that authorities are even less capable than usual of responding to situations of violence against women. This, in turn, only reinforces men's freedom to commit acts of violence against women with impunity. In such situations there are 'fewer options for women and fewer controls on men.'[26] This is so because 'permission is granted, metaphorically speaking, for men to assert or reassert their power and dominance.'[27]

In the Oceanian context, this dynamic is clearly in evidence in settings such as post-coup Fiji. On the simplest level, 'the general

24. Susan Boyd, keynote address, Third Regional Meeting of the Pacific Women's Network on Violence Against Women, Fiji Women's Crisis Centre, Korolevu, Suva, Fiji, 19 February–2 March 2001, p. 4.

25. Fiji Women's Crisis Centre, *The Impact of the May 19 Coup on Women in Fiji* (Suva, Fiji: Fiji Women's Crisis Centre, 2001), p. 1.

26. McWilliams, 'Violence Against Women', p. 138.

27. McWilliams, 'Violence Against Women', p. 138.

breakdown in law and order following the coups has tended to see it [violence against women] placed much lower on the police force's priorities, since there are always more "serious" cases of violence and other law and order problems to tackle first.'[28] But additionally, given the routinization of violence in society, police and other authorities are even less disposed to address violence against women since they have become some of its worst perpetrators. The Fiji Women's Crisis Centre has attempted to expose the high levels of involvement of the police and military in acts of violence against women,[29] and Halapua further discloses how acts of violence against women have 'intensified' in a social environment in which 'police are embroiled in lawlessness ... and can escape their crimes ... [and] the military can get away with illegalities.'[30]

This mentality is aggravated in societies which have traditionally sanctioned aggressive male behavior. We are well aware that there is not one monolithic construct known as Oceanian culture. Oceania obviously comprises many cultures, some more or less aggressive than others. However, it is fair to state that male aggression has played a significant role in the history of inter-tribal warfare in many Pacific Islands cultures. This tradition continues today in the violent outworkings of the various socio-political conflicts referred to earlier, and even perhaps in the near obsession of at least some of the Polynesian cultures with the violent sport of rugby. This heritage of male aggression, in turn, is reflected in the upsurge in acts of violence against women in the Oceanian societies facing the greatest social stress today.

This observation, regarding the interplay between the negative effects of contemporary social stress on women and pre-existing cultural conventions, is a perfect example of how the various strands which weave together the fabric of violence against women complement each other. We certainly cannot hope to understand the context of violence against women in Oceania without a full and frank consideration of the role which culture plays in that context.

28. Hapalua, 'Militarism and the Moral Decay in Fiji', p. 113.
29. See Fiji Women's Crisis Centre, *The Impact of the May 19 Coup*, p. 26.
30. Halapua, 'Militarism and the Moral Decay in Fiji', p. 113.

The Impact of Culture on Oceanian Women

The guiding life principles of Oceanian cultures are the honor of the extended family and clan, respect for the traditional values of communal solidarity and reciprocity, and respect for origins (people, land and sea).[31] Pacific Islanders grow up knowing exactly what roles they are expected to play in the family and community. They reciprocate the love and protection they receive through a clearly prescribed set of obligations to family and community. Like most other non-Western peoples, their collective identity is much more important than their individual identity. It is this closely knit familial and communal matrix that defines Pacific Islanders.

The mutual web of obligations to others is treasured and embraced by most Pacific Islanders. The core Oceanian values of generosity, hospitality and respect for authority are ingrained into the very fiber of their beings. These obligations, however, can also be burdensome at times, and this is particularly true for women, who must maintain cultural responsibilities while also meeting the expectations of husbands (and elders) and being the primary care-givers and upholders of harmony in their families.

The status and roles of Oceanian women vary somewhat, depending on the cultural traditions of each island nation or ethnic group. Hence the treatment of women in some Oceanian cultures is more respectful than in others.[32] Women themselves hold different stances regarding their status in their respective cultures. While some emphasize the central role they play in their culture—for instance, the Samoan woman's respected role in the sister-brother covenant (*feagaiga*)[33] and occasionally even as a chief (*matai*)[34]—others

31. The latter has been integrated into theological reflection by Oceanian contextual theologians such as Ama'amalele Tofaeono (Samoa), Sevati Tuwere (Fiji) and Cliff Bird (Solomon Islands).

32. This is detailed in Vanessa Griffen, *Development and Empowerment: A Pacific Feminist Perspective* (Suva, Fiji: Star, 1989), p. 24.

33. For an elaboration on the concept see Penelope Schoeffel, 'The Samoan Concept of *Feagaiga* and its Transformation', in J. Huntsman (ed.), *Tonga and Samoa: Images of Gender and Polity*, (Christchurch, NZ: Macmillan Brown Centre for Pacific Studies, 1998), pp. 85–105. *Feagaiga* is also discussed from a theological perspective by Faatauva'a Tapuai, Roina Tapuai Faatauva'a and later Michiko Ete-Lima in their theses or research projects at Pacific Theological College.

34. This has been discussed by, among others, Fetaomi Tapu-Qilio, in 'Singing the Lord's Song in a Strange Land: The Theological Quest of Young Exiles of the Pacific', in Johnson and Filemoni-Tofaeono (eds.), *Weavings*, p. 178.

question the viability or applicability of the cultural values that appear to hold women in high regard.[35] What can be asserted unequivocally is that all Oceanian cultures are patriarchal, even though there are matriarchal elements in some sub-cultures and clan groupings. The following section characterizes this Oceanian strand of patriarchy in relation to its implications for the problem of violence against women.

The Cultural Face of Patriarchy in Oceania

An underlying premise of Oceanian cultures is that women's status and roles are circumscribed by the dictates of natural law. Akuila Yabaki, reflecting on the relationship between Oceanian culture and violence against women, has stated that,

> Traditional gender roles in many Pacific societies have been premised on women's biological capacity to bear children, and a division of labor believed to be dictated by nature and divine decree... Violence against women and children is a serious consequence...[36]

This 'natural law' argument for women's lower status in relation to men, and their restriction to inferior domestic roles, is echoed across the region. Mine Pase has analyzed how this inferior status is manifested in Samoan culture (even where, as noted above, there is ostensibly high regard for the sister):

> Samoa is a male-oriented culture, and women still hold a sub-dominant place in society. In a traditional cultural event... it is not uncommon for a woman of esteemed calibre or high social standing to be serving from the back, unrecognized. In a political setting, she may be the boss, but in her own village among chiefs' wives, she is a mere servant. ... In some severe cases, women are not even supposed to be seen, as in a royal *'ava* (kava) ceremony. Women are looked down upon as not good enough to prepare or serve, let alone partake of it. ... In short, as children are in some cultures, so are women in our Samoan culture — they are to be seen but not heard.[37]

---

35. This is explicated by Fana'afi Aiono, 'Western Samoa: The Sacred Covenant', in Cema Bolabola *et al.* (eds.), *Land Rights of Pacific Women* (Suva, Fiji: Institute of Pacific Studies/University of the South Pacific, 1986a), pp. 96–115.

36. Akuila Yabaki, paper presented, Pacific Regional Workshop on Strengthening Partnerships for Eliminating Violence Against Women, Pacific Forum Secretariat, Suva, Fiji, 17–19 February 2003.

37. Mine Pase, 'Gospel and Culture: Samoan Style', in Johnson and Filemoni-Tofaeono (eds.), *Weavings*, p. 72.

Other Oceanian women have pointed out that, although women do have some influence in certain contexts, especially in the few matrilineal sub-cultures of Oceania, this influence is limited, since it is still men who make the final or important decisions.[38] Hence, while many island cultures claim that women are important, the practical benefits of that 'importance' are negligible.[39] Oceanian women are 'valued' primarily for their role as helpers to men; they are overwhelmingly seen as derivative of men.[40]

There is therefore often a huge gap between the cultural rhetoric of praise for women and the reality 'on the ground.' In analyzing violence against Kanak (Melanesian) women in the New Caledonian (Kanaky) context, Yandro Pelletier has questioned why 'there is such a disparity between public praise of women, or rather of their traditional role, and the harsh reality of the courtroom or medical clinics.'[41] She continues:

> Official rhetoric pays lip service to Kanak women's traditional role, but when a more in-depth analysis of the social relationships between the sexes is made, it soon becomes apparent that they are based on an unequivocal ideology of male domination that sanctions inequalities in relationships between men and women, in both symbolic and physical terms.[42]

This analysis is echoed by other Oceanian commentators who have noted that gender relations in the region are 'characterized by inequalities of power, opportunity, and access to resources ... these relations are closely linked to cycles of violence that maintain low levels of status and high levels of victimization of women and girls.'[43]

38. Alice Pollard, 'Solomon Islands', in Taiamoni Tagamoa (ed.), *Pacific Women: Roles and Status of Women in Pacific Societies* (Suva, Fiji: Institute of Pacific Studies/ University of the South Pacific, 1988), p. 43.

39. Keiti Ann Kanongata'a, paper presented, EATWOT Consultation, Southern Cross Hotel, Suva, Fiji, 1994.

40. Kanongata'a, 'A Pacific Women's Theology of Birthing and Liberation', p. 6.

41. Yandro Pelletier, 'Qualitative Study on Domestic and Sexual Violence Against Kanak Women in New Caledonia: Or, Violence Against Women as a Social and Cultural Symptom, Viewed from a Gender-based Perspective', *Report, IEDES Attachment* (Paris: University of Paris, in collaboration with the Pacific Women's Bureau of the Secretariat of the Pacific Community, Noumea, New Caledonia, 2002), p. 3.

42. Pelletier, 'Qualitative Study on Domestic and Sexual Violence', p. 3.

43. 'Overview of Efforts to Eliminate Violence Against Women in the Pacific', in *Strengthening Pacific Partnerships for Eliminating Violence Against Women: A Pacific Regional Workshop Report, Suva, Fiji Islands, 17–19 February 2003* (Suva, Fiji: Commonwealth

In some Oceanian cultures this subordination of women is quite striking. This is evident in Fiji, for instance, where women are frequently 'seen but not heard'—and at times not even seen—in traditional ceremonies and other important gatherings.[44]

Women grow up knowing clearly that men are the leading figures, and that women are the mute supporters through their roles as child-bearers and home-makers.[45] In other Melanesian cultures, the customs of arranged marriage and bride price are still firmly entrenched, 'reinforc[ing] the belief that women are the property of men.'[46]

Oceanian women are not only subordinate to men in the domestic sphere, but in politics and other social institutions, including the church. They rarely take part in key institutional decision-making,[47] and hence they must live with political decisions made by male leaders.[48] Even in the few instances where women are allowed a decision-making role, they are often co-opted by the patriarchal system.[49]

In many cases this means meekly accepting their token role, remaining quiet and deferring to the males in authority. This opens the door to their being manipulated by the men in charge. A few of these 'token women' who are allowed a seat at the male table may choose to act and think like the men who have the ultimate control over the institutions. As a result of being co-opted into the male leadership system, some of these women leaders come to enjoy

Secretariat, UNDP/UNIFEM, Pacific Islands Forum Secretariat, Secretariat for the Pacific Communities, 2003), p. 82.

44. See, for example, Cema Bolabola, 'Fiji: Customary Constraints and Legal Progress', in Cema Bolabola, *et al.*, (eds.), *Land Rights of Pacific Women* (Suva, Fiji: Institute of Pacific Studies, University of the South Pacific, 1986a), p. 5.

45. This has been elaborated by Meresiana Soronakadavu, 'The Traditional Role of Fijian Women, with Reference to Christian Justice', in Johnson and Filemoni-Tofaeono (eds.), *Weavings*, p. 161.

46. Ethel Sigimanu, paper presented, Pacific Regional Workshop on Strengthening Partnerships for Eliminating Violence Against Women, Pacific Forum Secretariat, Suva, Fiji, 17–19 February, 2003.

47. See the discussion by Mosikaka Moengangongo, 'Tonga', in *Pacific Women: Roles and Status of Women in the Pacific Societies*, ed. Taiamoni Tagamoa (Suva, Fiji: Institute of Pacific Studies, University of the South Pacific, 1988), p. 61.

48. Slatter, 'Political and Economic Status of Women in the Pacific'.

49. This is analyzed by Imrana P. Jalal, in *Law for Pacific Women: A Legal Rights Handbook* (Brisbane: Watson Ferguson, 1998), p. 14.

being on a pedestal and are unwilling to 'go out on a line' and take a public stand on issues of injustice. They treasure their role as historic 'firsts' — even as tokens — more than the opportunity to fight for the oppressed, including other women.

This Oceanian outworking of patriarchy has created what Fijian Lisa Meo has called an Oceanian women's *culture of silence*.[50] Following interviews conducted with a number of women at Pacific Theological College, Meo reported that these women identified the following as the root causes of this culture of silence:

- In the authoritarian, sometimes dictatorial upbringing in the family, women are ordered to keep quiet and denied an adequate education and opportunities to participate in doing important things;
- Women are dominated by men's masculinity and are thus afraid of saying the wrong things which will be laughed at;
- They lack support and encouragement from both males and females, and there is a general negative attitude toward women among leading people, including ministers and other church leaders.[51]

Clearly the consequence of this culture of silence is that most Oceanian women who are victims of violence are unable to 'name' this violence and thus they are incapable of challenging it.

The common response by men (and even some women) to the concerns noted above by Meo is that it is 'our culture' that determines the clear gender role divisions in Oceanian societies, and that since culture is sacred it cannot be questioned. This type of argumentation has been questioned by Zohl de Ishtar: 'When we challenge traditional attitudes to women [in Oceania], some people say, "Oh, but our identity, we mustn't lose our identity!" So we have to tell them that ... some traditional things should be accepted, others rejected, depending on whether they improve our society.'[52]

Finally, the patriarchal worldview that is the norm throughout Oceania has been 'strengthened by Christianity, thereby further legitimizing the oppression of Women ... [It is] because of this oppressive status [that] women are the primary victims of

---

50. See Ilisapeci Meo, 'Why Do Women Remain Silent in Meetings and Discussions with Men?', *Pacific Journal of Theology* II:3 (1990): pp. 45–47.

51. Meo, 'Why Do Women Remain Silent', p. 45.

52. Zohl de Ishtar, *Daughters of the Pacific* (Melbourne: Spinifex Press, 1994), p. 103.

violence.'[53] The church, as the most influential social institution in all Oceanian societies, has supported the culturally sanctioned gender power imbalance, and this has 'led to the view that women [who are] subject to violence should stay with their husbands'[54] because they are under men's authority by the will of God.

This interweaving of cultural and Christian patriarchy has been noted by commentators such as Judy Towandong of Papua New Guinea, who asserts that 'traditional values and norms, as well as the Judeo-Christian tradition which we have inherited with the coming of Christianity, have had a big impact on how men view women and define their role in Papua New Guinean society.'[55] Winston Halapua has further highlighted the extent to which the 'cultural construction of gender roles, sanctioned by a particular religious orientation which conditions women to take a subservient status,'[56] has exacerbated the problem of violence against women in Oceania.

In other words, Oceanian culture and Christianity have colluded to support the patriarchal foundations upon which violence against women rests. One consequence is that violence against women in Oceania has been privitized, because it cannot be openly challenged on the basis of either cultural or religious values. In Aquila Yabaki's words,

> Violence against women—rape, incest, prostitution, dowry, burning, battering, pornography—has been seen as personal violence and as a domestic problem, and thus privatized and individualized. These are crimes against half of humanity, violations of the human rights of women and a total negation of the right to be human, yet they are tolerated publicly in all social systems and ... cultural contexts.[57]

This extremely important religious strand of the fabric of violence against women will be examined in greater depth in Chapter Four. Against the backdrop of the above general description of the cultural characteristics of patriarchy in Oceania, attention is focused in the

53. Ilisapeci Meo, 'Asserting Women's Dignity in a Patriarchal World', in Johnson and Filemoni-Tofaeono (eds.), *Weavings*, p. 151.

54. 'Overview of Efforts to Eliminate Violence Against Women in the Pacific', p. 82.

55. Judy Towandong, 'Papua New Guinea: Violence Against Women', in Aruna Gnanadason, Musimbi Kanyoro and Lucia Ann McSpadden (eds.), *Women, Violence and Non-Violent Change* (Geneva: WCC Publications, 1996), p. 119.

56. Halapua, 'Militarism and the Moral Decay in Fiji', p. 114.

57. Yabaki, paper presented, Pacific Regional Workshop.

following section on the ways in which cultural myths serve as a prop or sanction for attitudes that can contribute to violence against women.

The Role of Sacred Myths in Upholding Cultural Patriarchy

Myths and legends have functioned over many generations to preserve the stories of ancient gods and spirits, heroes, heroines and ancestors in all Oceanian cultures. These stories are still told to convey and sustain the traditional life-ways of island communities. Some stories attempt to uphold core values by reminding people of the origins of things. Other narratives are told to reinforce the memories of a people's identity-forming experiences throughout history. Such narratives are considered living accounts for they are retold and reinterpreted from generation to generation.

While myths and legends have been positive sources that have defined and shaped the identity of Oceanian people, it cannot be denied that they also document and support the patriarchal foundation of Oceanian cultures. The following myth is one example of how the underlying values of a myth can be humiliating rather than life-affirming for women. In other words, even our most sacred stories can be internalized and utilized as an exploitative tool of patriarchy.

The Myth – Origin of the Rain

There lived once upon a time on one of the islands of Samoa, Tui Manua,[58] the sacred chief of the island of Manua. Tui Manua and his wife had two daughters named Sina and Aolele. Their beauty was admired by the people of Samoa and the other neighboring islands. These two young women grew up in a very protective environment. This was due not only to their being daughters of the paramount chief but also to their beauty. It was the hope of the parents that they would one day marry either a son of a sacred chief or a chief himself.

One of the sisters was so outstandingly beautiful that the news of her beauty raised the curiosity and challenged the manhood of many South Seas men, especially the sons of the sacred chiefs, if not the paramount chiefs themselves. As a result, many of them paddled over to Samoa in their canoes to contest for Sina 's hand in marriage. Among them were the Tui Tonga, Tui Fiti (Fiji),

58. The real first name is not recorded in the story. Rather, Tui, a form of address for a sacred paramount chief, indicates that this person reigned over Manua, the far-eastern islands of Samoa. The honorary address given to sacred chiefs, traditionally venerated by Samoans, has been transformed and is now known as 'king' today in the Samoan chiefly structure.

Fotuna and so forth. Despite the wealth, status and prestige which these men offered, none of them won her heart. Instead, she was attracted and fell in love with a young Samoan man who was a farmer and a nobody, whose family background was no match for hers. This made her father, the sacred chief, furious as his daughter had not only disgraced the family but also the kingship. Despite the opposition from her chiefly family, Sina insisted on marrying the man she loved. To avoid her eloping with him, the family hesitantly agreed to their marriage.

The situation became more complicated when Sina, after the wedding, informed her family of her decision to live with her husband and his family. Again, to keep the waters calm, Sina was allowed to travel with him to his island and stayed there with his family. It was a very tough experience for her as she was exposed for the first time to the life of the commoners where she had not only to provide for herself but also to serve her in-laws. She was no longer served as a princess of her islands, but she had to be a server herself, a role that is often not pleasant for married women living with their in-laws. Slowly she got used to her new lifestyle and her love for her husband helped her endure the hard challenge of being a daughter-in-law.

One day, Tui Manua dreamt of his daughter Sina. This troubled him so much that he eventually sent his other daughter, Aolele, as a messenger to tell Sina to come back home. It was believed in those days that bad luck would haunt a person who repeatedly disobeyed the sacred chief, elders or parents. Sina had to go back to her family. Before departing, Sina farewelled her husband with assuring words of her love by saying, 'my dear, it is hard but it has to be done because the consequences of disobedience will be greater than the pain of separation. I shall leave, otherwise the curse of the divine (from the sacred chief) will fall on us and the whole family. But please be assured that my heart will always be with you no matter what. Remember that I will always think of you. Whenever it rains, be reminded that those raindrops will be my overflowing tears. I will keep in touch and remind you of my love through my tears.' So, whenever it rains, the people claim that Sina is crying for her husband, and thus the origin of the rain is believed to be from the tears of Sina.[59]

In traditional societies, oral traditions were the primary means of record-keeping of important historical events and genealogical information. Myths and legends were mostly transmitted by the leaders of families and clans, who of course were predominantly men. Consequently, the way the stories were told and the characters

59. This English translation of the myth by Joan Filemoni-Tofaeono is adapted from the unpublished Samoan writings of the late Reverend Elder Filemoni Tuigamala. This is one of the versions of this particular myth. The Samoan myth traces the origin of the rain to the tears of Aosina (literally, 'white clouds') but this has been shortened over time to Sina. Rain (her tears) is believed to be a seal of Sina's love for her husband.

portrayed was a reflection of male constructions of what was important.[60]

Inevitably, then, the messages behind most of the cultural myths are belittling to women, when re-read through a feminist lens. This realization is particularly shocking when one applies a conscientized interpretive framework in analyzing the standard interpretations of these myths.

The story of the origin of the rain presents a hierarchical, patriarchal worldview. Its social, political, psychological and religious value structure was not only typical of the old Samoa but is still commonplace in most Oceanian cultures today, whose corporate well-being is assumed to be dependent upon clear distinctions between gender roles. This framework has defined the whole cultural system, in its threefold manifestations: ideational (spiritual or religious), practical (performances in terms of art or artifacts, rituals and celebrations) and material (things used to express the culture, such as pigs, fine mats, whales' teeth, and so on).

One can thus uncover through an analysis of the myth of Sina from a feminist perspective how women's stories have become instruments of patriarchal oppression in Oceanian cultures. Beneath the surface or between the lines of the story one can detect the sanctioning of the objectification and domestication of women. The following sections will elaborate how this is the case.

The Power of the Patriarch: Tui Manua, Sina's father, is the patriarch in the story, representing the center of power and authority for the family and society. His role clearly depicts the structure of traditional island society, where sacredness or divinity was vested primarily in the male chiefly figure. This is still typical of Oceanian patriarchal societies, in which women appear almost always as objects for decoration and domestication.

The almost unlimited power of the patriarch is unfortunately used as a weapon to silence any dissent or challenge to the status quo. This extreme social control may have been deemed essential in ancient island societies, as they were settled over a long period of time by successive waves of migration, which made them vulnerable to external attack and in need of strong internal social

60. For a discussion of the ways in which women have been the subjects of the sexual fantasies of men in oral traditions, see Phyllis Trible, *God and the Rhetoric of Sexuality* (Philadelphia: Fortress Press, 1978).

cohesion. However, this rationale is no longer justified today, as Oceanian societies are a part of a world community of nations, subject to international laws and safeguards.

Although a superficial reading of the myth of Sina may lead one to conclude that Sina did succeed in defying her chiefly father, by insisting on marrying the man she loved, a critical analysis makes it clear that the story is structured in such a way that, at the end of the day, the patriarch's ultimate power is reasserted. In the end, Sina must obey him.

Gender Socialization and Stereotyping: The roles of the three women in the story (Sina, Aolele, and their nameless mother) are an accurate depiction of the living reality of the majority of women in Oceania. The Tongan theologian Keiti Ann Ka'anongata'a has articulated this reality aptly:

> Traditionally, our women have been regarded as derivative. They have been considered 'natural followers' rather than leaders, supporters rather than administrators, dependents rather than providers. Even when they are praised it is usually in terms of achievement in an ancillary role. ... More often than not women are first identified as daughter of, wife of, mother of, widow of. ... In contrast, men are defined by their titles and what they do. ... Stripped of a husband's name and title, stripped of parents' names and titles, Pacific women are considered as leftovers...[61]

The women in the myth are all reared to fulfill their assigned roles: the *daughterly* role (to be meek, beautiful, and a beautifier of the home and surroundings); the *wifely* role (to be procreators of life for their husbands and caretakers for the children), and the *womanly* role (to be laborers supporting the men). The three female characters in the myth present these derivative roles very clearly. And, again, while Sina initially rebelled in defying her father's wishes, it was only to move from one subservient, derivative role (as daughter) to another (as wife). At no time did she assume any role other than a derivative one.

The Objectification of Beauty: In almost every cultural myth in Oceania, young women are 'valued' primarily in terms of their physical beauty. Having the bewitching power of beauty, however, is not a passport to freedom but a passport into the patriarchal system, for

61. Kanongata'a, 'A Pacific Women's Theology of Birthing and Liberation', p. 6.

it does not entitle one to be an equal partner in decision-making, but an ornament to be used for social decoration. From a feminist perspective, the problem in the myth of Sina is not that she happens to be beautiful, but that she is valued only for her outward appearance, rather than as a person capable of accomplishing something other than being beautiful.

This objectification of women is still the norm today in the cultures of Oceania. It can be seen, for example, in the practices of cultural dancing. Women's dance has unfortunately come to be associated with erotic enticement. The graceful, gentle movement of islander women in dance has been sold as a commodity for the pleasure of male tourists, even as an asset for the sex industry.

When women are thus objectified as sex objects, they become even more vulnerable to the violence of sexual exploitation. Just as, in the myth, it was acceptable for men to row their canoes from across the South Pacific in response to the beauty of Sina — who was to be 'sold to the highest bidder' by her father — so today sanction is given for men to come to the South Pacific from all over the world, to procure sexual favors from island women on the basis of their beauty. Like Sina, they are not valued for their intrinsic worth as human beings.

The Horizontal Oppression of Women: The daughters in the myth were beautiful, but one daughter was more beautiful than the others. This commonplace language of comparison instills and fosters jealousy and envy amongst women. Sina's status was determined by her beauty's potential as a weapon that could be used to attract and acquire fame and wealth for her father. Her extraordinary beauty and her status as a daughter of a powerful chief were convenient tools to be exploited by her father for conquest; they were vital to the strategic power plays inherent in the patriarchal system. Sina was merely a useful instrument to bring greater glory to her important family.

In contrast, Sina's sister Aolele was inevitably the second best, a comparably inferior object in relation to her more beautiful sister. She is thus automatically given the role of messenger, doing as she is bidden to serve the larger purposes of the family. She becomes nothing more than a passive agent of the oppressive system. The 'lesser' sister is unable to support Sina's desire for freedom in any way, much less to act in support of her own freedom.

The sisters' roles in the story are representative of the ways in which island women are often placed in competing positions to tame them as docile cultural persons. As we have seen previously, women's limited social roles, lack of access to education, and other restrictions prevent them from networking with and empowering each other. Women often end up fighting against each other for recognition in situations where they face extremely limited possibilities. This in-fighting shifts the focus away from the real enemy — patriarchy. Women end up contributing to their sisters' oppression by their competition for scarce domains of power.

The Internalized Submission of Women: In the myth, Sina had no option but to fulfill her domestic feminine duties of either living out her father's expectations or being obedient to her husband. In her husband's family's home, she was in some respects even less free than she had been in her privileged chiefly home. But she had learned well to internalize her submission to the culture that gave her an identity and sense of belonging.

Oceanian women are still experts in this internalization of submission. This is evidenced in the culture of silence described earlier. This is why many women feel extremely threatened when they see the rare woman break out of the patriarchal mold and assume a leadership or other high-profile role. As long as this identity of submissiveness to patriarchal authority remains internalized for most Oceanian women, they will remain powerless victims of violence, whether physical or psychological.

The Glorification of Sacrifice: In the end Sina chose to play the role of servitude to her father, sacrificing her own happiness and love. The *mana* (sacred power) of the Tui Manua was a force of fear rather than comfort or blessing. Sina sacrificed everything she desired to return to her father's home out of fear of the patriarch's power.

Oceanian cultures still glorify the sacrifices people make for the sake of the family and community, especially the sacrifices of women. Women who are victims of domestic violence are often told by male authority figures (especially male clergy) that they should be happy to sacrifice their own desires for the sake of their husband's happiness. (This 'theology of sacrifice' will be critiqued in the following chapter.)

Sina's sacrifice has been praised as an idealization of womanhood. Yet this glorification of sacrifice sidesteps the way in which the very same story devalued the worth of Sina as a human being. One may argue, again, that Sina at least initially got what she wanted. Yet when the story is unraveled, one unearths the hidden reality that Sina in actuality was only allowed to marry the man she loved to save the face of the monarchy and protect the name of the family from the embarrassing scandal that would have ensued had she eloped. What was most at stake was the father's and family's prestige. In the end Sina had to submit to the demands of her father, acting out her expected daughterly role of obedience, sacrificing her own love in the service of her family.

This sacrificial nature of women's love continues in many relationships today, as women transfer their internalized submission to their fathers (as the head of the family of origin), to their husbands (as the head of the family through marriage) and to God (the male head of the Christian patriarchal family). Because of the inhibitions imposed by this cultural expectation, the woman is often the first to blame herself for any problem within the family, as well as to accept any form of violent punishment from her husband or father.

Silencing of the Invisible Woman: The mother in the myth is a silent visage who is only there in her child-bearing role, as the mother of the two daughters. She was not even worth mentioning by name as she had no part to play, no activity in which to be involved. She is the unknown being whose contribution remains invisible. What does this say about the position of women? Woman's worth is mostly limited to being the birth-giver and it is thus determined by the fruitfulness of her womb.

The silencing that comes with invisibility is a form of violence that violates the dignity of the woman as a human being created in God's image. Yet women's invisibility still remains a commonplace reality even today in many Oceanian settings. Important gatherings of chiefs, politicians, business leaders, church leaders, academics, and theological educators are all gatherings primarily or exclusively of men. The women are invisible; if they are around at all they are out of sight, most likely in the kitchen, preparing to serve the men. They are not only 'seen but not heard,' they are usually not even seen.

This analysis has attempted to bring a fresh interpretation to what has been overlooked or downplayed for far too long, namely, the role of our sacred Oceanian myths and legends in perpetuating the oppression and exploitation of women. While it is painful for Pacific Islanders to critique their sacred myths, this is a necessary step in the understanding of the deeply ingrained cultural beliefs that can unwittingly sanction discrimination and violence against women. It is only as we unravel the cultural strand fully that we can assess what it is made of and extract those fibers which are poisonous. Having begun that preliminary process, we focus attention now on the actual shape of violence against women — the patterns created in the mat when the various patriarchal strands are woven together.

Patterns in the Fabric of Violence Against Women in Oceania

Identifying the Threads

Few attempts have been made to date to define or categorize acts of violence against women in Oceanian societies.[62] Many islanders claim that accepted international definitions are inappropriate because they are influenced by Western thinking, or that they are false allegations which debase the cherished cultural values of the island nations. Violence against women has also not been a priority for researchers in the region because it is, on the one hand, so normalized and, on the other hand, such a taboo topic.

As a result, 'there has been previously little qualitative or quantitative research conducted [in Oceania] to objectively identify the various determinants of violence [against women] in the community setting or even at home.'[63] This lack of attention to the problem of violence against women has also been attributed to the particular complexity of this issue in the Oceanian context, with its 'huge interplay between traditions, culture, religion, education … power imbalances and decision-making.'[64]

62. One of the few academic reflections is Dorothy A. Counts, 'Domestic Violence in Oceania', *Pacific Studies* 13 (1990): pp. 22–27. Other more recent public discussions are referred to in this chapter.

63. Jimmie Rodgers, opening address, Pacific Regional Workshop on Strengthening Partnerships for Eliminating Violence Against Women, Pacific Forum Secretariat, Suva, Fiji, 17–19 February, 2003. It should be noted that the South Pacific Commission has collaborated with the United Nations Population Fund and the Ministry of Women in Samoa to conduct the first ever national study on violence against women in Samoa, from 1999–2000.

64. Rodgers, opening address, Pacific Regional Workshop.

However, at the 2003 Pacific Regional Workshop on Strengthening Partnerships for Eliminating Violence Against Women, violence against women was first publicly defined by concerned Pacific Islanders, primarily as a violation of human rights. This view was summed up in the address by Asenaca Caucau, Fiji's Minister for Women, Social Welfare and Poverty Alleviation, who stated:

> Violence against women is a violation of human rights that can never be justified. Such violence reflects a breakdown in family values, and has been recognized internationally as a major cause of women's lack of participation in the social, economic and political arenas. … When we talk about violence against women, we tend to limit ourselves to physical violence. There are other forms of violence against women that are … just as destructive. These include abusive language, as well as psychological and intellectual abuse inflicted by family, partners [and others].[65]

This same gathering identified domestic violence as 'the most common form of violence against women and girls in the Pacific.' The term 'domestic' was defined as

> violence by a husband against a wife or by a boyfriend against a girlfriend, although it can also encompass violence between other members of a household or extended family. It is often accepted as normal, with both women and men believing that violence by men against their female partner is justified under certain circumstances.[66]

In the one study which had previously been undertaken in Oceania on violence against women (in Samoa), it was found that factors contributing to domestic abuse ranged from men's use of alcohol and drugs to economic problems, lack of communication, and gender role expectations. Such abuse was found to be acceptable in situations where the victims failed to perform domestic duties, were disobedient, or refused to have sex with their husbands or partners.[67]

65. Asenaca Caucau, keynote address, Pacific Regional Workshop on Strengthening Partnerships for Eliminating Violence Against Women, Pacific Forum Secretariat, Suva, Fiji, 17–19 February, 2003.

66. 'Overview of Efforts to Eliminate Violence Against Women in the Pacific'. This report is part of an assessment by UNIFEM of global efforts to eliminate violence against women and girls.

67. Faasili Afamasaga and Kuiniselani Tago presented an update on the joint project by the South Pacific Commission, United Nations Development Program, and the Ministry of Women in Samoa, 'Family Health and Safety Study of Violence Against Women in Oceania', Pacific Regional Workshop on Strengthening Partnerships for Eliminating Violence Against Women, Pacific Forum Secretariat, Suva, Fiji, 17–19 February, 2003.

The Scope of the Problem

It is an understatement to assert that violence against women is one of the most significant social problems in Oceanian communities. It is sickening to read in the leading newspapers[68] on a daily basis about cases of violent sexual brutality, rape and attempted rape, child molestation, and incest. In addition to the two most common and serious forms of sexual and domestic violence, harassment of women is also endemic in urban areas, workplaces and social institutions. What follows are just a few representative chronicles of these myriad forms of violence against women.

The intermingling of sexual and other forms of physical violence or threatened violence, while rare in the past, is becoming increasingly prevalent, as in the following account: 'B is alleged to have raped a 24-year-old American tourist while she was taking a walk … the victim was repeatedly raped at gunpoint during the night and was only able to escape after B fell asleep in the early morning.'[69] The most common form of rape, however, is still that committed by a family member, as in this typical case: 'The Suva Magistrates Court yesterday jailed a 66-year-old grandfather found guilty of indecently assaulting and raping his two granddaughters over a period of eight years.'[70]

There are also many reported (and many more unreported) cases of attempted rape and sexual assault. Consider the following common scenario: 'A 37-year-old man was yesterday sentenced to four years imprisonment for abducting a girl under the age of 18 years with intent to have carnal knowledge and indecently assaulting her; (he) confronted her by closing her mouth with his hand and dragged her to a nearby vacant house. At the house he forced her to remove her clothes, laid her down and touched her private parts. He took off his trousers and tried to have intercourse with her.'[71]

There has also been a marked increase in recent years in gang rape (or 'pack rape') in those countries experiencing the greatest social stress, such as Papua New Guinea, the Solomon Islands and

---

68. The incidents presented in this section are taken from the three major Fiji newspapers: *The Fiji Times*, *The Sun* and *The Daily Post*.

69. *The Daily Post*, 12 September 2002, p. 7.

70. *The Daily Post*, 26 July 2002, p. 1.

71. Charlotte Peters, 'Sexual Offender Cops 4-year Term', *Fiji Sun*, 12 November 2002, p. 2.

Fiji. As Halapua's research confirms, in post-coup Fiji, 'not only have gang rapes increased, but they are taking on more horrific forms. A November 2002 case of a gang rape of a woman by three masked men, in front of her husband and two children, is an example of this trend.'[72]

Reports of girl-child sexual abuse also proliferate in the media. A typical newspaper account reports that 'a villager was sentenced to 10 years ... for sexually abusing eight (female) children ... between the ages of four and nine. The 64-year-old said he had reconciled with church elders and parents of the victims and was forgiven.'[73] Another familiar scenario is echoed in this account: 'A man was jailed for two years for indecently assaulting his 10-year old neighbor. The accused had gone to the victim's house and told her to send her younger sister to a neighbor's house. When the victim's sister left, the accused then undressed the victim and touched her private parts. He also undressed himself, rubbed his private parts against the victim's thighs and left the house.'[74]

All too often, child sexual abuse takes the form of incest, clearly a serious problem in several Oceanian societies, but one almost always hidden because of cultural taboos. It is extremely rare for incest cases to be reported to the authorities, much less for the perpetrators to be brought to trial, and even rarer for the perpetrator to be punished, as in the following cases: 'A Lautoka (Fiji) father who has ... sexually assaulted his two daughters yesterday pleaded guilty on rape and two counts of indecent assault before the Lautoka Magistrates Court.'[75] And, again: 'A father raped his partially crippled daughter for a period of almost three weeks until she could not hide it anymore and broke the sick news to her mother ... who then reported the matter to the Fiji Women's Crisis Centre. She (the victim) is partially crippled from the waist down. ... This is probably the sickest and biggest sexual offence ever committed in Fiji.'[76]

There are virtually no studies documenting the incidence of harassment in Oceania. However, international studies have found

72. Halapua, 'Militarism and the Moral Decay in Fiji', p. 115.

73. *The Fiji Times*, 28 June 2002, p. 3.

74. Avinesh Gopal, 'Child Molester Goes to Prison', *The Fiji Times*, 24 April 2002, p. 8.

75. *Fiji Sun*, 12 November 2002, p. 2.

76. Raymond Singh, 'Father Rapes Crippled Daughter', *The Daily Post*, 2 October 2002, p. 1.

that 'where domestic violence is rife, sexual harassment is even more prevalent.'[77] Even in the absence of hard statistics in the region, the anecdotal evidence is alarming. The authors' first-hand experience and analysis of complaints shared in confidence by victims confirm that it is routinized and only very rarely challenged.

The incidence of all of these forms of violence against women is clearly on the rise across the region. For example, a recent survey undertaken by the Fiji Women's Crisis Centre found that 'sixty-six per cent of women in Fiji had been beaten by their partners.'[78] In Suva alone (the capitol of Fiji and largest urban hub in the region), according to a newspaper report, 'police statistics reveal reported sexual offences rose by 20 per cent this year compared to last year, with incest having the highest figure in the category.'[79] While this documentation applies only to one city, it is fair to conclude that the situation in Suva is similar to that in other urban centers throughout Oceania. The true picture is also much more severe than the statistics indicate, as it is well known that the vast majority of cases of domestic violence and harassment are never reported to anyone, so that what is heard about is only the tip of the iceberg.

One of the very few reliable sources of information on and analysis of violence against women in Oceania is the Fiji Women's Crisis Centre. One of the Centre's annual reports states:

> Violence against women and children continues to be a serious issue of concern in Fiji and the Pacific region. ... In particular there has been a marked increase in the number of cases of incest and sexual assault being reported to the police. In Papua New Guinea, cases of pack-rape and in particular that associated with organized hold-ups, have also increased. In Vanuatu serious cases of domestic violence, including those leading to the deaths of several women, have been reported over the past year.[80]

Another more recent regional study by the Crisis Centre has highlighted several clear trends quoted below:

- the increased brutality of the acts (of violence against women);
- the increase in physical violence associated with sexual violence;

---

77. Webb, *Global Impact of Sexual Harassment*, p. 90.

78. Cited in Kotoisuva, 'Domestic Violence', p. 42.

79. Imran Ali, 'Father Under Probe for Sex Crimes', *The Fiji Times*, 15 November 2002, p. 3.

80. Fiji Women's Crisis Centre, 'Annual Report', October 2002.

- the increase in gang rapes;
- the increase in young offenders.[81]

We alluded in Chapter One to an international survey of acts of violence against women which estimated that fully two-thirds of wives in Papua New Guinea are victims of domestic violence.[82] The Fiji Women's Crisis Centre has also found that in Oceania, as in many other parts of the world, violence against women is usually 'committed by a man she [the woman] is well acquainted with, such as her husband, father, brother or father-in-law...'[83] Indeed, an FWCC survey found that 80% of female victims of violence were abused in their own homes, and that 'of the 88 murders [in Fiji in a two-year period], these included 26 females murdered by their partners.'[84]

Shamima Ali also contends that, 'in no Pacific country does the law protect women or provide women with justice.'[85] Merilyn Tahi, Director of the Vanuatu Komiti Agensem Vaelens Agensem Women (also known as the Vanuatu Women's Counselling Service), has further confirmed that, in a society where 'violence [against women] has been getting worse since independence, women are still silent for fear of being beaten or sent back to violent husbands, and few are aware of their rights before the law.'[86]

Legal expert Joni Madraiwiwi has confirmed that the legal systems of most Oceanian countries have actually 'reinforced the disadvantaged status' of women by privatizing and de-criminalising violence against women.[87] Legal authorities tend to use 'the sanctity of the home' as an excuse not to intervene in, or punish domestic violence, 'allowing men free rein to assault women in the home.'[88] Consequently, even in Fiji, where there is probably the highest level

81. Cited in Kotoisuva, 'Domestic Violence', p. 43.

82. Webb, *Global Impact of Sexual Harassment*, p. 90. Kotoisuva also cites this study, noting that it identified as victims of domestic violence 67% of women in urban areas, and 54% of women in rural areas. See Kotoisuva, 'Domestic Violence', p. 43.

83. Shamima Ali, 'Violence Against Women', in *Women's Theology: Pacific Perspectives* (Suva, Fiji: SPATS, 1996), p. 59.

84. Ali, 'Violence Against Women', p. 59.

85. Ali, 'Violence Against Women', p. 59.

86. 'Combating Violence Against Women: The Campaign Continues', *Women's News* 8 (Pacific Women's Resource Bureau, Noumea) (May 1993): p. 22.

87. Joni Madraiwiwi, 'Domestic Violence and the Law', *Pacific Journal of Theology* II: 30 (2003): p. 46.

88. Madraiwiwi, 'Domestic Violence', p. 47.

of advocacy for, and awareness of, women's rights, it is estimated that three-quarters of the victims of domestic violence never report their abuse to the police or even to medical authorities.[89] In the very few cases which reach the courts, offenders found guilty are usually given extremely lenient sentences.

Even though some Oceanian governments have made incremental improvements in their policies and laws to increase protection for women against male violence, this has not thus far been an effective deterrent against male violence toward women.[90] A police inspector involved in the development of community-based policing in several Oceanian nations has noted that domestic violence in the region is still generally regarded as an inevitable part of life. He observed that, because island societies support the established view that men have the right to beat their wives—and thus friends and relatives often support the men who commit such acts of violence—it is extremely difficult for police to investigate allegations of domestic violence or to intervene in people's homes.[91] The abused women are unwilling to file a complaint with the police because they fear their problems will be aggravated if the police become involved.[92]

Ethel Sigimanu, Permanent Secretary of the Department of Foreign Affairs in the Solomons Islands, has reported that the primary reason it is almost impossible to determine the extent of violence against women in the Solomons is that most women still do not recognize their abuse as a crime and thus do not report it.[93] As a result, violence against women continues to be tolerated in Solomon Islands society.[94] The causes of such violence in the Solomons context are complex and have been compounded by the recent ethnic armed conflict and subsequent lawlessness.[95] Anecdotal

89. Fiji Women's Crisis Centre, *The Incidence, Prevalence and Nature of Domestic Violence and Sexual Assault in Fiji* (Suva, Fiji: Fiji Women's Crisis Centre, n.d.), p. 42.

90. This is borne out, for instance, in J. Cribb and R. Barnett, 'Being Bashed: Western Samoan Women's Responses to Domestic Violence in Western Samoa', *Western Samoa and New Zealand: Gender, Place and Culture* 6 (January 1999): pp. 49–65.

91. Rob Veale, paper presented, Pacific Regional Workshop on Strengthening Partnerships for Eliminating Violence Against Women, Pacific Forum Secretariat, Suva, Fiji, 17–19 February 2003.

92. Veale, paper presented, Pacific Regional Workshop.

93. This mindset is at times also related to the widespread belief that women 'deserve' to be raped, noted in, for example, Kotoisuva, 'Domestic Violence', p. 43.

94. Sigamanu, paper presented, Pacific Regional Workshop.

95. Sigamanu, paper presented, Pacific Regional Workshop.

evidence indicates that, during and after the latest ethnic conflict, rape, sexual abuse and other forms of violence were inflicted on women by warring factions as a form of revenge.[96]

There is not space here to address in detail the seriousness of the problem of violence against children, as the focus of our study is on the struggles of adult women. However, it is important to note that violence against female children is just as serious a problem in Oceania as violence against women, if not greater. Therefore, some cases of sexual abuse of female children have been cited to indicate the seriousness of the problem.

In order to concretize the experience of violence against women in Oceania, it will be helpful to further analyze several cases reported in the Fiji media. Specific case studies from the theological school setting will be highlighted in Chapter Six, as a part of our analysis of violence against women in Oceanian churches and their institutions.

Case Studies from Oceania

Case One

Two young girls who were raped and assaulted by their father submitted letters of reconciliation in court. Proceedings at the Lautoka [Fiji] court were closed to the public after the 47-year-old man told the court that his daughters and wife had forgiven him and produced the letters… He said he was very stressed and in financial difficulty when he committed the offences. The alleged offences began almost six years ago when his elder daughter was 15-years-old. He admitted raping his elder daughter and trying to rape and indecently assaulting the younger one, who was 12-years-old. The matter came to light when the older daughter told a neighbor of the alleged incidences.[97]

This is a typical example of those few cases of sexual abuse in Oceanian families which are actually reported. Many more such cases remain unreported and are kept hidden in family closets. Most of those which do end up in court are incest cases where the perpetrators are a brother, father, uncle, cousin, or grandfather. The victims of incest are as young as three months and as old as eighty-plus years old. Most cases of incest are safely kept in secrecy to safeguard the name and the reputation of the family and the perpetrators. Victims are often forced to reconcile with the

96. Sigamanu, paper presented, Pacific Regional Workshop.

97. Seema Sharma, 'Daughters Give Letters of Reconciliation', *The Fiji Times*, 20 November 2002, p. 5.

perpetrator, or the families seek a means of reconciling with each other without taking the children's feelings into consideration at all.

It is noteworthy that even in the above extreme crime of incest, the perpetrator made excuses for his actions, as though economic stress were somehow a justification for his violent assaults on his own daughters. It is telling that this man's wife and daughters publicly 'forgave' him. This is a commonplace response once such cases of domestic violence reach the courts: Women are conditioned to 'smooth over' the offences committed against them or their children by a family member, whether out of fear of further violence, fear of the loss of the family breadwinner if he is imprisoned, or simply shame that they have brought their family name into disrepute.

Case Two

A 34-year-old soldier appeared before the Chief Magistrate … for assaulting his wife … The complainant approached the accused to discuss family problems. During the discussion an argument developed between the couple whereby the accused allegedly started punching the complainant. The complainant suffered injuries as a result and reported the matter to police.[98]

Case Two speaks of an experience which all too many Oceanian women share in common. Only a very few have the courage to report such an assault to the police or to seek support from a care-giving agency. Many islander women have at one time, if not many times in their lives, experienced an assault resulting from a relationship, marital or de facto. Such men often resort to physical violence to 'resolve' conflicts in relationships.[99] In so doing, however, the relational problems are not resolved or dissolved. They only become suppressed, such that one partner must bail out of the disagreement. It is almost always the woman who is silenced in such disputes, through her fear of further violence. The mere threat of a repeat of the violence is sufficient to keep her quiet, obedient and submissive.

---

98. *The Daily Post*, 22 March 2002, p. 3.

99. Often both partners contribute to the misunderstandings in the marriage or a relationship. Both are victims of other forms of violence such as emotional, psychological or verbal violence. The issue here is not who or what caused the problem. The point is that men are more prone to resort to physical violence to deal with relational difficulties. As a consequence, the women are almost always the victims of violent physical abuse.

We are not aware of the existence of any studies detailing the results or long-term effects in the rare cases such as the one in the above newspaper account, in which charges are brought against the perpetrators of domestic violence. However, from our years of observing the reporting of these types of court cases in Fiji, it is clear that sentences, if any, tend to be extremely light. Even in cases of rape, perpetrators are often given sentences of only a few years in prison. Most domestic violence cases, of course, never come to trial.

Case Three

A domestic dispute between a couple living in a de facto relationship turned tragic when the man threw a punch intended for his wife, who was breastfeeding their three month-old son. It landed on the infant, killing him almost instantly.[100]

This case is an extreme example of how domestic violence intended for a woman can create an ever-expanding spiral of violence that affects everyone else in the family. In this tragic incident, a couple's baby died as the result of the father's misplaced blow. Even when the children are not physically assaulted, however, they are emotionally damaged and scarred through witnessing acts of brutality against their mothers.

This is more likely to be the case in traditional Oceanian homes which are typically small in size, with one shared living space. What goes on in the home is not easily hidden from sight, with the result that acts of domestic violence against women are imprinted on the consciousness of the children. In such families, boys often grow up to copy their fathers by relating to women violently, and girls frequently grow up to expect and accept that they will be on the receiving end of violence from their partners. Thus the cycle of violence spreads like an unchecked virus, dehumanizing everyone.

Violence against women in Oceania cannot be viewed as something that goes away once the triggering dispute is over. It is a deadly disease that continues to suck up its victims and perpetrators alike in a vicious cycle as it moves from one generation to another. Perpetrators falsely believe that once the tears are dried and the bruises disappear the problem is also over. Victims internalize their woundedness and fear and remain silent.

100. Tanya McCutchen, 'Drunken Dad Kills Son With One Punch', *The Daily Post*, 14 October 2002, p. 1.

There is now, however, a growing consciousness amongst at least a few Pacific Islanders that violence against women is a serious and unjustifiable evil affecting society at all levels. There is also an increasing awareness that many interrelated factors have contributed to the increase of violence against women in Oceania — the interwoven strands of growing social stress and instability; rising poverty, thanks in large measure to globalization; greater exposure to violence in all forms of media; and acceptance by the churches of the cultural patriarchy that condones male domination and control of women.

*   *   *

Despite positive social changes taking place in various parts of the world, the social constructions of patriarchy continue to relegate women to secondary and inferior status in many societies, including the island nations of Oceania. Oceanian Christians need to be reminded that social and cultural values are not divine mandates but the creations of flawed human beings. The ways in which patriarchy has manifested itself in Oceanian societies must be challenged as morally unacceptable forces that have denied women the fullness of life and dignity and left them particularly vulnerable to the most violent forms of male power and control.

Some living conditions have improved in Oceania in recent decades, but the marginalization and domestication of women continues, at times assuming new forms and faces. A paradox exists, in which Oceanian societies have become more affirmative in their rhetoric but more deadly for women in reality. Life is more poisonous now than ever for all too many Oceanian women, as many of the ruling patriarchs, especially those in the church, have learned to speak and use the language of liberation for women to their own advantage. These men are the worst practitioners of the patriarchal system because they are wolves clothed in sheepskin waiting to consume unsuspecting, unprotected women.

Now that we have disclosed the strands of both cause and effect in the fabric of violence, violence against women, and violence against women in the Oceanian context, the following chapter shifts our attention to the particular strand of patriarchy that is at the very heart of Oceanian life: that of the church. If we are to be able to reweave the mat of relationality, we need first to unravel the sub-strands that presently characterize the Oceanian churches' theology, biblical interpretations, church traditions and practices, and understandings of the clergy. All of these, woven together, have created an ecclesial fabric which has contributed to or condoned violence against women.

Chapter Four

RELIGIOUS STRANDS IN THE FABRIC OF VIOLENCE AGAINST
WOMEN: THEOLOGICAL MISCONSTRUALS

Because we approach the problem of violence against women
theologically, as Christian women with a personal stake in the
Oceanian ecclesial and theological community, it is imperative that
we attempt to understand the interrelationship between patriarchal
appropriations of Christianity and the reality of violence against
women.

Our major focus in this chapter will be on problematical
interpretations of Christian theology, particularly in the Oceanian
context. It will be helpful to begin, however, with a brief framing
of the larger religious worldview (in relation to violence). Religious
influences in diverse traditions are not entirely discontinuous with
what is happening in our own Christian tradition. In briefly
sketching the contours of the major religions' track records on
violence, we acknowledge that we do so as lay people rather than
as scholars of world religions. Our intent is to open the door to an
understanding of how construals of religious traditions by adherents
can become toxic fibers in the fabric of violence, including violence
against women.

Religion(s) and Violence: The Larger Mosaic

As an integral part of the life-ways of all societies, religion plays a
major role in shaping what people define as acceptable behavior.
The justification of violence by reference to religious teachings has
unfortunately become an underlying contributor to many forms of
violence. Religion is often used by perpetrators of violence to
convince themselves and others that their actions are just and
ethically defensible.

The sacred scriptures of various religions in particular have been used — and are used increasingly in the current world climate of terrorism and fear of terrorism — to justify war, ethnic cleansing, suicide bombings, genocide, and gender-based violence. The scriptures of the world's religions are replete with texts which can be interpreted in such a way as to condone violence. In some sacred texts, violence is considered justifiable if it is deemed necessary for God or initiated by God, for the well-being of human communities, or to protect the particular religious faith. Yet this use of scriptures to justify violence is not often analyzed by religious leaders or adherents, either within their own religious communities or in interfaith dialogue, as the emphasis is usually on fine-tuning the strengths and empowering aspects of each religious tradition.[1]

This does not mean that the world religions have done nothing to condemn violence or to challenge sacred texts that appear to justify violence. Credit must be given to the religious leaders who have been constant in their efforts to work for peace amongst the various religious traditions. The point is that such efforts have not stopped adherents of these religious traditions from using their scriptures or traditions as a pretext for acts of violence. In other words, there appears to be a gap between the peace-loving teachings of many religions and their practitioners' violence-affirming appropriation of those teachings. As Hans Ucko has observed,

> It is true that *Om Shanti, Shantihi* is the emphatic Vedic blessing. It is true that Jesus greeted people with the gift of peace, "Peace be upon you." It is true that there is an absolute emphasis on compassion and *ahimsa* in Buddhism. It is true that Judaism has given the world the word and concept *shalom*. It is true that in many cases, based on their ideals, religions seek to contribute to building peace. However …, religions are more than often related to the powers that be, which seem to provide the legitimization for violence. There are groups within our religious families who seem to need violence to affirm their own beliefs. We cannot run away from the effect of religious language such as "Onward Christian Soldiers," and acts such as the Crusades, the Holocaust or apartheid … We have to ask the penetrating question about the role of religion in violence.[2]

---

1.   Hans Ucko, 'Introduction to the "Thinking Together" Consultation on Religion and Violence', *Current Dialogue* 39 (June 2002), http://www.wcc-coe.org/wcc/what/interreligious/cd39-01.html.

2.   Ucko, 'Introduction to the "Thinking Together" Consultation'.

Space does not permit a thorough examination here of the many ways in which followers of the world's major religions have justified their embrace of violence through appeals to particular interpretations of their religious beliefs. It will suffice to mention briefly several pertinent examples.

Judaism and Violence

Deborah Weissmann's research on violence in Judaism has shown how the interpretations of sacred texts have directly or indirectly contributed to the acceptance of violence in the Jewish tradition. She contends that Israel's self-identity as the Chosen People and consequent claim to sovereignty over the Promised Land have become a warrant for the exclusion of others, legitimizing state-sanctioned violence. She further suggests that 'Jews have been victims for so long … [that] it becomes difficult for us to recognize that we are also victimizers, and to assume moral responsibility for our actions.'[3]

Although Judaism advocates for justice and *shalom* (peace) in the world, the Hebrew Bible is also filled with violent encounters of people with God, nature and others. Metaphorical depictions of God acting violently and images of God as warrior and conqueror are plentiful.[4] As André Wénin puts it, 'God is constantly involved in it [violence], and often as an agent.'[5] The generalization of such God imagery, and ultra-nationalist Jewish interpretations of the concept of Israel as the 'chosen people' of God can clearly contribute to a culture of violence.[6]

Islam and Violence

Recent world events and their association with Islamic extremism, especially in the West, have painted a stereotypical image of Islam as a religion which legitimates violence. This perception is heightened when radical Muslims call for *jihad* (typically translated

3. Deborah Weissmann, 'The Co-existence of Violence and Non-Violence in Judaism', *Current Dialogue*, 39 (June 2002), http://www.wcc-coe.org/wcc/what/interreligious/cd39-07.html.

4. See, for example, the book of Exodus, in which God clearly has a warrior role (e.g., Exod. 15:3).

5. André Wénin, 'La Bible pour démasquer la violence', *Bulletin de Pax Christi* 19:3 (September 1996), cited in Wim Beuken and Karl-Josef Kusher (eds.), *Religion as a Source of Violence* (London: SCM Press; Maryknoll, NY: Orbis Books, 1992), p. 2.

6. Weissmann, 'The Co-existence of Violence'.

as 'holy war') in defence of Islam. The *Qur'an* does indeed sanction 'just war' in order to counter persecution and defend Islamic values. Yet despite its teaching that *jihad* is a comprehensive concept embracing peaceful persuasion (*Qur'an* 16:125), passive resistance (13:22; 23:96; 41:34), as well as armed struggle against oppression and injustice (2:193; 4:75; 8:39) which is not directed at other faiths (2:256), *jihad* has been radically reinterpreted by extremist Muslim fundamentalists.[7] This stream of Islam has embraced opportunistic acts of violence, targeting innocent persons.

Other less political expressions of Islamic fundamentalism also justify violence to uphold patriarchal Islamic teachings, such as beating or even murdering women who have committed adultery. Although such legalistic interpretations are in part a reflection of honor codes embedded in the Arab culture from which Islam emerged, they are also expressive of Islam's historic placement of a higher value on justice than on love. As a result, in the words of Ali Mazrui, Islam has by and large 'offered little resistance to the tendency of certain groups to appeal to the attribution of this justice in their use of violence.'[8] These interpretations of the *Qur'an*, in turn, have become stereotypes of Islam, fueling antagonism in other religious adherents, which leads to further violence—both by and against Muslims.

Hinduism and Violence

Mahatma Gandhi is perceived by many as the embodiment of the Hindu worldview and ethic. He made *ahimsa* (non-violence) 'the cornerstone of his philosophy and practice and spoke of it as constituting the essence of Hinduism.'[9] Yet the use of violence is nonetheless clearly sanctioned in some traditions of Hinduism. For example, there is the *purusa Sukta* hymn in the *Rgveda*, the most ancient scripture of Hinduism, which authorized the *ksatriyas* (warrior kings) to use armed force to safeguard the community

7.   This argument has been articulated by Imam A. Rashied Omar, 'Islam and Violence', *Current Dialogue* 39 (June 2002), http://www.wcc-coe.org/wcc/what/interreligious/cd39-01.html.

8.   Ali Mazrui, cited in Sohail H. Hashi, 'International Society and its Islamic Malcontents', *The Fletcher Forum on World Affairs* (Winter/Spring 1996): p. 23.

9.   Anantanand Rambachan, 'The Co-Existence of Violence and Non-Violence in Hinduism', *Current Dialogue* 39 (June 2002), http://www.wcc-coe.org/wcc/what/interreligious/cd39-01.html.

and to defend *dharma* (ritual order).[10] The most popular scripture of Hinduism, the *Bhagavadgita*, states that it is the personal duty of *ksatriyas* to participate in this defense of *dharma*, as a means of bringing about justice and righteousness, and to maintain the security of the community.[11] The Law of Manu 'establishes a hierarchy in which the Brahmin, ontologically situated at the top of the scale of castes, is easily justified in the violent defence of its position...'[12]

These influential traditions within Hinduism have been cleverly used by Hindu extremists in recent years to support their own militant nationalistic agenda. This has resulted in an acceleration of acts of violence in India today, in which these extremists target Muslim and even Christian sacred sites and communities, inviting violent retaliation in return.[13]

Buddhism and Violence

Ahimsa, the philosophy and practice of non-violence, is as significant in Buddhism as in Hinduism. The life of Buddha, the model whom all Buddhists aspire to emulate, is epitomized by the value of selfless compassion. Buddhist sacred texts are a living witness to 'the pacifist image of Buddhist teachings and historical practices of non-violent actions in Buddhist communities.'[14] Buddhist teaching does not ostensibly accept violence as a means to solve conflicts and disputes.

This mandate for non-violence, however, is not as clear-cut as it may first appear. Buddhist ethics stresses 'intention,' and although violence 'is not sought,' neither is it actually prohibited.[15] Buddhist individuals and communities have deviated from the non-violent foundation of Buddhism by engaging periodically in acts of

10. Rambachan, 'The Co-Existence of Violence'.

11. Rambachan, 'The Co-Existence of Violence'.

12. François Houtart, 'The Cult of Violence in the Name of Religion: A Panorama', in Wim Beuken and Karl-Josef Kusher (eds.), *Religion as a Source of Violence* (London: SCM Press; Maryknoll, NY: Orbis Books, 1992), p. 2.

13. As Houtart reminds us, this violent Hindu nationalism 'finds political expression today above all in the BJP (Barattya Janaty Party), whose recent history shows that non-violence is not its cup of tea.' Houtart, 'The Cult of Violence in the Name of Religion'.

14. Mahinda Deegalle, 'Is Violence Justified in Theravada Buddhism?', *Current Dialogue* 39 (June 2002), http://www.wcc-coe.org/wcc/what/interreligious/cd39-05.html.

15. Mark Juergenmeyer, 'The Terrorist Who Longs for Peace', *The Fletcher Forum for World Affairs* (Winter/Spring 1996): pp. 7–8.

orchestrated violence, especially during civil upheavals where their communities or way of life may be threatened.[16] The violent actions of nationalist Buddhists have been substantiated by reference to a 'genre of post-canonical literature (which) gives the impression that in certain circumstances … the use of certain degrees of violence is not going to harm the Buddha's doctrine of non-violence.'[17]

In all of these major religious traditions, the problem is not necessarily the fundamental tenets of the particular body of religious beliefs. It is true that the monotheistic religions of Judaism, Islam and Christianity are all deeply embedded in patriarchy, which in itself provides a warrant for using force to achieve a 'just' end.[18] But the larger problem is that it is all too easy for adherents of any religion to choose to interpret their beliefs in a way that sanctions violence. Even underlying theologies of non-violence and justice can be construed in such a way as to condone believers' desires to have their own way at any cost. And where violence in general is condoned, violence in specific cases becomes much more palatable. As we have seen, the more violent the society, the more violence against women tends to be tolerated and even to flourish.[19]

But what about our own religion? We come to the problem of violence against women as followers of the Christian faith. It is the relationship between Christianity and violence, and particularly its relationship to violence against women, which is the primary concern of this chapter and this work. Our next task is thus to highlight the strand of Christianity in the fabric of violence against women, so that we can unravel it from its conjoined cultural and social strands, and then reweave a new mat of relationality.

Christianity and Violence

Outsiders looking in for the first time by perusing the pages of the Old/First Testament of the Christian scriptures might be shocked

16. Deegalle, 'Is Violence Justified'.

17. Deegalle, 'Is Violence Justified'.

18. For an in-depth discussion of the paradoxical role of religious traditions as partners in cultural violence, see Cheryl Kirk-Duggan, *Misbegotten Anguish: A Theology and Ethics of Violence* (St. Louis, MO: Chalice Press, 2001).

19. See the discussion of the specific correlation between religious dogmas and violence against women in Hedwig Meyer-Wilmes, 'Excessive Violence against Women in the Name of Religion', in Wim Beuken and Karl-Josef Kusher (eds.), *Religion as a Source of Violence* (London: SCM Press; Maryknoll, NY: Orbis, Books, 1997), pp. 55–63.

to discover that it overflows with violent narratives and imagery. These narratives provide graphic details of a God who sanctions violence and acts violently, of nations or individuals at war with each other in the presence, at the direction, and under the protection of God, of brutal acts of violence carried out by the people of God.

Observing Christians' behavior down through the centuries, these outside observers might also conclude that, despite the countervailing pacifist message of Jesus in the New Testament—who calls on the faithful to 'love their enemies,' to 'turn the other cheek' when attacked, to 'do good to those who hate you' and to 'love others as you love yourself'—many Christians have embraced not only the presumed justice of war but violence as a legitimate means of righting wrongs.

The triumphalistic Warrior God has in fact been a common metaphor, or image of God, throughout Christian history.[20] This warrior God was a convenient guide in the Crusaders' conquest of Islam, as in other successive conquests. Such violent metaphors continue to be used in our time to describe and limit God, as in the current American president's frequent references to the Christian God to justify American aggression in any country deemed to be associated with terrorists.

Many Christian fundamentalists have interpreted these judgmental metaphors for God as normative descriptions that sanction many forms of violence, both militaristic and personal. The contradictions between peace-loving Gospel and aggressive Christian history require us to examine the questions, 'Is Christianity a religion of peace or not?' And 'What are the implications of our answer to this question for the church's role in relation to violence against women?'

Since our primary concern is the religious context in which violence against women has evolved in Oceania, it will be important to examine the particular shape and form of the Christianity that found its way to and took root in the island communities of Oceania. The introduction of Christianity in Oceania in the late eighteenth and early nineteenth centuries had a profound impact on Oceanian communities' religio-cultural worldview. The proclamation of absolute biblical truths, the inculcation of patriarchal theology, and

20. Sallie McFague, guest lecture, 'Ecological Theology of Oceans', Dr. Ama'amalele Tofaeono, Vancouver School of Theology, 16 September 2003.

the veneration of the clergy as 'holy men' all became thoroughly impregnated in the Oceanian worldview.

In order to unravel the complex religious strands that characterize Oceanian Christianity, it is essential that we examine the roles which the theological, biblical and ecclesiastical traditions that took hold in Oceania have played in upholding patriarchy. This investigation will uncover the underlying theological presuppositions that have legitimized violence against women. After diagnosing the problems with these prevailing Christian traditions, alternative interpretations embedded in the same traditions can be suggested. This will be the beginning of our reweaving—a first step in liberating our inherited traditions so that our religious fabric is transformed from a mat of violence to a mat of peace.

We must unravel and examine each major strand in our inherited Oceanian Christian tradition in turn, beginning in this chapter with the strands of patriarchal theology and biblical interpretations, and moving on in the following chapter to the strands of patriarchal church traditions and male clergy power.

The Problem with Patriarchal Theology

The Christian church has had an ambivalent response to violence against women because, as established previously, violence against women is about the abuse of power and, as Christine McMullen puts it, 'the church has had an ambivalent attitude to power.'[21] Because the church is itself trapped in a patriarchal construal of power, it has become complicit in the perpetration of a theology that engenders and legitimizes violence against women.

Feminist theology asserts that the 'confusion of the Gospel with the ideology of patriarchy'[22] is at the very heart of the problem with the church's teachings and practices. Until recent decades, most of what has 'counted' as Christian theology has assumed that a patriarchal worldview is divinely constituted. This patriarchal structure rests on the premise that God is male, the Father of all humankind. The maleness and fatherhood of God is promoted by the language of the 'overwhelming majority of worship services,

21. Christine McMullen, 'One Day I Went to a Theological Consultation on Domestic Violence', *Feminist Theology* 11:2 (2003): p. 198.

22. Louise Schottroff, *Lydia's Impatient Sisters: A Feminist Social History of Early Christianity* (Louisville, KY: Westminster/John Knox Press, 1995), p. 19.

liturgies, creeds, statements of theology, Bible readings, sermons, canon laws, hymns and prayers.'[23]

In other words, Christian orthodoxy has 'accepted patriarchal patterns ... and has understood God's relationship with humanity through that lens.'[24] It has proclaimed:

> the god of patriarchy, who is in control of everything. Though this god might allow freedom, he would be very much in command ... a patriarchal god would relate to his creatures by command and decree, expecting a response of submission and obedience, giving protection in exchange for obedience and either punishment or mercy when obedience was denied.[25]

Feminist theologians have analyzed the ways in which the patriarchal ideal of *father-rule* has monopolized the Christian image of God. Rosemary Ruether, for example, has shown how the God who is encapsulated by the image of father-rule becomes 'Sovereign, King, Warrior, God of Power and Might ... (who) cannot be imaged in the faces of women, or children.'[26] She continues: 'Men are the proper and fitting image of this mighty God, especially powerful men — rulers who command, warriors who kill, judges who punish. These are the ones who ... most exemplify the image of God. To see them is to see God.'[27]

This patriarchal God, in turn, is determinative of a hierarchical understanding of relationality — often referred to as the relational pyramid. This is a 'pyramid of graded subordinations and exploitations [that] specifies women's oppression.'[28] At the top of the pyramid is Yahweh, the male God described above. Just beneath 'Him' are males, who are the 'heads' of households and societies. Their characteristics and prerogatives mirror those of the patriarchal God. Church teaching that man is the head of the family just as Christ is the head of the church has thus 'raised no eyebrows,

23. Helen Hood, 'Speaking Out and Doing Justice: It's No Longer a Secret but What are the Churches Doing about Overcoming Violence Against Women?', *Feminist Theology* 11:2 (2003): p. 220.

24. McMullen, 'One Day I Went to a Theological Consultation', p. 199.

25. Brian Wren, *What Language Shall I Borrow? God-Talk in Worship: A Male Response to Feminist Theology* (London: SCM Press, 1989), p. 56.

26. Rosemary Ruether, *Women-Church: Theology and Practice* (San Francisco: Harper & Row, 1985), p. 70.

27. Rosemary Ruether, *Women-Church*, p. 70.

28. Letty Russell, *Authority in Feminist Theology: Household of Freedom* (Philadelphia: Westminster Press, 1987), pp. 33–34.

because men were used to behaving in their own family in a similar way to a patriarchal god.'[29] Historically, Christian theology has, at least until challenged by feminism, accepted the view that women are below men in the relational pyramid, since they are 'emotional, irrational and need to belong to a man in order to survive.'[30]

Although many Christians have claimed that masculine God-language does not adversely affect the way they experience God, mainstream feminist theology challenges this assumption. It insists that this is where our discussion of issues like violence against women must begin, because although we know that God is not male, 'we have absorbed male language for God into our very selves … (and) when male language is combined with images of authority such as Father, Lord and King, it is even more difficult to escape from the picture of God as a male authority figure.'[31] In the extreme, God has even been portrayed metaphorically as a domineering, battering husband, particularly in the prophetic tradition seen in Hosea, Ezekiel and Jeremiah.[32] How can such imagery have a liberating effect on women?

As long as males are, consciously or unconsciously, viewed as being *more* in the image of God than females (despite the inclusion of women in God's image in Gen. 1: 27), the negative effects on women will be inevitable. And as long as Christians accept male-dominated God language and theology, they 'will find it difficult to empathize with women who have experienced violence (at the hands of men), and hard to understand when such women do not wish to join the worshipping community.'[33]

In a nutshell, the absolutism of the theology of father-rule has fostered a hierarchical dualism that appeals to the divine right of the Heavenly Father to rule over all, earthly fathers to rule over households, kings to lord over subjects, and males in general to be

29. McMullen, 'One Day I Went to a Theological Consultation', p. 200. See, Eph. 5: 23.

30. McMullen, 'One Day I Went to a Theological Consultation', p. 200. See, Eph. 5: 23.

31. Hood, 'Speaking Out and Doing Justice', p. 220.

32. For an elaboration of this view, see Renita Weems, *Battered Love: Marriage, Sex, and Violence in the Hebrew Prophets* (Minneapolis, MN: Fortress Press, 1995). Weems reveals the rootedness of violence in the language, images and symbols used by many of the prophets. She demonstrates how many biblical texts portray a degree of acceptability of a violent God, and violent action by God and for the work of God.

33. Hood, 'Speaking Out and Doing Justice', p. 221.

responsible for females who are dependent on them. Christians have, through the centuries, internalized this hierarchical dualism, such that the 'theocratic fatherhood of God'[34] has been replicated in the assumed power of men over women, children and creation.

Although Jesus' messianic movement radically turned the social order upside down and offered equality and liberation for all from every form of enslavement, the outworking of that movement in the church, particularly in terms of the treatment of women, has not been very faithful to Jesus' vision. The father, whether in reality or in symbolism, is still the central figure in Christian households and institutions. The father on earth as representative of the heavenly father remains normative in much of Christian theology and practice.

At the heart of the problem of patriarchal theology, then, is a misconstrual of power that provides sanction for males to practice 'power-over' relationality. Men have seized upon the granting of 'dominion' in Gen. 1: 28 as blanket permission to have dominion over women, as well as the rest of creation. Yet 'power-over' relationality is evil because it 'harms the power of life itself within the relational web … and stifles the possibility of mutuality and interdependence.'[35] It is a 'denial of communion and a denial of freedom for self, others and God.'[36] It undercuts the essence of the fullness and wholeness of humanity that is at the very heart of the Gospel. Nonetheless, it has been the rock-solid theological ground upon which the church's sanction for male 'power-over' ways of relating to women has rested for centuries.

Historically, this patriarchal theology has had innumerable ill effects on women, despite Jesus' implicit transformation of patriarchy in his teaching and ministry. In the first few centuries of church history, patriarchal constructions of power and authority were smoothly accommodated into the church. This accommodation became entrenched in ecclesiastical institutions after the first few centuries, through the Middle Ages, and into the Reformation era.[37]

34. A term explicated by Paul K. Jewett, *Man as Male and Female* (Grand Rapids, MI: William B. Eerdmans Publishing Co., 1975), p. 129.

35. Poling, *The Abuse of Power*, p. 31.

36. Poling, *The Abuse of Power*, p. 31. Poling also analyzes male abuse of power in the more recent *Understanding Male Violence: Pastoral Care Issues* (St. Louis, MO: Chalice Press, 2003).

37. For a feminist reading of the evolution of patriarchy in church history, see, for example, Genevieve Lloyd, *The Man of Reason: 'Male' & 'Female' in Western Philosophy*

Although the Reformation sought to recover the prominence of the doctrine of the 'priesthood of all believers,' patriarchal theology was never seriously challenged by Protestant theology or churches. Hence, for example, in the Victorian era, Christian women were honored for a type of 'saintliness' which was closely associated with the raising of children in Christian moral values and devotion to domestic duties in the home.[38] Repercussions of this view of the ideal Christian woman have carried over even into the present era, and continue to be evident in many churches' theology today.[39]

The legacy of the patriarchal theology imported to Oceania by European missionaries has further contributed to the plight of women there. The merging of the transplanted father-rule theology with the patriarchal values of indigenous Oceanian communities reinforced and intensified the peripheral status and unequal treatment of women. This accommodation of Christianity can only be viewed as an almost total failure of the liberating power of the Gospel, at least for women.

The consequence of this assimilation of patriarchal theology is that, rather than being a seedbed for women's liberation, Christianity in Oceania has driven women further into insignificance. Oceanian Christian women have been expected to be dependent on and obedient to their male counterparts.[40] The hierarchical dualism of father/mother, king/subjects, male/female, strong/weak, and so on, enhanced by the patriarchal way of thinking about God, has not assisted in bringing about equity in gender relationships. Since patriarchal theology has been inextricably linked to dualistic philosophy,[41] which espouses male supremacy

(London: Methuen & Co. Ltd., 1984), pp. 25–37; Gillian Cloke, *This Female Man of God: Women and Spiritual Power in the Patristic Age* (London: Routledge, 1995); Jane Dempsey Douglass, *Women, Freedom and Calvin* (Philadelphia: Westminster Press, 1985); and Rosemary Radford Ruether, *Christianity and the Making of the Modern Family: Ruling Ideologies, Diverse Realities* (Boston: Beacon Press, 2000).

38. Ruether has elaborated on this in Chapters 3, 4 and 5 of *Christianity and the Making of the Modern Family*.

39. Ruether differentiates here between the domestication of white middle-class European women and Black enslaved women.

40. James Poling extensively analyzes family violence and the perpetuation of a dependency syndrome in victims due to their economic vulnerability, and challenges the church's role in this problem in *Render unto God: Economic Vulnerability, Family Violence, and Pastoral Theology* (St. Louis, MO: Chalice Press, 2002).

41. Lloyd, *The Man of Reason*, pp. 25–37. Reference is made here to the historical development of the Western philosophical tradition within the framework of Christianity.

in nature and rational thinking,[42] it has been a breeding ground of women's oppression.

In short, patriarchal theology has had devastating effects on women in Oceania, as in many other parts of the world, in terms of erecting an edifice of support for Christian men's 'power-over' ways of relating to women, and Christian women's acquiescence or silence in the face of these chauvinistic behaviors. Included in these theological distortions have been one-sided biblical interpretations, sexist liturgies, and any number of theological dogmatisms that have downplayed or denied women's full humanity. In the following sections we will highlight just a few of these patriarchal theological premises which have been particularly detrimental to women, and which have even been used as a justification for committing or condoning acts of violence against them.

Theology of Headship

An especially devastating source of male abuse in patriarchal theology is its assumption that the man is the 'head' of the family. Grounded in the mandate in Gen. 3: 16—'he shall rule over'—this male headship principle has been largely accepted in mainstream Christian theology.[43] Central to the conventional interpretation of Gen. 3: 16 is the importance of the 'difference' in men's and women's respective functions, especially the male's intrinsic right to rule.[44]

There is nothing inherently problematic about the concept of *difference* between males and females. What is problematic is the focus on men's right to 'rule over' females, which relegates the

Aspects of dualistic thinking include the male as the most capable, morally good and rational being, over against the female as incapable, morally weak, irrational, and affiliated with the material world, temptation and evil.

42. Lloyd, *The Man of Reason*, pp. 25–37. This can be traced back to Philo of Alexandria who viewed woman as a 'symbol of sense perception' (and) a 'source of man's wretchedness.' His philosophy was based on the ancient Greek 'theme of female passivity' which provided a foundation for his allegorical view of woman as a 'non-rational' human being. This has led to male-female distinctions in which 'passion' is, by nature, feminine, whereas 'noble affection … marks the masculine traits.'

43. Although certain historical eras, such as the Industrial Revolution and the Enlightenment, began to place greater emphasis on human equality, the mainstream theology emanating from those eras made no effort to refute the 'man to rule over' dictum so as to elevate the status of women.

44. Other interpretations have identified Genesis 1 and 2 as presenting a more complementary view of the man-woman relationship, emphasizing the ontological equality of both man and woman.

female partner to that of listener and follower. This principle has been reinforced through conservative references to man being 'created first,' which is linked to woman's 'dependence' on him, by virtue of the man's 'naming' or 'identification' of the woman.[45] As a result of these divine mandates, authority is vested in the man, who becomes the sole ruler in the relationship.[46]

This Old Testament theological underpinning for male headship was not thoroughly eradicated in the early church, despite the egalitarian ethic of Gospel relationality.[47] This is vividly expressed in the theology of the apostle Paul regarding women's submissive roles in the church as well as in marriage. In contrast, there is of course also Paul's manifesto in Gal. 3: 28—that, in Christ, *there is no longer male or female*—a statement cited by feminist theologians as a theological basis for the equality of men and women. However, it is clear from the historical evidence that the living out of this exhortation was not fully realized in the church.

In both the Catholic and Protestant traditions, theological positions that support male headship and female submission have never been adequately rejected, certainly not by the most prominent theologians. For example, it is evident that the exclusion of woman from the imagery of the Godhead in St. Augustine's *De Trinitate* is deliberate.[48] In referring to 'Man' as the 'image of the Trinity,' he asserts that a male 'is like the Trinity in that he: (1) is, (2) knows that he is, and (3) delights in his being and in the knowledge of this being.'[49] Augustine spoke of a certain 'spiritual equality' of men and women but emphasized woman's 'natural subordination.'[50]

St. Thomas Aquinas makes no mention of the male/female relationship in the nine articles in the *Summa* in which he deals with

45. See Genesis 3, particularly Adam's saying, 'This, at last, bone of my bones and flesh of my flesh.' Here the woman is the by-product of the man. This passage will be analyzed further in the next section.

46. David M. Scholer, 'The Evangelical Debate over Biblical Headship', in Catherine Clark Kroeger and James R. Beck (eds.), *Women, Abuse, and the Bible: How Scripture Can Be Used to Hurt or Heal* (Grand Rapids, MI: Baker Books, 1996), p. 37.

47. In addition to Genesis 1–3, Scholer examines four New Testament passages which are normally used to support man's headship (*kephale*) and authority (*authentein*) and woman's submission: 1 Cor.11: 2-16; Eph. 5: 21-33; 1 Tim. 2: 8-15—especially vs.12; and I Cor. 14: 34–35.

48. Cf. Lloyd, *The Man of Reason*, pp. 28-33.

49. Cited in Jewett, *Man as Male and Female*, p. 29.

50. Cited in Lloyd, *The Man of Reason*, p. 30.

the creation of 'Man' in the divine image.[51] Although he worked toward a 'more integrated view of human nature,' Aquinas still perceived the male as 'the principle of the human race' and the woman as his 'helpmate.' His treatment of the theology of male headship is formed out of an 'array of Aristotelian distinctions between "actualities and potentialities," "powers and functions." '[52] Woman's subordination in Aquinas' theology is grounded in the presumed predominance of 'reason' in the male. Since the male was created in the image of God—which is associated with the *mind* of God—man:

> … symbolizes human vital functioning, including Reason; he is the principle of the race, that in which its nature can be identified. Woman, separately created, symbolizes generation (which is) the perpetuation of that nature summed up in man. It is her role in creation … that makes her man's helpmate.[53]

The Protestant Reformer John Calvin likewise describes the male in the *Institutes, I, xv,* as 'a diversity of soul and body, a being endowed with free will,'[54] and says almost nothing about women except with reference to the values of chastity and obedience in marriage. Neither Calvin nor Luther[55] have much to say about women at all, other than to support the primacy of male headship and the natural suitability of women for subordinate domestic roles.

Mainstream Christian theology, then, has taken for granted the patriarchal tradition of male headship and it is still rare, with the exception of feminist theologies, to find the male headship ideology radically challenged or rendered invalid. We can only assume that the fundamental reason for this is that it is painful for patriarchal theology to let go of its position of dominance atop the pyramid inherited from the historical traditions.

Whatever the avenues taken by the church to justify the appropriateness of headship theology, they will never bring about liberation for women. Headship theology perpetuates the supremacy

51. Cited in Lloyd, *The Man of Reason,* pp. 35–36.
52. Cited in Lloyd, *The Man of Reason,* p. 34.
53. Cited in Lloyd, *The Man of Reason,* p. 36.
54. Cited in Jewitt, *Man as Male and Female,* pp. 28–29. See also Douglass, *Women, Freedom & Calvin,* especially her discussion of Calvin, pp. 41–65, and Luther, pp. 15–19 and pp. 88–90.
55. Jewett discusses Calvin's and Luther's positions on women in greater depth in *Man as Male and Female,* pp. 66–70.

of male over female, rational man over irrational woman, powerful male over weaker female, man as reason over woman as body, and so on.

Theology of Marriage

The Christian tradition has affirmed an ideal of marriage as a divinely sanctioned mirror of the model of Jesus' intimate relationship with the church. This model suggests reciprocity and mutuality in terms of commitment, sharing, providing, caring and nurturing. Procreation is not the sole focus in this model of marriage, although it is naturally an important dimension. As long as each partner seeks to nurture life in the other, Christian marriage is meaningful.[56]

Unfortunately, however, Christian marriage has developed less along the lines of Jesus' intimate relationship with the church than along patriarchal lines.[57] In many contexts it has become reduced to a patriarchal model. Christianity has 'provided the ideological and moral support for patriarchal marriage, rationalized it, and actively taught men and women to fit into this form of marriage.'[58] In this framework, wives are largely restricted to procreating and nurturing roles, whereas husbands give orders and make decisions, imitating at home what they do out in the world.

Paul Jewett has noted that, since 'understanding "Man" as an androgynous Subject, transcending the duality of male and female, has been generally rejected in Christian theology, it has seldom occurred to the theologians even to mention the fellowship of the sexes.'[59] The theological emphasis has been more on the hierarchical division of roles, rather than on both husband and wife being made in the divine image of God. The wife has been viewed as a helper given to the husband, primarily for the purpose of procreating.[60]

56. See Lisa Sowle Cahill, 'Marriage', in Letty Russell and J. Shannon Clarkson (eds.), *Dictionary of Feminist Theologies* (Louisville, KY: Westminster/John Knox Press, 1996), p. 172.

57. Cahill, 'Marriage', p. 173. Cahill notes how the Christian tradition has 'enshrined women's maternal, nurturing, and self-sacrificial roles and encouraged women to be submissive to men in the name of Christ.'

58. Rebecca E. Dobash and Russell P. Dobash, *Violence Against Wives: A Case Against the Patriarchy* (New York: Free Press, 1979), p. 44.

59. Jewett, *Man as Male and Female*, p. 29.

60. For further discussion of the notion of women as helpmates, see Alice Ogden Bellis, *Helpmates, Harlots, Heroes: Women's Stories in the Hebrew Bible* (Louisville, KY: Westminster/John Knox Press, 1994).

A theology of marriage thus framed has driven women not only to confinement in domestic service but also to a secondary and dependent position in the relationship. This creates an unhealthy dualism wherein the lesser partners (women) have been denied their own rights and potential as equal participants in a covenantal relationship. As lesser beings in marriage, women must be submissive and obedient to their male partners, who are the supervisors. The high value placed on procreation means that barren women can be labeled as worthless beings whose wombs must have been cursed by God.

This kind of theology considers women only on the basis of their biological, child-rearing and serving functions, over against respect for their integrity as human beings equally created and loved by God. Sadly, this patriarchal theology of marriage is still the unquestioned norm in Oceanian Christian communities. It is deeply rooted in the consciousness of Oceanian Christians, particularly the men, who cannot conceive of the equality and true complementarity of partners in marriage.

This boils down to a violation of the personhood of women and feeds directly into Oceanian Christian men's justification for the acts of violence they commit against their wives. This violence becomes institutionalized in the very structure of the patriarchal family, 'supported by economic and political institutions and by a (religious) belief system … that makes such relationships seem natural, morally just and sacred.'[61]

In particular, researchers who have studied violence in Christian marriages have found that biblical warrants for the submission of wives are used as a justification for wife abuse.[62] Battered wives who are devout Christians are therefore prone to:

> interpret their experiences of abuse according to the Genesis story of creation and the Fall; the New Testament 'household code' admonitions to wives to be subject to their husbands; the sayings of Jesus about divorce; and assorted other Gospel texts which urge meekness, self-abnegation, suffering and sacrifice as marks of the Christian life.[63]

61. Dobash and Dobash, *Violence Against Wives*, p. 34.

62. See, for instance, Susan Brooks Thistlethwaite, 'Every Two Minutes: Battered Women and Feminist Interpretation', in Letty Russell (ed.), *Feminist Interpretation of the Bible*, (Philadelphia: Fortress Press, 1985), p. 105. This case is also made by various contributors to Carol J. Adams and Marie M. Fortune (eds.), *Violence Against Women and Children: A Christian Theological Sourcebook* (New York: Continuum 1997).

63. Thisthethwaite, 'Every Two Minutes', p. 105.

To summarize, the bonding of husband and wife in Christian marriage, in the all-encompassing embrace of God-given love, should ideally enhance each partner's enrichment and growth. Theoretically, Christian marriage is not merely a procreative union (since procreation is not always possible), but first and foremost a partnership of mutual care and encouragement between two people. Where such mutual nurturance is affirmed, neither partner can dominate, and no form of violence can be tolerated. It is tragic that this originary theology of marriage has been overshadowed by a patriarchal construction of marriage in Christian tradition.

Theology of Sacrifice

Central to the teachings of the Christian faith is the theology of the sacrifice of Jesus Christ, although the language of sacrifice itself is not common in the New Testament. (In fact, the earliest liturgies avoided sacrificial language and did not even mention the Last Supper.[64]) Jesus' willing suffering and death on the cross was God's ultimate gift of love for humanity. The Old Testament concept of sacrifice was reformulated in this pivotal moment in the Jesus story to express the sacrificial love of God in Jesus.

Lamentably, this theology of sacrifice has been glorified over the centuries to the detriment of women. Suffering women have been exhorted to accept their suffering in imitation of the suffering of Christ ('Christ suffered on the cross; can't you bear a little suffering too?'[65]). Women have been counseled to 'carry the cross they have to bear' as a sacrifice on behalf of others. Many Christian women who are victims of male violence have in fact been told by their male pastors or priests that they should accept their abuse and 'willingly share in the sufferings of Christ.'[66]

This traditional theological focus on sacrifice is vigorously critiqued by feminist theologians, particularly in the light of its connection with violence against women.[67] They point out that Christian women who suffer from male abuse have often been undermined by a patriarchal reading of the theology of sacrifice.

---

64. See Andrew Brian McGowan, *Ascetic Eucharists: Food and Drink in Early Christian Ritual Meals* (Oxford: Clarendon Press; New York: Oxford University Press, 1999).

65. Gnanadasen, *No Longer a Secret*, p. 49.

66. Hood, 'Speaking Out and Doing Justice', p. 221.

67. See Rachel Fulton, *From Judgment to Passion: Devotion to Christ and the Virgin Mary 800–1200* (New York: Columbia University Press, 2002).

They assert that the theology of sacrifice has in fact been specifically directed toward women and other oppressed groups. Women, in particular,

> have been exhorted to enter into the destiny and vocation that belong to them through their superior capacity for self-sacrifice, self-denial and suffering that has been thought ... to belong to their "proper nature." ... Women have been invited to participate in and conform themselves to the suffering of Christ by remaining passive and powerless because it is these qualities that will humanize the children they raise and the men for whom they provide a home.[68]

Mary Daly puts the case even more strongly when she insists that:

> qualities that Christianity has idealized, especially for women, are also those of a victim: sacrificial love, passive acceptance of suffering, humility, and meekness. Since these are the qualities idealized in Jesus, 'who died for our sins,' his functioning as a model reinforces the scapegoat syndrome of women.[69]

What is forgotten in the traditional glorification of sacrifice is that, while Jesus voluntarily sacrificed his life for others, the victims of violent abuse do not voluntarily offer themselves to be punching-bags to relieve the aggression of their partners or other men.[70] Female victims of male violence 'do not choose to suffer and there is little sense that they are suffering in order to achieve a greater good.'[71]

Yet Christian women who are victims of domestic abuse have routinely been counseled to take 'the sacrificial suffering of Christ ... as a model and reason for them to stay in abusive relationships.'[72] The intrinsic worth of the 'good Christian woman' has been posited as her willingness to inculcate the 'suffering servant' mentality into her self-understanding. But, as Sheila Collins points out, by 'accepting that particular interpretation of the Christ event as normative for their lives, women have participated in their own crucifixion.'[73]

68. Scholer, 'The Evangelical Debate', p. 32.

69. Mary Daly, *Beyond God the Father: Toward a Philosophy of Women's Liberation* (Boston: Beacon Press, 1973), p. 7.

70. For a fuller discussion of voluntary versus involuntary suffering, see Marie M. Fortune, 'The Transformation of Suffering: A Biblical and Theological Perspective', in Adams and Fortune (eds.), *Violence Against Women and Children*, pp. 85–91.

71. McMullen, 'One Day I Went to a Theological Consultation', p. 200.

72. McMullen, 'One Day I Went to a Theological Consultation', p. 200.

73. Sheila Collins, *A Different Heaven and Earth* (Valley Forge, PA: Judson Press, 1974), pp. 88–89.

For women, this perversion of the theology of sacrifice is dangerous and morally disastrous, when sacrifice becomes self-negation. Marjorie Proctor-Smith argues that the 'glorification of suffering in Christian thought and practice has contributed to the difficulty of those who need to claim their own right and need to live without suffering inflicted on them by others,' and that 'the interpretation of Jesus' death as a redemptive sacrifice is deeply problematic for survivors of violence, whose own suffering saves no one.'[74]

The giving of oneself for the good of the other is, of course, a Christian mandate for all believers, male and female. But when sacrifice dehumanizes the sacrificer, it is meaningless. It simply allows the suffering of one party to benefit the other. If the Christian value of 'giving up something valuable for a better spiritual and material growth and development' is to be framed in a more life-affirming way, it must be construed such that it is for the mutual benefit of 'the offerer as well as the receiver.'[75]

An Indian Christian women's group has asserted that, rather than continue to trumpet our distorted crucifixion theology, what women need to reclaim for themselves is 'the resurrection ... as a step towards the discovery of their power.'[76] Marie Fortune and other female theologians have issued similar challenges, in an attempt to remove any theological justification for women's suffering at the hands of men through appeals to Christ's suffering on the cross. In Fortune's words, 'Rather than the sanctification of suffering, Jesus' crucifixion should be a witness to the horror of violence. It is not a model of how suffering should be borne, but a witness of God's desire that no one should have to suffer violence again.'[77]

This distorted Christian theology of sacrifice was adopted wholesale by Oceanian Christians. All too many Oceanian women have sacrificed their own self-development for an existence

74. Marjorie Proctor-Smith, 'The Whole Loaf: Holy Communion and Survival', in Adams and Fortune (eds.), *Violence Against Women and Children*, p. 473.

75. Elizabeth Amoah, 'Sacrifice / Self-Negation', in Russell and Clarkson (eds.), *Dictionary of Feminist Theologies*, p. 254.

76. 'The National Situation: A Biblical Response from Women', *Stree Reflect Series* 1 (All India Council of Christian Women/National Council of Churches in India) (1986): n.p., cited in Gnanadason, *No Longer a Secret*, p. 50.

77. Marie Fortune, *Family Violence: A Workshop Manual* (Seattle, WA: Center for the Prevention of Sexual and Domestic Violence, 1980), p. 3.

narrowly confined to child-rearing and domestic service. They have internalized their self-negation in silence, because they were taught that self-sacrifice is what makes one a true Christian, and that their trials are in no way comparable to the suffering of the Savior who redeemed their sins.

Given the extent to which the theology of sacrifice has been used to further Oceanian women's passive acceptance of male violence, there is an urgent need for the churches of Oceania to radically rethink the whole theology of atonement.[78] It 'needs careful interpretation and proper understanding within the different traditions, so that in no denomination will there be those who can argue that women's submission to violence accords with God's purposes.'[79]

Since the suffering of Jesus has been used as a destructive tool for the oppression of women and other groups, new interpretations must be envisioned so that women can experience what it means to be fully liberated from the cross into the new life of the resurrection. Many new questions about the correlation of the theology of sacrifice with violence against women are already being raised by Western feminist theologians such as Rita Nakashima Brock, Marie Fortune, Rebecca Ann Parker, Joanne Carlson Brown, and others. Oceanian Christian women need to join their international sisters in addressing these questions in their own contexts, questions such as:

> How is it that the tortuous death of Jesus can be spoken of as initiating this new community? Do we need the death of God incarnate to show us that God is with us in our suffering? Was Jesus' suffering and death required for revelation to occur? Was God not with us in suffering before the death of Jesus?[80]

78. Among texts commonly used in teaching about the atonement in theological school classrooms today are John Driver, *Understanding the Atonement for the Mission of the Church* (Scottsdale, PA: Herald Press, 1986); Thomas N. Finger, *Christian Theology: An Eschatological Approach*, vol. 1 (Nashville, TN: Thomas Nelson Publishers, 1985); and the very conservative Millard Erickson, *Christian Theology*, 2nd edn. (Grand Rapids, MI: Baker Books, 2001). These more traditional interpretations are critiqued by feminist theologians, but they have also criticized the theology of atonement of Jürgen Moltmann, who has been accused of 'blessing the victims' of suffering in his *The Crucified God* (New York: Harper and Row, 1974).

79. Hood, 'Speaking Out and Doing Justice', p. 221. See also Denny Weaver, *A Non-Violent Atonement* (Grand Rapids, MI: William B. Eerdmans Publishing Co., 2001).

80. Joanne Carlson Brown and Rebecca Parker, 'For God so Loved the World?', in Adams and Fortune (eds.), *Violence Against Women and Children*, p. 48. Similar questions are raised in Rita Nakashima Brock and Rebecca Ann Parker, *Proverbs of Ashes: Violence, Redemptive Suffering, and the Search for What Saves Us* (Boston: Beacon Press, 2001).

Theology of Forgiveness

A further theological problem for Oceanian churches which impinges on the issue of violence against women is that women, including female victims of violence, are socialized by the churches to be meek, forgiving Christians. This expectation is related to the mis-appropriated theology of sacrifice discussed above. Jesus' sufferings are again brought into play, with church teachings arguing that, if Jesus could forgive those who crucified him, then women should likewise forgive their abusive husbands, partners, or others who discriminate against them. The cure for their woundedness, they are told, lies in 'following the pattern of Christ and forgiving their abuser, in keeping with Jesus' parable suggesting that there should be no end to forgiveness (Mt. 18: 21).'[81]

This appropriation of forgiveness is extremely problematic when it is used to justify the endurance of relentless violence against women. The standard counsel of many Oceanian clergy to female victims of domestic violence that they should respond to their abusers with forgiveness and unconditional Christian love only encourages more violence. It keeps female victims silent and allows male perpetrators to avoid accountability and atonement for their abuse.

Theologian Mary Hunt has condemned this 'forgiving and forgetting' theology as 'pathological advice in a culture of violence.'[82] A more fitting theological focus, she asserts, should be on justice. In a biblically sound theology, there can in fact be no forgiveness without justice. Using the injunction in Mic. 6: 8 as a guide ('what does the Lord require of you but to do justice...'), Marie Fortune has also commented,

> Truth-telling, acknowledgement of violation, compassion, protection of the vulnerable, accountability, restitution and vindication are the requirements of doing justice and mercy in the face of violation and injustice ... Vindication for victims is the substance of justice and mercy.[83]

Before the churches of Oceania instruct women to forgive the men who abuse them, they must begin their healing ministry by

81. Hood, 'Speaking Out and Doing Justice', p. 221.

82. Mary Hunt, 'Waging War at Home: Christianity and Structural Violence', *Miriam's Song* V (1992): n.p.

83. Marie Fortune, *Is Nothing Sacred? When Sex Invades the Pastoral Relationship* (San Francisco: Harper and Collins, 1989), p. 56.

declaring the church's unequivocal commitment to justice, which in this regard entails an intolerance of any form of violence against women. By brainwashing women to 'forgive and forget' the violence committed against them, the churches have sanctioned the double victimization of women, instilling in them the belief that, 'in addition to suffering violence, it is they and they alone who are required to meet the demands of the church' to forgive their abusers.[84] Justice for the church in Oceania must begin with deeper theological reflection and teaching about the interrelationship between justice and reconciliation.

All too often the churches of Oceania have relied upon the tenets of patriarchal theology such as those highlighted in the preceding sections as justification for minimizing or ignoring violence against women, blaming women for their own suffering, and sanctioning men's abuse of power. Certainly very few, if any, mainstream male theologians today, in Oceania or elsewhere, would attempt to construct a theological position that overtly justified violence against women. Yet the fact remains that many churches still continue to hold in esteem the patriarchal 'fathers' of church tradition. The basic assertions of their theology have been inculcated in our very beings — in both men and women — over many centuries. They have become, for many believers in the church worldwide, so taken-for-granted that they are like the air we breathe.

In order for a breath of fresh air to blow through the church, so that the strands of patriarchal theology can be unraveled and dismantled, our churches must first return to a reconsideration of their primary text, the Bible. While we do not claim to be biblical scholars, we do offer the following lay reflections on the problem of biblical interpretation, in relation to violence against women.

The Problem with Biblical Interpretation

The Bible is the primary source of enlightenment and guidance for all Christians. However, it has not only been, in Elisabeth Schüssler Fiorenza's words, 'interpreted by a long line of men and proclaimed in patriarchal churches, it is also authored by men, written in androcentric language, reflective of male religious experience, and

84. Fortune, *Is Nothing Sacred*, p. 56.

selected and transmitted by male religious leadership.'[85] As such, it has been manipulated and twisted by men to validate the objectification of women.

Historically, it was understood that women were meant only to hear the Bible, and perhaps to read it, but certainly to accept men's interpretations of its meanings and import. This limited role for women in relation to biblical interpretation stemmed from the widespread perception of women as inferior intellectual beings. Since there was thus no need to educate women theologically, their knowledge of biblical languages and traditions remained limited throughout much of church history.[86]

More recent interpretations of the Bible from feminist perspectives have brought about a new awareness of how female interpreters approach scriptural texts and contexts. While, on the one hand, viewing the Bible as a source of liberation and inspiration, many women have also critiqued the ways in which the Bible has been used as a patriarchal tool to their disadvantage.

Kwok Pui-Lan claims that the Bible is 'doubly problematic for Third World women because it has been used not only against their cultures but also against their women.'[87] Another non-western feminist voice, Elsa Tamez, asserts that the 'time has come to acknowledge that those biblical texts that reflect patriarchal culture proclaim women's inferiority and their submission to men and are not normative.'[88] Feminist interpretations of the Bible have posed

85. Elisabeth Schüssler Fiorenza, 'The Will to Choose or Reject: Continuing our Critical Work', in Letty Russell (ed.), *Feminist Interpretation of the Bible* (Philadelphia: Fortress Press, 1985), p. 130.

86. Reference is made here to the late nineteenth and early twentieth centuries' movement in which a 'clear sense of the need for women to read the Bible self-consciously as women' emerged. This indicates that, for many generations, women's active role in terms of interpretation was not recognized. See Carol A. Newsom and Sharon H. Ringe, 'Introduction to the First Edition', in Carol A. Newsom and Sharon H. Ringe (eds.), *Women's Bible Commentary: Expanded Edition with Apocrypha* (Louisville, KY: Westminster/John Knox Press, 1998), pp. xix–xxiv.

87. Kwok Pui-Lan, 'Racism and Ethnocentrism in Feminist Biblical Interpretation', in Elisabeth Schüssler Fiorenza (ed.), *Searching the Scriptures: A Feminist Introduction*, (New York: The Crossroad Publishing Company, 2001), p. 101. See also, Kwok Pui-Lan, *Discovering the Bible in the Non-Biblical World* (Maryknoll, NY: Orbis Books, 1995).

88. Elsa Tamez, 'Women's Re-reading of the Bible', in Virginia Fabella and Mercy Amba Oduyoye (eds.), *With Passion and Compassion: Third World Women Doing Theology* (Maryknoll, NY: Orbis Books, 1988), p. 176.

radical challenges to the prevailing patriarchal assumptions about what constitutes biblical 'truth' and normative moral precepts.

In the history of the Oceanian churches, traditional patriarchal interpretations of the Bible have been and remain unquestioned. The uncritical imposition of this approach to biblical hermeneutics can be partly claimed as a contributing factor to the problem of violence against women in Christian Oceanian communities. It is through the influence of this tradition that the inferior status of women has been reinforced.

For the most part, Oceanian Christian women have yet to emerge from the cage of patriarchy to 'liberate the Word'[89] for themselves. The majority of women in the Oceanian churches still interpret biblical passages literally. This literal interpretation is synonymous with a fundamentalist approach to the Bible. Such an approach sees claims of ultimate truth embedded in every text. These truths are treasured and appropriated without question. Any exegetical attempt to explore alternative meanings or contextual implications is considered a serious heretical offence and a distortion of the 'truth-reality' presented by the text itself. Most Oceanian women's knowledge of biblical texts, even when gleaned from their private devotional reading, is informed primarily by their male pastors or priests, whom they trust as the only qualified persons to interpret the Bible.

Feminist interpretation of the Bible, in contrast, has as its starting point a critical stance, whereby the final form of the scriptures presented to us is opened up for questioning. Women's critical task is seen to be that of engaging in a 'self-conscious' reading of the Bible in order to both engage the larger (patriarchal) context in its wholeness and also to hopefully discover alternative interpretations of selected biblical texts that uphold oppressive attitudes toward women.

With the Oceanian context of patriarchal biblical interpretations in mind, the following sections briefly examine a few selected texts which have been used most frequently in Oceanian churches to justify the subjugation of women—and thus, indirectly, violence against women.

89. This term has been explicated in Letty M. Russell (ed.), *Liberating Word: A Guide to Non-Sexist Interpretation in the Bible* (Philadelphia: Westminster Press, 1976).

Old Testament Text: Gen. 2: 4b – 3: 24

The conventional interpretation of the second creation story in Genesis is a prime example of how the Bible can be used to reinforce the subjugation of women. Gen. 2: 23 ('out of man this one was taken') has often been distorted to justify violence against women, the rationale being that if woman was created 'out of' man, then she must be inferior to him and must submit to his control. Instead of upholding the creation of woman for the sake of partnership and companionship, the emphasis is on ownership and possession.

Almost all of the Oceanian men and women asked about this passage as a part of this study responded that the first woman was created solely to be the helper to the man. This view upholds the standard of female submission set by the church and affirmed by culture, leading to the ongoing sanction of domestic violence as a way of 'teaching' women to remember their 'proper place.'

The standard interpretation of the second creation story maintains that the origin, sexual status and role of Eve all point to her 'derivative' and 'secondary' identity in relation to the man.[90] These derivative attributes are an intrinsic part of the larger design of the Yahwist narrative itself. (Adam was himself 'derived' from the earth, for example.) The story reaches its penultimate climax in the garden, with the derivative formation of Eve—a woman who is to created to be a helpmate for the man.

The final climax, of course, depicts the banishment of both the man and the woman from the garden. In traditional interpretations this has been blamed on the woman, as the temptress of the man and thus the source of original sin. In her exposition of the Genesis creation accounts, Susan Niditch comments:

> The tale explaining the departure from Eden into a real world of work, birth, and death in Genesis 3 is taken to be an even stronger indictment of woman as a gullible, unworthy partner who lets loose sin and death. Her biological function as conceiver and bearer of children is perceived as confirmation of her fall, a punishment shared by all women who come after her.[91]

90. The 'derivative' elements of the creation accounts are evidenced in the closing phrase of the first creation narrative (Gen. 2:4a) and the opening statement of the second creation story (Gen. 2:4b). The transitional sentence indicates the shift of focus of procreative activity from the heavenly to the earthly sphere. See Susan Niditch, 'Genesis', in Newsom and Ringe (eds.), *Women's Bible Commentary*, p. 16.

91. 'Genesis', in Newsom and Ringe (eds.), *Women's Bible Commentary*, p. 16.

The larger contention of the patriarchal reading of this story, of course, is that the inferior status of women has already been confirmed by her being 'formed out of' the man in the first place. Here the man is viewed as the one who conceives and the woman as the by-product. She was created as an 'after-thought' of the Creator.[92] This is evidenced in Adam's definitive exclamation: *'This at last is bone of my bones and flesh of my flesh; she shall be called Woman, because she was taken out of Man'* (Gen. 2: 23).

Adam's statement is the seedbed of traditional interpretations that mandate the secondary place of women in every sphere of life. This rendering has been used not only as incontrovertible evidence of woman's lower status, but also as justification for male attempts to control and punish women for 'stepping out of line,'[93] even if this involves violence.

Interpretations which dwell on Eve as a derivative by-product confine the meaning of this story to a face value reading (viewed through a patriarchal lens), without probing other possible meanings which may lie beneath the surface.[94] In an extensive exposition of Gen. 2: 23 in *God and the Rhetoric of Sexuality*, Phyllis Trible provides an alternative interpretation that points to the hidden reality of God's creative activity.

Trible presents the episode in the garden as the story of a significant shift, from the creation of living beings out of *ha'adamah* — earth — to a 'creative act (that) comes out of the earth creature itself.'[95] This creaturely being now performs the function formerly assumed by the earth. Trible then points to the uniqueness of the woman's creation outside the ordinary order of 'landed' activities (creation out of the ground), and refers to the woman as 'belong[ing] to a new order that will by itself transform the earthly creature [man].'[96]

This feminist interpretation demonstrates that even biblical texts which emerged out of patriarchal contexts, and which have thus

92. Gayle Graham Yates, *What Women Want: The Ideas of the Movement* (Cambridge, MA: Harvard University Press, 1975), p. 69.

93. Newsom and Ringe, 'Introduction', *Women's Bible Commentary*, p. 16.

94. Note that the early church theologians understood Mary, the mother of God, as the new Eve, and Jesus as the new Adam. Mary, the well-spring of her son who delivers salvation, and Jesus, the child of God, become the new Eve and Adam who restore life in paradise for all humanity.

95. Phyllis Trible, *God and the Rhetoric of Sexuality: Overtures to Biblical Theology* (Philadelphia: Fortress Press, 1978), p. 96.

96. Trible, *God and the Rhetoric of Sexuality*, p. 97.

easily lent themselves to continuing patriarchal constructions, can at times be freed from interpretations that restrict the intended liberating love of God for all creation.

New Testament Text (I): I Cor. 11: 2–16

St. Paul's writings on women's status and roles in the church are paradoxical — a reflection of the tension that existed between Gospel and culture even in the early church. One finds Paul's approach to women in some texts liberating, while in other Pauline passages one is met with more confusing or even contradictory attitudes that appear to deny women's equality. One of the texts cited most frequently to support the secondary status and submission of women is found in Paul's first Epistle to the Corinthians 11: 2–16.

Since the text is quite extensive, our discussion will focus on the key themes of women's head-covering and headship. The covering of women's heads in worship was taken for granted in the cultural tradition which was assumed by the Christian congregation in Corinth. Upholding this tradition, Paul writes in I Cor. 11: 2–5:

> (2) I commend you because you remember me in everything and maintain the *traditions* even as I have delivered them to you. (3) But I want you to understand that *the head of every man is Christ, the head of a woman is her husband, and the head of Christ is God.* (4) Any man who prophesies with his head covered dishonors his head, (5) *but any woman who prays or prophesies with her head unveiled dishonors her head* — it is the same as if her head were shaven. (Italics added)

On the one hand, Paul appears to be asserting the headship of Christ as the model for the husband-wife relationship. On a more practical level, he may also have been attempting to accommodate the widespread belief that head coverings were a protection from the evil forces or demons which attacked women.[97] His upholding of the model of headship becomes distorted, however, when the headship image is applied in a way that diminishes women's value in comparison with men.

Imaging the man as the head of woman indicates Paul's capitulation to a patriarchal understanding of male-female relationships. In this view, the exposure of a man's head is a sign of

---

97. This and other fascinating insights are disclosed in a feminist essay on the relationship between veiling and the sexuality of women in Elizabeth Castelli (ed.), *Women, Gender, Religion: A Reader* (New York: Houndmills; London: Palgrave, 2001).

his headship. For a woman to do likewise would be a disgrace, given the social conventions of the time, in which she could never, or rarely, be the head of anything. In simpler terms, the woman does not belong to the triad of headships: the headship of God the father, Christ the Son, and man the husband.

This text has been the central focus of many scholarly debates regarding the concept of headship. Some have argued that Paul speaks here of 'head' to mean 'source,' while others emphasize 'rank and authority.'[98] Both concepts are found in the later parts of the text itself. For example, in 1 Cor. 11: 14–15, Paul dwells on the image of the head as source rather than authority.[99]

However, his reference in 1 Cor. 11: 7 to the man being closer to the godhead and made in the image of God, while the woman is only a 'reflection' of the man's glory, simply indicates, again, that Paul is unable in this instance to escape his entrapment in the patriarchal mindset—despite his ability to transcend it in other passages such as Gal. 3: 28. This mindset reaffirms women's secondary status, and gives the impression that 'woman was created from and for the sake of man, and not vice-versa'[100] (I Cor. 11: 8–9).

A literal reading of this text thus undermines and invalidates women's integrity, and serves as a medium of oppression rather than liberation. More critical interpretations are needed in order to locate the text in its cultural context (of patriarchy), so that readers can be reminded of the contrasting liberating thrust of Jesus' gospel. Otherwise, this passage only reinforces patriarchal attitudes that undermine women's freedom and oneness with men 'in Christ.'

It is worth noting, in light of the inherited orthodox reading of this passage, that many churches in Oceania still require women to cover their heads in church, by reference to I Cor. 11. Especially during important church meetings and Sunday morning worship services, women are told—at least in most Polynesian church contexts—that they must wear a hat, preferably white. Any woman

98. Scholer, 'The Evangelical Debate', pp. 39–44. See also Catherine Clark Kroeger, 'God's Purpose in the Midst of Human Sin', in Catherine Clark Kroeger and James R. Beck (eds.), *Women, Abuse and the Bible: How Scripture Can be Used to Hurt or Heal* (Grand Rapids, MI: Baker Book House, 1996), pp. 206–10.

99. See Jouette M. Bassler, '1 Corinthians', in Newsom and Ringe (eds.), *Women's Bible Commentary*, p. 417. This is generally viewed as a recitation of the Adam-Eve relationship in Genesis 2–3.

100. Bassler, '1 Corinthians', in *Women's Bible Commentary*, p. 417.

who disobeys this rule will not only be publicly scolded and embarrassed but will also have to pay fines to the Women's Fellowship.

Women, especially clergy spouses, must also wear dresses that are long enough to cover everything up to the neck, including the arms, and the legs down to the toes. In short, many Oceanian churches have taken the above passage from Corinthians farther than even Paul intended and have held on to the Victorian model of womanliness imposed by the early missionaries, using the weapon of biblical infallibility and authority.

The Oceanian husband assumes the role of enforcer, instructing his wife to be obedient to church rules and the Bible by wearing her hat in church. On occasions where the wife neglects to follow this custom, his function is to instill in her the validity of the inherited tradition through reminding or commanding. The wife in return must obey. The problem, in the context of Paul's teaching to the Corinthians, is that the liberating love of the Gospel is overtaken by the cultural underpinnings of patriarchy.

New Testament Text (II): Eph. 5: 21–24

St. Paul addresses the husband-wife relationship in marriage in this part of his letter to the Ephesians. In its simple literary form, it is clear that Paul is validating the husband's authoritarianism at the expense of the wife's subordination. This is indicated by his use of the two terms 'subject' and 'head.' Paul writes:

> (21) Be *subject* to one another out of reverence for Christ. (22) Wives, be *subject* to your husbands, as to the Lord. (23) For the husband is the *head* of the wife as Christ is the *head* of the church, his body, as he is himself its Savior. (24) As the church is *subject* to Christ, so let wives also be *subject in everything* to their husbands. [RSV] (Italics added.)

Some exegetes have argued that the emphasis of Paul's teaching here is the Christ-church model, in which the subjection of both husband and wife to each other through mutual care and service in marriage is an imitation of their loyalty to Christ.[101] It is contended that, in contrast to the Greco-Roman understanding of marriage, in

---

101. Some have argued that Paul might have been referring here to Jesus' model of servanthood, as well as to the teaching that the first must become the last. However, this kind of reading is slightly out of context as Paul is dealing with the immediate issue of the husband-wife relationship.

which wives must *always* submit to husbands, 'the cultural understanding of marriage [in this passage] is significantly qualified for those in Christ, so that the passage teaches an overarching concept of mutual submission.'[102]

This positive interpretation is debatable, however, in the sense that any *mutuality* in husbands' and wives' subjection is valid only in relation to the couple's reverence for Christ. In other words, mutual submission applies to the relationship with Christ but not to the actual husband-wife relationship. In addition, the translation of the Greek *kephale* as 'source' rather than 'authority'[103] does nothing to soften the image of an authoritative and dominating role for husbands as 'heads.'

The structure of verses 22–24 further suggests the deliberate subjection of wives to husbands. Women are told: 'Wives, be subject to your husbands…' This is a direct command. This message is then justified by the phrase that follows: 'as to the Lord.' A hierarchy of subjections is delineated: to the Lord, who has authority over husbands; and to husbands, who rule over wives. Since Christ is 'Savior' of the Body of Christ, and husbands imitate Christ's authority, the status of husbands becomes analogous to that of a savior, a role that is not valid in a mutual relationship.[104]

* * *

One can see from this brief overview how certain Pauline texts can be readily used by patriarchal biblical interpreters to encourage authoritarian men to behave in controlling ways over their wives and other women, in the name of maintaining the divinely sanctioned subjection of women. Even if Paul's intention in these passages was to nurture right relationships with Christ, the majority of Christians in Oceania do not read such texts beyond what they see on the surface. For husbands, what the biblical texts state must be executed. Most women are likewise blindfolded by St. Paul's exhortations, and meekly accept their subjection to men's control. These texts are

102. Scholer, 'The Evangelical Debate', p. 43.

103. Scholer, 'The Evangelical Debate', p. 43. Although Scholer argues that *kephale* is best understood here as 'source', even he eventually acknowledges that it 'could just as likely mean "authority over."'

104. See Elizabeth Johnson, 'Ephesians', in *Women's Bible Commentary*, p. 431. As Johnson notes, 'The logic of the analogy collapses because husbands do not die for their wives as Christ died for the church…'

cited as confirmation of the power invested in men by God to rule over women. They can even become devices used to defend the violence inflicted on women by abusive men.

Biblical interpretations, of course, are only part of the problem. The place where patriarchal theology and biblical interpretations are played out through preaching, policies and practices is the church. The church has a powerful hold over the lives of most Oceanians, and it is for that reason essential that we turn our attention in the next chapter to an investigation of the role which the church plays in the problem of violence against women. This will entail an unraveling of two major strands: church traditions and the power of the male clergy.

Chapter Five

ECCLESIAL STRANDS IN THE FABRIC OF VIOLENCE AGAINST
WOMEN: CHURCH TRADITIONS AND CLERGY POWER

The Patriarchal Captivity of the Church

It is necessary at this juncture to ask the following question: What
have been the consequences of patriarchal theology and biblical
hermeneutics, with their inherent warrant for 'power-over'
relationality, in terms of the church's response to violence against
women? For all too many churches around the world, violence
against women has been, until recently, largely a taboo subject. In
the worst case scenarios, it has been a non-issue. The African feminist
theologian, Musimbi Kanyoro, has noted that 'even though women
in North America and, to a lesser extent, in Europe are beginning
to speak out, there is still much reluctance in many churches in the
world to discuss issues of (gender) violence openly.'[1] This has
certainly been the case in the churches of Oceania until now.

Indeed, although some North American and European churches
now have anti-harassment polices in place, there are very few such
policies, or even church statements forbidding discrimination
against women, in the non-Western churches. At the Sixth Assembly
of the All-Africa Conference of Churches in Harare, Zimbabwe in
1992, for the first time a woman spoke out forcefully condemning
the churches' silence on this issue. Kenyan feminist theologian
Nyambura Njoroge said, in part, in her sermon to the Assembly,
'Violence against women is promoted by (male church leaders')
greed for power ... and desire to dominate and control others.'[2]
This critique has been echoed by Musimbi Kanyoro's statement that

1. Musimbi Kanyoro, lecture, Augustana University College, Alberta, Canada,
March 1992, cited in Gnanadason, *No Longer a Secret*, p. 41.

2. Nyambura Njorage, address, Sixth Assembly of the All-Africa Conference of
Churches, Harare, Zimbabwe, October 1992, cited in Gnanadason, *No Longer a Secret*,
pp. 44–45.

'the rude discovery that even church ministers are violent to women challenges the church to overcome the temptation to be trapped in its own culture. In its silence and non-action the church is compromising its prophetic call.'[3]

The key phrase in Kanyoro's statement is that the church is 'trapped in its own culture' — that is, the culture of patriarchy. This explains the ambiguities and contradictions in the church's witness regarding women: on the one hand, preaching that violence and domination are wrong, while at the same time turning a blind eye to issues such as sexual abuse and harassment of women. How can such a contradiction happen in the church? It happens because the pull of cultural and theological patriarchy that sanctions male 'power-over' relationality is stronger than the pull of the countervailing Gospel mandate of mutuality and equality.

The end result of the church's captivity in the snares of patriarchy is that, in relation to violence against women, it has all too often been 'as much part of the problem as an agent in the solution.'[4] Recent studies show that all forms of violence against women are found 'within Christian and church communities at the same sort of levels as in the secular world.'[5] This is a reality that prevails not only in local parishes but in church institutions such as theological schools.[6]

Another consequence of the patriarchal entrapment of the church is that many women in churches and theological institutions (whether students, staff or spouses) have been indoctrinated by their churches to 'trust male authority figures' in ecclesial settings. Hence they often find themselves not well equipped emotionally to 'resist advances or confront harassers'[7] who are in leadership positions in the church.

Because patriarchal theological and cultural values still hold sway in so many churches around the world — particularly in heavily

3. Kanyoro, lecture, cited in Gnanadason, *No Longer a Secret*, p. 42.
4. McMullen, 'One Day I Went to a Theological Consultation', p. 197.
5. Hood, 'Speaking Out and Doing Justice', p. 217.
6. One study of male faculty in theological institutions found that they were 'much less likely than female faculty to label jokes, sexual teasing or innuendo, gestures or suggestive looks as harassing.' They defended their attitudes and behaviors by complaining about being misunderstood or even persecuted by women, and by denying that any power imbalance existed between them and women in the seminary community. See: LeMoncheck and Hajdin, *Sexual Harassment: A Debate*, p. 15.
7. LeMoncheck and Hajdin, *Sexual Harassment: A Debate*, p. 14.

patriarchal contexts such as Oceania—men continue to hold almost all important positions of ecclesial power. It is therefore men's judgments about what constitutes violence against women, or about who is to blame, that prevail. In such environments, 'even the most articulate and well-reasoned women' find it difficult to challenge discrimination and abuse in the church.[8]

The silence of many churches on the issue of violence against women, particularly its more subtle forms such as harassment, is thus a reflection of ecclesial complicity in the perpetuation of patriarchal theology. The church's silence has contributed to the invisibility of Christian women's suffering from male abuse. James Poling has noted that 'the church has been very poor at placing accountability on those [in its ranks] who abuse power.'[9] Clearly the church will be unable to break through its silence on or acquiescence in violence against women until it has grappled with its larger embrace of patriarchal models of leadership which have marginalized and disempowered women, and thus made them more vulnerable to abuse.

The Patriarchal Captivity of the Church in Oceania

Like so many other churches around the world, the varied church traditions represented in Oceania are thoroughly entrapped in patriarchy. It is no wonder that these churches teach women that they must respect and obey men at all times, and that their primary purpose is to bear and raise children for the continuance of the lineage and to keep the household in order. This is such a central understanding in Oceanian church traditions that it must be viewed as a significant contributing factor to the problem of violence against women.

Oceanian churches' unquestioning appropriation of the traditional marriage rite is a prime example of how church traditions have become a source of bondage for women in abusive relationships. This outmoded marriage rite reinforces the understanding that the man is given the divine authority to rule over the woman, since the wife promises to obey the husband, but not vice-versa. Because he is given this divine sanction through the sacrament of marriage, it can never be challenged.

8. LeMoncheck and Hajdin, *Sexual Harassment: A Debate*, p. 17.
9. Poling, *The Abuse of Power*, p. 150.

This understanding of marriage is similar across denominations in Oceania and has had many negative effects on attitudes toward women in our churches, and on the way they are treated as marital partners. Jesus, of course, spoke highly of the value of marriage (see, e.g., Mk. 10: 5–9). However, as Helen Hood has rightly questioned, 'should church teaching on the sanctity of the marriage vow override *all* other considerations, including that of personal safety within a violent marriage?'[10]

We could re-frame this question in another way, in the Oceanian context: 'Where is the source of liberation for women caught in abusive marriages yet bound to their church traditions, if the church's teaching does not provide an affirmative alternative for abused women?' All too many Oceanian churches have unfortunately not been a safe haven or a source of liberation for such women.

Why is this so? It is because our churches' wholesale appropriation of patriarchal theology, with its insistence that the 'good' and 'holy' woman must be submissive to men, has too often had the effect of silencing abused women, even instilling feelings that they must deserve the 'punishment' meted out by their husbands. (Recall our reflections on Theology of Headship.) To make matters worse, the few abused women who confide in their pastors or priests often find themselves counselled to forgive their abusive spouses, on the basis of warped church teachings on forgiveness. (Recall our reflections on Theology of Forgiveness.) They are urged to return to their abusive spouses on the basis of the church's teaching on 'marriage as the permanent ideal.'[11] (Recall our reflections on Theology of Marriage.)

Many Oceanian women consequently endure being abused for life because their churches teach that, since marriage vows made before God are sacred, they must be kept 'till death do us part,' and that, regardless of the hardship, 'those whom God has joined together let no one put asunder' (Mt. 19: 6). This rigid church teaching denies the theological affirmation that God seeks wholeness for every human life, and cannot therefore condone any relationship in which one party rules over the other party. If marriage is not mutually life-affirming, the church should not impose it rigidly on those who suffer within its confines.

10. Hood, 'Speaking Out and Doing Justice', p. 221.
11. McMullen, 'One Day I Went to a Theological Consultation', p. 201.

We have painted a rather bleak picture of the failure of the churches of Oceania to provide a life-affirming sanctuary for women who are on the receiving end of male violence. This is of course not the whole story. There are any number of individual clergy in churches across Oceania who have a compassionate understanding of women's rights and needs, and who are joining with them in solidarity in their struggles for justice. The fact remains, however, that to date most Oceanian churches remain in captivity to patriarchy, which means that women cannot often turn to the church for solace and succor when they experience violence and abuse.

There is reason for hope, however. In recent years increasing numbers of church women around the world have begun to give voice to their condemnation of the sinfulness of the church's silent complicity in violence against women through its capitulation to patriarchy. As a part of the World Council of Churches' Decade in Solidarity with Women (1989–1999), and in response to the Platform for Action approved at the United Nations World Conference on Women (Beijing, 1995), eight regional WCC workshops were held around the world in the mid-1990s, focusing on the church's role in the problem of violence against women. Oceanian church women participated in one of these workshops, and this has been a springboard for the un-silencing of some church women from Oceania on this and other women's justice issues.

At the conclusion of one of these regional gatherings, in one of the most stinging critiques of the church, the San Jose Declaration of Latin American church women stated unequivocally that 'as a consequence of the tolerance of these situations [of violence against women], the Body of Christ is mutilated … In tolerating these injustices the church loses its moral authority.'[12] The Bali Declaration of Asian church women stated in part: 'In its most blatant form, violence against women in the church is experienced in many pastoral counseling contexts … There is a misconception that clergy represent God … and very often the victim is condemned and the [clergy]man's actions are condoned.'[13]

The Asian women's statement challenges us to consider one of the most painful manifestations of the church's captivity to

12. San Jose Declaration of Latin American Women on Violence Against Women, San Jose, Puerto Rico, 1996, cited in Gnanadason, *No Longer a Secret*, p. 71.

13. Bali Declaration of Asian Women on Violence Against Women, Bali, Indonesia, 1996, cited in Gnanadason, *No Longer a Secret*, p. 70.

patriarchy: the poisonous strand in the patriarchal mat which is the abuse of male clergy power. Because the (almost entirely male) clergy are perhaps more powerful in Oceanian churches than anywhere else in the world, this power has become one of the most toxic strands in the patriarchal ecclesial mat in Oceania. Since this clergy power has had a profound and far-reaching bearing on violence against women in the Oceanian churches, it merits serious and in-depth discussion.

Unraveling the Strand of Male Clergy Power

The Roots of the Problem

In the first instance, the problem with the male clergy stems from a very long tradition of male church leadership which was established fairly early in church history. Contemporary patterns in Oceanian churches cannot be extricated from historical errors made by patriarchal church authorities in the past. Despite the egalitarianism and inclusiveness of Christian ministry in the early church,[14] as the church evolved and made accommodations to its patriarchal surroundings, 'ministry' gradually became identified with 'ordained clergy,' who became exclusively male. The egalitarian theology of ministry of the early church—the 'priesthood of all believers' which had given extraordinary scope and latitude to women's ministries— faded away or went underground.

As a result, church teachings, decisions and leadership models came to be encapsulated by masculine instincts and thought forms. This masculinization of church leadership was already becoming prototypical before Christianity became the state religion of the Roman Empire in the fourth century, but from that time onward

14. Historical and theological studies of the equality of women in ministry in the early church include, for example, Karen Torjeson, *When Women were Priests: Women's Leadership in the Early Church and the Scandal of their Subordination in the Rise of Christianity* (San Francisco: HarperSanFrancisco, 1993); Linda Belleville, *Women Leaders and the Church: Three Crucial Questions* (Grand Rapids, MI: Baker Books, 2000); Elizabeth Clark, *Women in the Early Church* (Wilmington, DE: M. Glazier, 1983); Fran Ferder and John Heagle, *Partnership: Women and Men in Ministry* (Notre Dame, IN: Ave Maria Press, 1989); Elizabeth Schüssler Fiorenza, *Discipleship of Equals: A Critical Feminist Ekklesialogy of Liberation* (London: SCM Press, 1993); Anne Jenson, *God's Self-Confident Daughters: Early Christianity and the Liberation of Women*, trans. O.C. Dean (Louisville, KY: Westminster/John Knox Press, 1996); and Jean LaPorte, *The Role of Women in Early Christianity* (New York: Mellon Press, 1982).

the patriarchal power models of empire became firmly entrenched in the church. For centuries thereafter, until recent decades, women were never or only very rarely admitted into the all-male clergy domain. Male leadership and decision-making were the unquestioned norm in the life of the worldwide church, and this is still the case in Oceania, where the majority of denominations still do not accept women in ministry.

Needless to say, it is extremely problematic for women in the church when 'it is the (male) ordained clergy who interpret Scripture and tradition, determine church policies, and furnish leadership in the parish and the church hierarchies.'[15] In such an ethos, 'even as ministers talk humbly about servanthood, they may still be exerting power manipulatively and collusively.'[16] They exercise authority in churches that remain enmeshed in patriarchal constructions of authority. Once again, the problem is one of 'power-over' relationality.

The Outworkings of Patriarchal Clergy Power

The problem with male clergy power — specifically, their 'power-over' way of relating to women — has been analyzed by a number of theologians.[17] Our analysis draws largely on the work of feminist theologians such as Pamela Cooper-White and Marie Fortune. Cooper-White has shown how the authority of the male clergy has traditionally extended from his spiritual role as the *Man of God*, to his worldly role as a male *authority figure* who 'protects and dominates,' to his professional roles as *teacher/expert* with 'special knowledge,' and *counselor* with the 'wisdom and experience' to deal with all situations.[18] Marie Fortune has also pointed out that, because of the patriarchal ministry paradigm still adopted by most churches, there is a huge power differential between ministers or priests and

15. Mary Daly, *The Church and the Second Sex* (London: Geoffrey Chapman, 1968), pp. 15–25. See also, Gayle Graham Yates, *What Women Want: The Ideas of the Movement* (Cambridge, MA: Harvard University Press, 1975), p. 67.

16. McMullen, 'One Day I Went to a Theological Consultation', p. 198.

17. See, for example, Marie Fortune, *Clergy Misconduct: Sexual Abuse in the Ministerial Relationship* (Seattle, WA: Center for the Prevention of Sexual and Domestic Violence, 1992), and *Is Nothing Sacred;* Nancy Poling, *Victim to Survivor: Women Recovering from Clergy Sexual Abuse* (Cleveland, OH: United Church Press, 1999); and Peter Rutter, *Sex in the Forbidden Zone: When Men in Power — Therapists, Doctors, Clergy, Teachers and Others — Betray Women's Trust* (Los Angeles: Jeremy Tarcher, 1989).

18. Cooper-White, *The Cry of Tamar*, pp. 129–30.

their parishioners – and of course the power differential is greatest where women are concerned.[19]

First, as *Men of God* male clergy are seen as God's special representatives and are hence enshrouded in a protective aura of inviolability. This is especially the case in Oceania, where clergy are seen as divinely sanctioned mentors and protectors. Their word is law and is not open to question. The honor formerly granted to the sacred high chiefs in ancient Oceanian cultures simply shifted to the ordained minister following the missionary conquest of Oceania, and in many Oceanian cultures the sacredness and immutability of the authority of the clergy have even surpassed that of the traditional chiefs.

Now the Oceanian church finds itself entrapped in a system which makes male clergy the honorific messengers of God. When there is a need for a prophetic witness from these messengers of God, they are handcuffed within the system. They are caught between their loyalty to the people who have elevated them so highly and who provide them prestige and nurturance, and their calling to speak out and act for justice. Nowhere is the veneration of male clergy more problematic than in relation to women. For how can a woman already conditioned to be submissive to men question the counsel of a Man of God to remain submissive – much less to challenge her abuser when he happens to *be* that Man of God?

In addition to the theological paradigm which equates male clergy with the other masculine authority figures in the patriarchal theology pyramid (God, Jesus, prophets, priests, rulers, teachers, judges, etc.), clergy are also viewed in the contemporary church as *professionals*. In the modern era they have become specialists, and all specialists enjoy a clear power differential over their constituents (such as doctors over patients, for example). This distantiation has been exacerbated by the creeping historical separation of clergy from laity (mentioned earlier), with its corollary diminution of the priesthood of all believers throughout the course of church history. As the specialist domains of the clergy have increased over time, their spheres of authority over parishioners have multiplied exponentially.

As ecclesial 'jacks-of-all-trades,' contemporary male clergy thus have a huge range of contexts and opportunities in which their

---

19. See: Marie M. Fortune, 'Is Nothing Sacred?', pp. 351–59.

parishioners (the majority of them female in most churches worldwide) come under their authority. Examples include but are not restricted to the following: as leaders of worship, as teachers, mentors or supervisors (including their roles as theological educators), as chaplains in various settings, as pastoral care or counseling 'experts,' as confessors, as persons offering healing ministries, as officiates at rites of passage, and at times as employers.[20] When we recall that institutional abuse of women is most commonplace in male-dominated institutions with a great deal of male-female interaction, and when nowhere is that relational configuration more prevalent than in the church, the potential for clergy abuse becomes obvious.

To summarize, the combination of the spiritual authority accorded to the 'Man of God' and the worldly authority inherent in being a 'specialist' creates a heady concentration of almost unlimited power that serves as a huge temptation to male clergy to make the most of their freedom to have 'power over' the women under their control. This confluence of arenas of 'specialness' gives them unique access to female parishioners, especially to those who are already vulnerable. This has proven time and time again to be a dangerous equation. It demands that we undertake an honest examination of the reality of clergy abuse—an all too common reality in Oceanian churches.

Clergy Abuse: Why and How it Happens

The problem of clergy abuse has in recent years achieved a high profile in the worldwide media due to the increasing numbers of lawsuits and other forms of legal action being brought against members of both Roman Catholic and Protestant male clergy. No part of the world is exempt from these horrific revelations, which appear in the media on an almost weekly basis. Yet while the paedophiliac abuse of young boys and men by Catholic priests has received the most widespread media coverage, the vast majority of clergy abuse cases are in fact heterosexual harassment or sexual abuse of girls and women.

The incidence of clergy abuse in most non-Western churches, including those of Oceania, is still largely undocumented. By far

20. Margaret Kennedy, 'Sexual Abuse of Women by Priests and Ministers to Whom They Go for Pastoral Care and Support', *Feminist Theology* 11:2 (2003): p. 227.

the greatest amount of research in this area has taken place in the United States. Reliable statistics are hard to come by even there because, even when male clergy's participation in research efforts is protected by confidentiality, they are often incapable of admitting that their behaviors in fact constitute abuse or harassment. Nonetheless, in the available studies, somewhere between one-eighth and one-third of male clergy admit crossing the boundary into abusive or harassing behaviors with their female parishioners.[21] The actual incidence is deemed to be higher by most researchers, and significantly higher in many non-Western churches where female victims are much less likely to take legal action or expose clergy abuse.

We are certainly not making the claim that the majority of male clergy participate in abusive or harassing behavior with their parishioners. We have no intention of painting all male clergy with the same condemnatory brush, and we commend all who are honorable and respectful in their relationships with their female parishioners. The issue we are addressing is this: What is it that predisposes some male clergy to cross the boundaries of appropriate clergy-female parishioner relationality?

We have seen that violence against women emanates from the power imbalance intrinsic to patriarchy, a power imbalance still accepted by many churches (their liberative theological pronouncements notwithstanding). Clergy abuse is a particularly virulent manifestation of that power imbalance — of 'power-over' relationality. Recent research has uncovered several profiles of the types of male clergy who tend to succumb to the temptation to abuse the trust of the women under their care in their churches or church institutions.

One such study has identified two major types of clergy abusers: the 'wanderers,' who wander unthinkingly back and forth across the boundaries of appropriate behavior, and the 'predators,' who are more intentional in their manipulative, controlling approach to their female parishioners.[22] Other studies have found that clergy abusers are particularly skilled at 'minimizing, protecting and redefining their behavior in the most favorable light.'[23] If exposed,

---

21. Cooper-White, *The Cry of Tamar*, p. 128.

22. Fortune, *Clergy Misconduct*, pp. 20–21.

23. Cooper-White, *The Cry of Tamar*, p. 135. For a fuller discussion of clergy abuser/harasser profiles, see Karen Lebacqz and Ronald G. Barton, *Sex in the Parish* (Louisville,

they often appeal to the church's 'culture of optimism,' acceptance and forgiveness.[24] They also tend to see themselves first and foremost as 'special' (again, they are Men of God), such that the normal rules regarding relational boundaries do not apply to them.

Clergy abuse may be triggered by stress, over-commitment, or lack of supervision. There are at times attendant danger signs as well, other evidences of boundary violations: Clergy abusers often abuse power in a variety of ways—perhaps through breaches of confidentiality, creating their own inner circle of cronies 'in the know' while keeping others in the dark, financial improprieties, and in general not leading in a transparent, accountable fashion.[25]

But whatever the triggering mechanisms or psychological difficulties in clergy abusers' lives, these are no excuse for their behavior. They know that the pastoral relationship is meant to be a 'sacred trust, a covenantal place of safety'[26] between clergy and parishioner. Even if we accept the notion of the minister or priest as a representative of God and Jesus, his use of power should then be in imitation of Christ—Spirit-infused power that empowers others, not 'power-over.' When male clergy cross the boundary from 'power-for' or 'power-with' to 'power-over,' they are 'stealing from her [the female victim] the appropriate ... sustaining relationship of spiritual guidance and support'[27] which should properly characterize the clergy-parishioner relationship.

What is particularly troubling is the preponderance of evidence that, once these boundaries have been breached, clergy abusers tend to use theological support to justify their behavior. Most clergy abusers tell their female victims that what is happening between them is divinely sanctioned—it is God's will. Indeed, many clergy abusers use God and faith as the 'hook' with which to ensnare vulnerable women. These women are persuaded to have sex through the usage of entrapment language such as: ' "God tells me that this will be good for you;" "God made sex, it's holy and OK for you and me to have sex;" "I am ordained and a holy person, I could not hurt

KY: Westminster/John Knox Press, 1991), especially 'Sex, Power and Ministry', pp. 36–48; and Marie Fortune, 'Violating the Pastoral Relation', review of Lebacqz and Barton, *Sex in the Parish*, *Christianity and Crisis* 51: pp. 16–17 (November 18, 1991): pp. 367–68.

    24. Cooper-White, *The Cry of Tamar*, p. 135.
    25. Cooper-White, *The Cry of Tamar*, p. 141.
    26. Cooper-White, *The Cry of Tamar*, p. 130.
    27. Cooper-White, *The Cry of Tamar*, p. 131.

you as that would offend God." '[28] Many clergy abusers convince their counselees that their sexual encounters will in fact be salvific for them.[29] This is a hideous perversion of Christian relationality.

Thus far our discussion has centred on the world of the clergy abuser. We move now into the world of the women who end up as the victims of clergy abuse. What happens to them and what are the repercussions once they have experienced abuse at the hands of their ministers or priests?

Women's Vulnerability to Clergy Abuse

We are by now well aware of the many different types of behaviors that constitute abuse or harassment of women. All of these, with the exception of street harassment, are practiced by clergy abusers. But what happens in clergy abuse that is distinctive? And what is it that makes women particularly vulnerable to clergy abuse?

What makes clergy abuse especially tricky is that it frequently starts out as friendship—as 'grey area behaviors'—and only gradually slips over into behaviors that are clearly inappropriate and recognized as such by the victim. Holding a woman's hand in prayer may be innocent enough behavior, but graduation to other forms of touching, prolonged visitations, impingement upon a woman's physical or psychological space—all of these constitute a violation of the boundaries and a shattering of the sacred trust that should characterize the clergy-parishioner relationship.

Most sexual abuse of women by male clergy in a parish occurs while they are undergoing counseling with him or are under his pastoral care. The forms of abuse vary from inappropriate remarks and fondling to sexual intercourse; 'some are clearly criminal offences of sexual assault, others more subtle exploitation.'[30] Some clergy abusers are extremely adept at maintaining 'grey area' behaviors just on the very edge of the boundary of inappropriateness, such that the woman will not have enough 'hard evidence' to accuse them of misconduct.

Most women who go to their clergy for pastoral care are already in a vulnerable state and are seeking reassurance, acceptance, and wise counsel. Such women may develop an emotional attachment to their minister, which in psychological terms results in a kind of

28. Kennedy, 'Sexual Abuse of Women', p. 231.
29. Kennedy, 'Sexual Abuse of Women', p. 231.
30. Kennedy, 'Sexual Abuse of Women', p. 227.

transference. This transference makes them more susceptible to inappropriate advances from clergy, and they may eventually 'accede or comply (not consent) because they do not want to lose what is important and valued in the relationship—namely, affirmation and support ... [But this] should never be seen as meaning the woman is consenting to a fully adult and equal sexual relationship.'[31]

These women's vulnerability, in conjunction with their ingrained trust of the clergy, makes it extremely difficult for them to resist unwanted sex or sexual advances. They can easily be coerced into having unwanted sex as a favour, in return for the free 'help' given to them by their respected minister or priest. These vulnerable women, 'especially those who have experienced ... abusive relationships in the past, may not be able to discern an abusive sexual boundary violation by a clergyperson, and it is such women who are most at risk—and indeed are deliberately targeted'[32] by clergy abusers.

Challenges and End Results for Female Victims

The scenario described above opens up what has been a thorny issue in the study of clergy abuse—the issue of consent. Clergy abusers routinely defend their behaviors by insisting that the women 'consented freely.' Our critique of patriarchy, however, has shown us that such an answer is far too simplistic. While it is true that a few women do intentionally set out to seduce their pastor or priest, 'what is crucial [in situations of clergy-parishioner relationships] is the imbalance of power. In such relationships the professional [the minister] always holds more power.'[33] The critical point to be made is that:

> *There can never be true consent when there is imbalance of power.* [Italics added] [Women] seeking help [from clergy] may need assistance in coping with a life crisis. The clergy professional who is helping them in a pastoral relationship is expected not only to possess skills but also to be completely trustworthy. ... The balance of power lies solely with the clergy professional. It is therefore [his] responsibility to set the boundaries of the relationship. Should these boundaries be breached the blame lies solely with the clergy.[34]

31. Kennedy, 'Sexual Abuse of Women', p. 230.
32. Kennedy, 'Sexual Abuse of Women', p. 230.
33. Kennedy, 'Sexual Abuse of Women', p. 227.
34. Kennedy, 'Sexual Abuse of Women', p. 230.

This assertion is not intended in any way to suggest that women are not to be held morally accountable in situations where they willingly consent to inappropriate relationships with clergy. As adult moral agents, they are accountable for their own behavior. We are only pointing out that the context of clergy abuse is not a level ethical playing field. Just as employees are not always 'free' to say no to their employers, and students are not 'free' to say no to their teachers, servants are not necessarily 'free' to run away from their masters. For all too many women in the church, especially in contexts such as Oceania, they are the servants and the clergy are their masters. Until the relational mat can be rewoven so that it is no longer a 'power-over' design, this will continue to be the case.

We have previously highlighted the multiplicity of negative effects of abuse and harassment on women. Here we wish to accentuate the distinctive repercussions of such abuse for women in the church and its related institutions, when the perpetrators are clergy or other men in positions of ecclesial authority.

We have seen that the ecclesial environment in which clergy abuse takes place is most often one of avoidance and cover-up. In such a milieu, as James Poling has pointed out, 'the experience of victims is excluded from the concern of the community.'[35] When female victims in the church or its institutions are not encouraged to give voice to their suffering—or when, in the few instances where their victimization is acknowledged, they are urged to 'forgive and forget'—and when clergy or other church leaders are not held to accountability, the consequences for these women are devastating. The very context in which their hope for justice and full humanity is most deeply grounded—the church—becomes, in a cruel irony, a context in which the seeds of betrayal, confusion and dehumanization are sown.

Indeed, one of the most appalling findings in recent studies is that the church fails to adequately address the injustice of clergy abuse to an even greater extent than is the case with abuse in secular society. Church leaders all too often seek to convince themselves and others either that breaches of sexual boundaries have not taken place (the women are making them up due to some psychological defect), or that whatever has taken place was innocent or consensual.

The tragic fact is that when female victims of clergy abuse do find the courage to seek redress in the church, many church

35. Poling, *The Abuse of Power*, p. 146.

authorities quickly come to the rescue of the abuser to avoid an embarrassing church scandal. Margaret Kennedy, who has years of experience working with the victim-survivors of clergy sexual abuse, has observed how 'the hierarchy and leadership of most Christian denominations commonly believe that these breaches of sexual boundaries were and are "affairs." They say the women are adults, with a full understanding of consent; therefore, there is no problem. This I dispute.'[36] The following stories of women sexually abused by clergy depict the church's denial and dissembling all too well:

> Evonne's Story: *I was a missionary nun in Africa; I was raped by (the priest who was) my retreat director. He said it was 'as God wanted for man and woman.' ... Whenever I resisted his advances, he displayed anger and insisted we had the 'highest of standards for growth and maturity.'*

> The priest who raped Evonne was found guilty of sexual abuse at an internal church hearing in England. However, he continues in ministry in Liverpool. The nun left her religious order after her superior requested she go for psychiatric evaluation and failed to offer Evonne the support she needed after this violation.

> Anne's Story: *I know I am far from being the only woman he has damaged. Yet he goes on as ever — and with the Bishop's knowledge and therefore acceptance. The Bishop merely shrugs his shoulders and says: 'I know, but what can I do if the man denies it and I have no direct proof?'*

> This Anglican priest was finally defrocked, not for professional misconduct [with Anne and other women in his parishes] but for adultery. The victim is in hiding due to threats to her life.[37]

The unwillingness of church authorities to hold clergy abusers accountable only feeds into and sustains victims' own self-negation and confusion. In a case known to us in a church setting in Oceania, a woman who went to her pastor for counseling felt simultaneously uncomfortable with his advances yet confused because she felt she ought to trust him since he was a minister. It never crossed her mind that higher church authorities might be called upon to intervene and stop the abuse that was taking place.

Women we know who have been prey to harassment in the theological school milieu in Oceania have experienced a similar disjunction between their own distress and their feelings of helplessness, even guilt, when they dared to report their harassment

36. Kennedy, 'Sexual Abuse of Women', p. 228.
37. Kennedy, 'Sexual Abuse of Women', p. 228.

to higher authorities, only to find themselves discounted or blamed for their own harassment.

The most devastating repercussion for the victims of clergy abuse appears to be, in fact, their enduring sense of inculcated shame. They internalize such shame because the church they love instills in them the travesty known as victim-blame. Such women experience 'a shame so deep that they become clinically depressed... and experience a breakdown of their world.'[38] This is corroborated in our knowledge of the experience of a student wife at Pacific Theological College who was so traumatized by the harassment she received from a faculty member (who was an ordained minister) that, once she returned home after her husband's graduation, she experienced a nervous breakdown. Only under the hypnotic spell of a traditional healer was she finally able to reveal the name of her harasser, and thus eventually to regain a measure of emotional health.

Why do so many victims of clergy abuse put up with such devastation of spirit? It is precisely because they know they have no recourse to justice and healing in the church. If clergy are held in such high esteem, if they have been placed on the highest rung of the patriarchal power pedestal, how can their abuse of power be challenged? When asked why they did not report the clergy who abused them, women in one study gave the following kinds of responses: that they couldn't bear to hurt their minister's career; that they knew they wouldn't be believed because their minister was so well-liked; that they were too attached to their church to cause trouble for the minister; or that they had been subtly threatened by the minister, especially if he was married.[39] Such is the intractable hold of clergy power over the women they abuse.

Clergy Abuse in Oceanian Churches

The case has already been made that male violence has destroyed the well-being of far too many women in Oceania, most of whom are church members. According to a respected secular counselor in Fiji, the majority of her female clients who are victims of sexual violence state that their ministers would be the very last persons they would consult about their abuse. This indicates not only the

---

38. Kennedy, 'Sexual Abuse of Women', p. 232.
39. Cooper-White, *The Cry of Tamar*, p. 138.

level of their inculcation of patriarchal church teachings, which instill guilt and self-blame, but their lack of trust of their ministers to actually help them with this kind of problem.

The venerated position of male clergy in Oceania undermines the ability of the church to address the problem of clergy abuse (and violence against women in general) because it is a well-known fact—though one almost never acknowledged—that there are Oceanian ordained clergy who are themselves perpetrators of sexual and domestic abuse against women. Most often, as in the worldwide trend, in the few cases when such clergy abuse is reported, the churches either transfer the abusers to other parishes (or countries), or to teach in a theological school. The incidents are generally covered up by the church authorities. Very few clergy abusers in Oceania are made to face the consequences of their acts. Achieving such accountability is especially problematic in the Oceanian context, where it is almost impossible to remove a minister or priest from his position of leadership.

Many of the ordained ministers in Oceania received their theological education in institutions that tolerated violence to discipline children, parishioners and even spouses. It was part of their theological training, at least in some Polynesian contexts, that the first-year students must be obedient to the final-year students. This obedience includes the humility (or, more accurately, humiliation) to tolerate abusive language and physical abuse imposed on them by their senior comrades. They in turn get their chance to do likewise when they become final-year students.[40] Thus the cycle of sanctioned violence continues.

This understanding of discipline is then appropriated by clergy at the parish level to keep the flock in line. While there are valid reasons for church discipline, violence should never be tolerated as a form of discipline. The use of strong language and physical force to silence and control others is a form of abuse. (The issue of church discipline will be explored in greater depth in the following chapter, when we discuss the role of theological education in the problem of violence.)

It is distressing that, while Oceanian clergy are meant to be care-givers for the souls and well-being of their parishioners, some of them are trapped in a culture of violence. Some are guilty of

40. This echoes similar hazing practices in the American college fraternity system, British boarding schools and military training.

physically abusing their Sunday Schoolers, parishioners and spouses. It is not a false allegation or an exaggeration to claim that a significant number of clergy wives in Oceania have experienced some form of physical abuse by their husbands. As alluded to earlier, in the few instances of physical violence committed by a wife, this is almost always out of self-defence. Most often clergy wives direct their anger at being abused not at their husbands but either toward themselves (through self-wounding) or toward their children (through beatings).

Acts of violence by clergy are connected not only to the cycle of violence associated with the ethos of 'discipline' described above, but also to the shaping of manhood within the culture. Male violence deemed justifiable is sanctioned in Oceanian cultures. At the same time, male clergy are so respected and honored by the people as the human representatives of God that it is important for them to be seen as free of faults. This is why most cases of clergy abuse are kept secret. Even if the parishioners know about it, as long as it does not take place before their eyes it is considered as not happening at all.

It is also the case that some Oceanian clergy are perpetrators of sexual abuse outside the family. While most of this abuse is hidden, in any given year several ordained clergy will be on discipline or temporarily stripped of their ordained status due to sexual abuse of a female parishioner (in church records, 'having an affair with a woman'). Unbelievably, there are still other clergy sexual abusers still currently serving the church in leadership positions and in parishes. In these cases the church authorities turn a blind eye, claiming that these clergy are innocent until proven guilty. Women who are impregnated by these clergy are forced to lie about the paternity of their children to save the men from being disciplined and thus publicly humiliated.

When it comes to the issue of clergy abuse, the church in Oceania is like the story 'The Emperor's New Clothes'. When the emperor made his grand entrance, a little child yelled repeatedly, 'the emperor has no clothes!' Yet the adults, although witnessing exactly the same thing as the child, chose to ignore reality, and pretended that the emperor was clothed. This is the sickness of the church in Oceania with regard to clergy abuse of women.

A final comment must be made about the relationship between clergy violence against women and the cultural role of the clergy in

Oceania as high chiefs. As mentioned previously, the patriarchal clergy system of imported Christianity was attuned to the institutions of the indigenous priestly and chiefly system. This is why ordained clergy, who are considered the earthly messengers of the Christian God, are treated with such awe and veneration.[41] The transference of sacred chiefly powers to the clergy allows them to rule as if they are high ranking chiefs themselves.

This concentration of power in the clergy remains the most compelling force sustaining the life of Oceanian communities. But what many clergy forget is that they are endowed with the power of the Gospel to liberate, rather than with worldly power to dominate. This forgetfulness is the reason clergy are so often unable to address the gravely critical issues pertaining to women's integrity and survival. For the Oceanian women who fall prey to clergy abusers, this misappropriation of clergy power is a dangerous weapon that only brings them helplessness and hopelessness.

* * *

It is a growing concern for many Oceanian women, and a few men as well, that the Oceanian churches have been neither prophetic nor pastoral in terms of social issues such as violence against women. Even if the churches have in some small ways spoken out,[42] they have not spoken loudly enough to be heard clearly and unequivocally, despite the fact that violence against women is a life-threatening reality for so many women, most of them church members.

The few victims who do have the courage to step forward, if they are very fortunate, can at times find refuge and solace in the care-giving services offered by the government,[43] civil societies[44]

41. The Samoan clergy are a typical example of this although the institutional practice is common throughout the region. See A. Tofaeono, *Eco-Theology*, pp. 131–38.

42. The now defunct Women's Desk of the Pacific Council of Churches (PCC) co-facilitated with the Women's Desk of the World Council of Churches a seminar on Violence Against Women in 1989. As the participants were chosen from among the spouses of the church leaders and women leaders themselves, this seminar was not known to the other 99% of Oceanian women and men. And since it was an initiative that came from women, the island churches never took it seriously. As a result, it was never followed up as an issue of importance for the church, nor was it mandated to be an important program of the PCC.

43. There are the beginnings of some small initiatives by governments, such as the following noted in a *Fiji Times* article (although it is of interest that the following initiative was for men rather than women): 'The Violence Against Women workshop training for men begins at the Naviti Resort on Sunday… In an earlier meeting members

and private sector groups, but only very rarely in the church. The ecclesial climate is one of avoidance, silence and non-accountability. Even in the most liberal church institution in the region, Pacific Theological College, whose leaders adopt a progressive stance with regard to issues of social justice, violence against women continues unabated. In the very few instances where it has been challenged by victims, they have, by and large, been blamed for having pursued their abuser, for being culturally insensitive, for being emotionally unstable, for misunderstanding their abuser's intentions, or all of the above.

This is a huge challenge for our churches. Where is the church's prophetic voice for women who are the victims of abuse? The following two chapters look to theological education as a natural arena for prophetic vision and action. Chapter Six grounds our examination of Oceanian theological education in the praxis of women's experiences of abuse in the theological school environment. The following chapter then explores the role which Oceania's theological institutions have played in the problem of violence against women, and examines how can they begin to address this problem more effectively. We will make the case that one of the most critical locations for the reweaving of the relational mat which is so essential for the churches of Oceania is in the theological schools where future church leaders are trained.

of the task force on eliminating violence against women discussed strategies to involve men from all levels of society. ... Permanent Secretary for Justice Alipate Qetaki said the aim of the project, which includes the training of male trainers, is the formulation of a bill on violence against women.' Seinimili Lewa, 'Men Discuss the Problems of Women', *The Fiji Times*, 15 November 2002, p. 5.

44. Civil societies in the Pacific have been very active in addressing social issues that are detrimental to the well-being of Oceanian people. Many have been the prophetic voice that is expected of the church, such as the Fiji Women's Crisis Center (FWCC) and the Mapusaga o Aiga (Family Haven, Samoa).

Chapter Six

THE PRAXIS OF VIOLENCE AGAINST WOMEN IN THE OCEANIAN
THEOLOGICAL SCHOOL SETTING

Theological institutions have become critically important church-shapers in the post-Enlightenment modern era, in which the clergy have become one of the 'professions' and so much of what is defined as 'ministry' emanates from and is determined by this professional cadre of leadership. It is this Western-imported paradigm of specialized ordained ministry—with its concomitant model of theological education—which took root in the churches of Oceania.

As a result, the small island nations of the South Pacific are awash in theological schools, and Oceanian Christians place a very high value on these institutions and on the status and prestige of their graduates. Given what has been disclosed in the previous chapter about the veneration of the male clergy in Oceanian societies, what they say and do, preach and practice, carries greater weight than is the case for clergy in any other part of the world of which we are aware.

Since the theology and praxis of ministry of Oceanian clergy are shaped so significantly by their theological education, and since they in turn shape the theology and praxis of their parishioners once they graduate, what happens in Oceania's theological schools has everything to do with the moral climate, ethical commitments and ingrained habits of Oceanian church communities. This includes, of course, their response to violence against women.

Until now, serious theological reflection/action around the problem of violence against women has been, for the most part, a non-issue in Oceanian theological education. This is so despite the fact that it is in the theological classrooms that future clergy are ostensibly being trained to deal with situations of conflict in their ministries. Any assumption that the mission entrusted to theological institutions encompasses all dimensions of ministry, therefore, is simply not born out in the actual formation of the region's theological students.

Theological educators have a central role to play in raising the awareness of their students regarding the ways in which social issues are a 'reality check' for the validity and applicability of the theology taught in the classroom. Yet, while the rhetoric is that theory and praxis are being integrated in our theological institutions, many of them are, regrettably, short on both theory and praxis when it comes to the application of theology to critical social problems such as violence against women.

Hence our discussion in the following two chapters of the interplay between theological education and violence against women in Oceania—the interweaving of these strands in the mat of patriarchy—is of vital importance. We begin by situating our analysis in the lived experiences of violence against women in the Oceanian theological school environment.

Women's Stories: Situating Violence Against Women in the Oceanian Theological School

One of the reasons for Oceanian theological institutions' failure to adequately address the issue of violence against women is that it has become part of the accepted culture in at least some of these institutions. Since the problem of violence against women extends beyond the student population to include even some faculty members, there has been little incentive for the almost exclusively male staff of the theological schools to raise awareness about, much less take action on, an issue which may implicate themselves or some of their colleagues.

In this context of denial or indifference, the only way to disclose the reality of violence against women in the Oceanian theological school setting is by means of actual case studies.[1] The sharing of these women's stories grounds not only our discussion in this and

---

1.   Because of the social, cultural and ecclesial realities described in previous chapters (especially the unquestioned power of the clergy), it is not possible to undertake a comprehensive or statistically accurate study of the prevalence of incidents of violence against women in the region's theological schools. A shield of protection surrounds the perpetrators in this setting. We have therefore had to rely on our first-hand knowledge and on stories shared in confidence.

the following chapter, but our overarching concerns in this entire work, in women's praxis.

These are all true stories (only a few of the many of which we are aware) which have taken place in Oceania's leading regional theological institution, Pacific Theological College. While this is only one theological school, because it is a regional and ecumenical institution, and because its students hail from the many denominational theological schools around the region, it can be said to be representative of the region as a whole. Both of us have had years of first-hand experience of Pacific Theological College, as a student and as staff members. This exposure enables us to state with confidence that the case studies included here are accurate characterizations of violence against women in an Oceanian theological education milieu.

This claim does not mean, however, that acts of violence against women are evenly distributed across the region's ethnic groupings. Because there is no way to conduct an accurate statistical survey, given the climate of secrecy and denial, we cannot scientifically verify our observations in this regard. What we can say is that the ethnic grouping with the least rigidly defined chiefly system in Oceania — Micronesia — exhibits the lowest levels of violence against women in the theological school arena. Indeed, in our collective fifteen years of association with Pacific Theological College, we have never heard of a single instance of violence against women by a Micronesian student or staff member. Perhaps significantly, it is also the major Micronesian denomination, the Kiribati Protestant Church, which has by far the best record in Oceania in terms of ordaining and placing women in ministry.[2]

The overwhelming majority of cases of violence against women of which we are aware at Pacific Theological College have been committed by Polynesians, with problems occasionally surfacing

2. Maleta Tenten has made a fascinating correlation between this church's unique position (in Oceania) on women's ministry and cultural values in I-Kiribati culture related to women's menstruation. See Maleta Tenten, 'The Relationship Between *Katekateka* and Women's Ordination in the Kiribati Protestant Church', in Johnson and Filemoni-Tofaeono (eds.), *Weavings*, pp. 32–42. As of 2002, the Kiribati Protestant Church had 18 ordained women ministers, 17 other women in the probational period, and a further 18 other women in theological training. Those numbers have likely increased in the intervening period. These are extraordinary statistics given the fact that the entire population of Kiribati is less than 80,000, and that the Kiribati Protestant Church has only around 29,000 members.

with Melanesians.[3] In the ten case studies in this chapter, all of the perpetrators were Polynesians except for two. Our hypothesis is that a correlation may exist between the more rigid manifestations of the patriarchal chiefly system in some Polynesian cultures and higher incidences of violence against women.

In other words, the stronger the grip of the system of social controls in a given culture, the greater the likelihood that the 'power-over' relational paradigm, coupled with pent-up frustration at the demands of 'fitting into' the system, may spill over the boundaries into violent behavior toward women. This hypothesis is certainly born out in our experience of violence against women at Pacific Theological College. While we cannot draw too many conclusions, the effect of particular cultural orientations on the likelihood of violence against women certainly warrants further research.

Although it is difficult for us to re-tell and re-live the painful experiences of women which occurred in an institution we love, and in which we have made a committed personal and vocational investment, it is necessary to ground analysis in truth. Even one case of violence against women in such a milieu would be cause for alarm. The many cases which have come to our attention are evidence of a serious problem. It is only as the strand of violence against women in Oceanian theological education is fully unraveled, exposed for what it is, that Oceanian Christians can begin to reweave the relational mat.

Case 1: Physical Abuse – A Husband's Duty

When a young student wife did not appear in morning chapel and was not seen outside her flat for several days, some on campus began to wonder what had happened. She was one of the student wives who had been beaten by her husband (already an ordained minister) several times before, and when this happened she always stayed in hiding until her facial bruises faded. Finally, a staff member suspicious of the possibility of another beating, decided to

---

3.   We have previously provided clear evidence that violence against women is a major problem in Fiji. Indigenous Fijians are ethnically Melanesian but their chiefly system is closer to that of Polynesia. The rest of Melanesia (Vanuatu, Kanaky/New Caledonia, Solomon Islands, Papua New Guinea) has a much looser, less rigid chiefly system. In our experience there have been a few problems at Pacific Theological College with some Melanesian students (who were sent to the college without their wives) frequenting prostitutes, but few known cases of domestic abuse. Since violence against women is a serious problem in Melanesian societies at large, this may indicate that a higher ethical standard is expected of Melanesian clergy and theological students.

confront the woman's husband directly. When pressed about why his wife had not been out of their flat for days, he admitted that she was nursing bruises. But he defended his actions, saying 'it was my duty as her husband to teach her a lesson. We had guests for dinner (the night that the latest beating happened), and she talked too much, even disagreeing with me in front of our guests. It was my Christian duty to teach her to behave as a proper wife and not embarrass me.'

Beating a wife out of a 'duty' to teach obedience and instill respect for the husband's authority has been an acceptable explanation for the bashing of many women in Oceania. As clearly spelled out in the above abuser's explanation, he was annoyed because his wife did not stay in her proper place—a place of submission and silence. It is the fear of many Oceanian women that taking a personal stance openly on an issue that differs from that of her husband may mean trouble for her later.

Since this beating happened in the private sphere, within the family, there were no disciplinary actions taken by the college against the abusive husband. Since there were no stated policies forbidding such behavior, it was not an issue for formal discussion at all. This has typically been the case in many other cases of spouse abuse at Pacific Theological College. The fact that the offender in this case was an excellent and well-liked student and an ordained minister led some staff members who knew of the incident to come to his defence in private conversations. Some questioned whether the beating had actually even happened. Consequently, those on campus who were troubled by the abuse felt they could do nothing, beyond personal efforts at pastoral care. Neither the victim nor the perpetrator were helped out of their cycle of violence.

Case 2: Abuse Under Pressure

A theological student (already an ordained minister) was feeling pressure trying to complete his thesis. His wife had recently given birth to their fourth child but was still in the hospital with complications, leaving the student to care for the other children at home — something to which he was not accustomed. He had begun losing sleep. One day he tried to check out a book in the college library but the library assistant refused to let him check it out, because he had other overdue books. The student first verbally abused the young woman, swearing at her and insisting that he had the right to check out another book. When she told him she could not bend the rules, he reached across the desk and slapped her hard on the face. She eventually forgave him after he and other representatives of his ethnic group visited her home, bringing gifts to her family as an act of apology, and after he apologized in morning chapel. He was not disciplined by the college and soon graduated, returning to a position of prominence in his home church and country.

This case is an example of an incident that happened in a public place, the college library, and thus became known to the whole college community within hours; yet no formal disciplinary action was taken by the college. The student involved, supported by other students and staff from his ethnic group, 'ironed things out' with the aid of traditional pardoning rituals from his culture. The message left for the college community was that violent outbursts directed at women can easily be pardoned with a cultural apology.[4]

Meanwhile, the library assistant was 'persuaded' by this cultural apology not to ask that the college expel or suspend the student, nor did she press charges against him. This woman had been courageous in the first instance, by insisting that she would not give the student special treatment. But her bravery turned lethal for her when the student, whose ego was insulted, punished her physically for denying him the privilege he demanded. Since she had no clout in the institution, as a female and a lower-echelon staff member, she had no recourse but to 'forgive' her abuser. Had she demanded that the college discipline him or reported the incident to the police, she would have had no choice but to resign.

Since the abuser was an ordained minister, he expected others to bend the rules in order to cater to his needs. Violence is often the counter-reaction if this does not happen. A number of male staff members and many students actually expressed sympathy for the student in this case, downplaying the seriousness of his violent actions on the grounds that he was under stress.

---

4.   We value the incorporation of traditional cultural practices of ritual pardoning as a means of bringing about reconciliation, as long as justice accompanies the performance of these rituals. The problem is that these rituals are sometimes abused or used lightly to let the perpetrators go free without making them accountable for their actions. This danger has also been noted by Fr. Seluini Akau'ola of Pacific Regional Seminary (Roman Catholic) in Fiji, who cautions that 'traditional forms of reconciliation (should) not be abused when dealing with violence against women and children … the danger is that … it will do more harm to the victims.' See Seluini Akau'ola, 'Violence Against Women and Children: A Theological Challenge', *Pacific Journal of Theology* II:30 (2003): p. 52.

Case 3: A Compounding of Abuses

One of the theological students had a habit of getting drunk when he felt academic pressures or when he was dissatisfied with the situation in his small student flat, where his young children were sometimes noisy when he was trying to study. It was well known on campus that he escaped by frequenting bars in downtown Suva and then picking up prostitutes. It was also well known that he often beat his wife, especially when he came home drunk. At times she was so frightened that she ran away from their flat and hid in the home of a faculty member. The principal did speak to the student after a particularly horrific beating, and he explained that he was sorry but could not be held responsible because he only beat his wife when he was drunk and not in control. Neither the drunkenness nor the wife-beating were ever dealt with, and the student graduated and went back home to assume a leadership position in his church.

This case exposes the troubling reality of another problem which is sometimes linked with wife abuse—substance abuse. Although the by-laws of Pacific Theological College forbid excessive consumption of alcohol by students on campus, abuse of alcohol by a minority of students is commonplace and discipline is applied only in the most extreme cases. This situation is not helped when some faculty members have been known to drink to excess, and some in authority even give liquor or money for alcohol to students from their ethnic group.

Many studies have detailed the correlation between abuse of alcohol or drugs and domestic violence. However, such abusers, including the theological student in the above case, have no grounds upon which to use their abuse of alcohol as a legitimate excuse for wife battering. As with many men who abuse both alcohol and women, drinking to excess was a convenient way for the student in the above case to bolster his ego. Being a weak and insecure student academically, he felt he needed to be drunk to feel 'on top of things.' But that only reinforced his need to control his wife by asserting his power over her.

The college failed both this student and his wife by only gently encouraging him to stop getting drunk and beating his wife. Some faculty members felt sorry for him because he was a weak student and experienced language difficulties. No one in authority dealt with any of the underlying causes of his abuse, and only the faculty wife who gave the victim sanctuary provided any appropriate care for the frightened and traumatized woman.

Case 4: Sexual Abuse: Trust and Obey

One of the student wives who came to the college with her husband as a newlywed found herself in a sexually abusive relationship. She was subjected to humiliating sexual experiences which were often tantamount to rape. Some of these experiences were physically painful. In desperation, she finally went to a female staff member for help. She in turn spoke to the leader of the young woman's Pastoral Advisory Group,[5] who was a senior minister from the victim's own ethnic group, hoping that he would admonish her husband. But this man's notion of 'pastoral care' only added to the young woman's trauma. Rather than speaking with the husband, he told the interceding staff member she should counsel the woman to comply with her husband's demands as her wifely duty, implying that she needed to grow out of her sexual naiveté. He then took perverse delight in sharing her problem with some of the male students from their ethnic group, and jokes began surfacing about her husband's virility and sexual prowess.

This is one of the most troubling cases of violence against women at Pacific Theological College which has come to our attention. This woman found herself with a husband who felt that it was his right to demand any kind of sex he wanted, regardless of how coercive, painful and humiliating. She had no idea that rape in marriage is a crime in some societies, and even if she had laid a charge of rape against her husband, it would have gone absolutely nowhere in the legal system.

Instead, through the intercession of another woman, she indirectly sought the help of a pastor and senior figure on campus who had the authority to ask her husband to be less violent. If her husband was likely to listen to anyone, it would be a minister from his own culture. Deplorably, this minister turned out to be almost as sick as her own husband. By appealing to the cultural and theological mandates for wives to be submissive to their husbands, he sought to advise this young woman to remain in a situation which was

---

5.   At Pacific Theological College all members of the community (academic and administrative staff, students and families) are assigned to Pastoral Advisory Groups, usually consisting of 10–15 members, each led by a faculty member. These groups meet periodically for fellowship, often around a potluck meal, and students and their spouses are encouraged to consult the leader of their group for pastoral care.

degrading in the extreme. Equally devastating was his trivializing of her abuse by turning it into a joke which had the effect of rewarding the husband for being abusive.

This tragic case points up the inability of even some of our most respected senior theological educators to provide effective pastoral care. In this case the staff member failed this victim of sexual abuse both pastorally and professionally. He allowed his captivity to a 'power-over' relational ethic to outweigh any genuine concern for a young woman's well-being. Moreover, he breached the boundaries of professional ethics by turning the victim's distressing situation into a joke which only fuelled other male students' own 'power-over' sexuality. The victim was left doubly shattered.

Case 5: Double Harassment

A woman on campus was being harassed by one of the workers, who stalked her and stared at her through the windows of her flat. When she told someone in authority whom she thought was in a position to help, he made light of her experience by joking, 'maybe he just enjoys seeing you with no clothes on!' This man is a prominent Oceanian theological educator who himself has a long history of sexual misconduct. Yet despite his inappropriate behavior with women, he is completely protected by the prestige of his position. His cavalier attitude extends to making jokes with students from his ethnic group about how hard it is to fight off all the women who adore him, and is evidenced in his dismissive and offensive remark to the woman who sought his help with a clear-cut case of harassment.

The woman in this case was doubly harassed because the man whose help she sought could get away with compounding her feelings of violation with absolutely no repercussions for himself. He was protected by his aura of invincible authority. As a well-educated theologian, he is skilled in making use of politically correct rhetoric, at strategic times and places. This means that he can 'make all the right noises' and appear publicly to condemn discrimination against women, while at the same time engaging in inappropriate behavior toward women himself and thus implicitly condoning it in others.

This theological educator's duplicitous behavior sends the message to the theological students under his tutelage that being a minister or church leader and treating women as sexual objects can go hand in hand. Such behavior makes a mockery of the high-minded liberationist rhetoric often espoused by such men, which rings empty in the consciousness of the theological students who are ostensibly being mentored by them.

Case 6: The Interweaving of Institutional and Physical Abuse

A married couple were living and working at the theological college, where patriarchal leadership and cronyism are the norm. The husband became a victim of this system and its dirty politics. The ensuing stress affected the couple's relationship at home and their frustration was taken out on each other. One day their pent-up frustrations culminated in a verbal argument that turned physically violent. The wife reported the incident to the principal, who met with the couple privately. They were told to go home, reconcile and pray about their problem. As soon as the couple left, the principal shared this incident, which had been revealed in confidence, with his closest confidantes, who in turn spread the news as a gossip to their colleagues, friends and students. The gossip got back to the couple, who then regretted going to the principal for pastoral support, as it became a source of destruction rather than a catalyst of healing for them.

Case 6 highlights the unpreparedness of many in positions of authority in the Oceanian theological school setting to play their pastoral roles adequately when presented with real-life conflict situations. In this case the college authorities were successful only in turning one couple's dilemma into a topic for community gossip. This is precisely the greatest fear of most women who are victims of domestic abuse on theological college campuses — that their family problems will become only the source of juicy gossip for the college community — hence, their silence. Almost no one offers to help or to raise the issue of domestic violence as a problem that must be dealt with pastorally and theologically by the theological institution. The lack of confidentiality and effective pastoral care in situations of domestic violence is a serious and ongoing predicament.

Case 7: The Cat and Mouse Routine of Harassment

One of the student wives in the college has been trying to avoid one of the male married students. Whenever she passes him in a corridor or on a footpath on campus, he makes a flirtatious comment that leaves her feeling extremely uneasy and embarrassed. He compliments her on her looks, or suggests she bring something to his flat while his wife is away. Several times he has stood so close to her that he has brushed against her breasts. She is too afraid to say anything directly to him, so she can only try to stay out of his way. This means constantly modifying her movements around campus, and trying to move quickly out of sight when she sees him coming from a distance. As a result of the tension which now characterizes her everyday life, she has begun to suffer from frequent headaches and stomach aches.

This is a classic case of harassment, in which the victim feels helpless to do anything to change her situation, for the variety of reasons we have outlined in our previous discussion of harassment. Although the woman in this case was otherwise a strong and confident young woman, she was completely disempowered when confronted with harassment. She did not dare report her harasser to the college authorities because she knew that both he and those in authority would dismiss her experience as a case of 'nothing really happened.' Her harasser was a popular student, an officer of the Student Body Association, and an ordained minister. He was highly respected in his church. No one was likely to believe that he was doing anything inappropriate.

In fact, had this student wife reported her harassment, the response she almost certainly would have received would have been along the classic lines of 'what have you been doing to provoke him; why have you been flirting with him in the first place?' In an environment in which harassment is so normalized (this case is just one of many examples known to us of harassment by male students or staff on campus), the only recourse for this woman was an internalization of her feelings of violation and humiliation. Like so many other victims of harassment, since she had no way to effect an end to the harassment, she began to get sick. Her reaction echoes other examples of harassment at Pacific Theological College, such as the one outlined in chapter five in which the victim ended up having a nervous breakdown after she returned to her home country (see, page 119).

Case 8: Harassment by Faculty: No Institutional Refuge

A female staff member became aware that a male faculty member at the college was paying undue attention to her. In public gatherings he always found a way to sit or stand next to her. He stood so close that he was literally 'in her face,' and began to touch her arm while speaking to her. He frequently stopped by her office when there was really no work-related reason to so do. At one event, when the staff were seated on the floor during a cultural ceremony he placed his hand on her thigh while everyone's eyes were closed in prayer. When the victim finally shared her distress with the principal and the harasser was confronted, he strenuously denied any wrongdoing, and blamed the woman for pursuing him ('she must have been attracted to me and is falsely accusing me because I didn't reciprocate').

In this case the victim of harassment was not a young, inexperienced student wife, but a woman with considerable awareness of women's rights. She felt uncomfortable with her colleague's way of relating to her from the very beginning. Yet she was unable to find any effective way of dealing with her situation of harassment. She was able to bring her problem to the attention of the principal but, although he was personally sympathetic to her plight, there were no effective institutional mechanisms for dealing with the harassment.

In fact, the victim in this case discovered that the college had no anti-harassment policy whatsoever, and that there was nothing in the college's constitution, by-laws, or terms and conditions of employment to address her situation or the others like it on campus. There was no grievance procedure to which she could appeal, no advocate to assist her, and no institutional source of pastoral care. The offender in question was admonished by the principal to cease his harassment, but he was not disciplined in any way, or even required to undergo counseling.

In the end, when the harasser's long-suffering wife stood by him, pleading tearfully with the principal not to believe any harassment had taken place, no further action was taken. This was despite the fact that, by this time, it had been revealed that this man had been accused of sexual harassment in previous employment situations and even in other settings off-campus in Suva. Once again, the harasser was protected while the victim continued to suffer.

Case 9: Street Harassment Along the Seawall

Many girls in the theological college community (teenage daughters of students and staff) like to take walks in the evening by the seawall opposite the campus. There have always been some problems with boys and men making catcalls and suggestive sexual remarks. But recently, in the aftermath of a coup and the resulting social upheaval, their experiences while walking have worsened considerably. Not only do men call out to them in ways that humiliate and embarrass them, but at times groups of teenage boys surround them, make unwanted and offensive comments, and brush up against them, touching them inappropriately. Sometimes men try to make them get into their cars. If the girls try to resist, even verbally, the men make threatening remarks to them. It is so unpleasant that some of them have stopped going on walks.

In this case, the problem is not with the theological school environment *per se*, but with the surrounding social context. The increased incidence of street harassment in Suva in recent years is a glaring example of how violence against women multiplies in 'societies under stress.' What is particularly sad about the above case is that these young women in the theological college have absolutely no recourse to avenues of assistance. There is simply nothing they can do. Reporting their harassment to the police would be laughable, in a social context in which males have been granted enormous leeway to 'take power into their own hands.'

But what makes this situation worse is that it would never occur to most of these girls to bring the issue of their harassment to the attention of the college authorities and community, or to expect that they might find a source of protection, advocacy or pastoral care in the college. Although a few individual fathers on campus might be counted on to accompany their daughters on their walks and provide personal protection, the issue of harassment itself is not on the institutional agenda.

Case 10: Subtle Violence in the Classroom

Some of the female students at the theological college are sharing informally with each other one afternoon on campus. At first they make jokes about their experiences being females in male-dominated classes. They begin to itemize the various ways in which their male counterparts subtly 'put them down' when they try to speak in class: for example, some of the men begin whispering, or opening and closing their books, staring out the window, sighing loudly, conspicuously reading while the women are speaking, scraping their chairs, or making insulting slurs in undertones which the women can hear but not the lecturer. After a time the women's laughter fades, and finally it turns into tears. 'Why do the men try to make us feel so stupid?' one asks.

The above scenario is not one which would be recognized by most Oceanian theological schools as an example of violence against women. Yet it too is another painful strand in the fabric of violence against women in the Oceanian theological school context. All of the examples cited above are patterns of harassment. These things do not happen to males in the theological school classroom. They happen only as a way of demeaning female students and asserting dominance over them.

As we noted in our earlier analysis of harassment, like other forms of violence against women it is a socially sanctioned way, in many cultures, for men to assert their superiority over women. In a theological school such as Pacific Theological College, where women have been accepted as students (which is still not the case in some other Oceanian theological schools), male students may feel particularly threatened by the presence of women in the classroom. Since they are accustomed to the church's corridors of power being an exclusively male domain, the presence of female counterparts at Pacific Theological College can be unsettling. Especially when some of the female students are outstanding academic achievers, some male students feel the need to reassert their dominance by subtly denigrating women's contributions. Although the bruising that results is less visible than that of women who are physically battered, it is bruising nonetheless. It is one more obstacle which women in theological education in Oceania have to struggle to overcome.

*   *   *

Almost all of the perpetrators and institutional administrators in the above cases are currently serving the churches of Oceania, in parishes, church headquarters or theological institutions. Some of the female victims may have been fortunate enough to find a way on their own to deal constructively with the abuse they have suffered. Others have learned from their experiences of abuse only how to be more adept at avoiding the next bashing, to defend their faces from visual bruises, or to internalize their harassment. The victims of spouse abuse who have never received assistance, and who are now working alongside their husbands in parishes or theological institutions, are no doubt coaching other victims in the survival mechanisms they know best from experience—that is, how to endure and hopefully avoid the most painful consequences of violence.

It is extremely important to keep these cases in mind as we move to a more in-depth analysis of how the strand of theological education in Oceania impinges on the problem of violence against women. These women's stories are the raw material out of which the theological institution strand is constructed, and out of which a new mat of relationality can ultimately be rewoven.

In the following two chapters we will critique the patriarchal theological education paradigm which is taken for granted in the Oceanian context; provide an example of how theological students have internalized patriarchal biblical interpretations that have a negative bearing on women; and suggest an alternative relational paradigm and several consequent proposals for Oceanian theological education which can counter the legacy of patriarchy. Both the critique and the proposals are a small first step in the transformation of the institutional ethos which has ill-equipped Oceania's theological schools to confront the evil of violence against women in their midst, in their churches, and in their societies.

Chapter Seven

UNRAVELING THE STRAND OF PATRI-KYRIARCHAL
THEOLOGICAL EDUCATION IN OCEANIA

The women's stories described in the previous chapter demonstrate indisputably that violence against women is as much a reality in the Oceanian theological education arena as it is in the larger church and society. It is a sad commentary that even some of those in positions of leadership in the region's theological institutions continue to tolerate violence against women through their silence, cover-ups, passive attitudes, ineffective counsel, and in some instances abusive behavior.

If our theological colleges continue to do almost nothing to prevent or deal with cases of violence against women in the theological learning community, then such violence—often excused as momentary lapses, or as 'nothing really happened'—will continue to be condoned by clergy for generations to come as something that is culturally, religiously and socially acceptable. If theological students are not equipped with the analytic and pastoral skills to respond adequately to situations in which women are demeaned, the age-old pattern of controlling women with the use of force or coercion will continue to be applied.

One of the greatest hindrances to the call to combat violence against women lies in the failure of theological educators to locate the problem in the ethos of the theological institution itself. There appears to be a mindset amongst some Oceanian theological educators that theological education can legitimately be separated from serious engagement with social issues. These educators contend that social issues, while perhaps important, have no direct pertinence for theological education,[1] whose primary agenda is the intellectual

1. This example is just one case in point: Following the military coups in Fiji in the late 1980s, students and staff at Pacific Theological College were instructed not to make any public comment, or to be involved in any protest action. Again, following the

study of the traditional (Western imposed) academic disciplines. Yet these same theological educators do not need to even turn their heads to look for the connections between the theology they teach and the lived experience toward which that theology is meant to be directed. These connections can be found every day right where they are—in the praxis of the theological school.

In relation to our primary concern in this work, the claim we are making is that the reality of violence against women is rooted in and reinforced by the patriarchal assumptions upon which Oceanian theological education rests. While our theological institutions are concentrating so single-mindedly on breeding theologically sophisticated academics, as defined by the Eurocentric model of theological education which they have inherited and continue to adopt (despite efforts at contextualization), they overlook the inevitable link between this patriarchal model and its outworkings.

Their students, in turn, become transporters of the theoretical seeds planted in the classroom to the various ministry contexts in which they will be placed following graduation. The fruitfulness of the theological nursery is tested when the planters are dispersed to work in the soil and with other gardeners. Often these theological graduates struggle to deal with the harsh realities they encounter after they are placed in the field, for no viable link has been made in their theological training between faith and life. The link that has been made is more between patriarchal theology and 'power-over' relationality than between Gospel and liberation for all.

Theological institutions are laboratories that must be constantly involved in creative and critical action/reflection—in *theological praxis*—if they are to be able to engage the 'real world' with the Gospel of liberation. Where traditionally accepted theological foundations have no efficacy, no moral warrant in the light of the liberating thrust of the Gospel, they must be transformed.

The following critique of the theological education status quo in Oceania will hopefully suggest an alternative foundation for the transformation of theological education. We hope through critique

latest coup in Fiji in 2000, Pacific Theological College did not take any public stance, despite the clear ethical issues at stake. The point is that, in general, theological institutions in the region tend to steer clear of social activism or prophetic proactivity. College authorities claimed that 'speaking out' would have jeopardized Pacific Theological College's standing with the government and safety, but prophetic social action always entails such risks; and silence becomes complicity in an unjust social system.

to contribute to the search for a culture and theology of peace and empowerment for all, centred in the church-shaping milieu of theological education.

A Critique of the Oceanian Theological Education Ethos

In the first instance, one of the underlying reasons for the failure of Oceanian theological education to adequately address the problem of violence against women is that it has been conveniently deemed a 'private' matter. This presumption has been challenged vigorously by health professionals, social activists and feminists. Yet despite persistent calls by these experts and by many Christians worldwide for a theological repudiation of violence, including violence against women, most theological schools in Oceania have passively allowed it to be 'off-limits' in theological education because it is said to belong in the private sphere. This is the easy route of avoidance, which commonly occurs when confrontation would require uncomfortable self-examination.

The end result of this passivity and avoidance is an unwillingness of theological schools to incorporate a pastoral/prophetic response to social issues — a living praxis grounded in critical analysis — into their program of theological formation. These institutions continue to accept the traditional (many would say outdated, even in the West) Eurocentric paradigm, in which theological education is fragmented into the discrete academic disciplines of systematic theology, church history, biblical studies, and pastoral theology.[2]

These disciplines, as they have been traditionally taught, are in no way grounded in praxis; rather, the *applicability* of knowledge in this paradigm becomes a 'second-order' concern, a rather fuzzy after-thought: It is simply hoped that students will somehow apply their academic knowledge after they graduate. The fact that the traditional theological disciplines or 'departments' have always operated out of a patriarchal framework undermines any serious quest for the integration of theory and praxis with regard to equipping students for a prophetic/pastoral response to problems such as violence against women. A critical analysis of such problems

2. For a description of how this fragmentation occurred historically, and its implications for theological education today, see Edward Farley, *Theologia: The Fragmentation and Unity of Theological Education* (Philadelphia: Fortress Press, 1983).

would shake patriarchy from its foundations and turn it on its head, threatening the entire theological education paradigm.

The root problem with the patriarchal framework of theological education, as explicated in our previous critique of patriarchal theology, is that women are treated as peripheral beings in the exposition and interpretation of most theological teachings. If Oceanian theological school students and graduates were surveyed to ascertain the percentage of female theologians studied, required textbooks and other readings authored by women, and female teachers and administrators encountered during their theological training, the percentage would be extremely low to non-existent. What 'counts' in our theological schools continues to be male theology and male leadership models.

In such a learning context, issues such as violence against women are naturally irrelevant subjects for serious theological discourse. This is reflected in the attitude of many students and faculty, as indicated in the earlier case studies, when actual cases of violence against women occur in the theological school setting. Even when such violence is occasionally condemned from the chapel pulpit, there are no effective policies in place to counter it. Where there are occasionally unwritten policies (i.e., what those in authority publicly espouse), they are vague, not consistently enforced, not applied to 'private' situations, or undermined by the authorities' own behavior.

As a result, students who have been theologically trained in institutions where violence was never adequately addressed inculcate the mentality that such violence is a normal part of life, if regrettable in its more extreme forms. Common reactions to violence by theological students such as 'no human is free of violent acts and thoughts,' or 'throw the first stone if you have not thought, spoken or acted in any violent way' are routinely used even in the worst cases of violence to protect the perpetrator and downplay the severity of the act itself.

Theological students who have been perpetrators of violence against women during the time of their theological formation, where this was never dealt with, will continue to commit such violent acts in the future. Violence will be viewed as a problem-solving device, not only at home but also in the parishes or church institutions where these theological graduates will be working. The theology they preach or teach will maintain the submission and obedience of women to men. The necessity of physical violence as a form of discipline will continue to be validated. It will be claimed that the Bible and culture clearly justify this understanding, and thus there can be no argument against it.

To further substantiate the need for transformation in Oceanian theological education, it may be helpful to refer to the results of a study conducted elsewhere which highlights the necessity for urgent change in the way clergy are trained. This study attempted to determine the numbers and severity of domestic violence cases which 'were encountered by individual ministers within (a given) year, how or whether the church officials were prepared or trained to deal with such cases, the church policy concerning such cases, and what was done in them.'[3] The responses, across the denominational spectrum, concurred in drawing the following conclusions:

> (1) Formal church policies and pastoral knowledge of this (domestic violence) are problematic; (2) specific training for family violence problems and counseling is for the most part absent from denominational training curricula; (3) pastors say they would report cases brought to their attention to ... authorities, as mandated by ... law, but only 3 percent of 1,200 actual known cases were reported (pastoral use of community resources is minimal); (5) ministers and pastors believe family violence problems to result from alcoholism and individualist factors.[4]

Although the above study was conducted in another context, the outcome also reflects the situation in Oceania. To our knowledge, none of the theological schools in Oceania have operative zero-tolerance policies related to violence against women, with established grievance procedures and mechanisms for enforcement,[5] nor does the curriculum in the theological institutions address this issue. Of the many cases of violence against women of which we are aware at Pacific Theological College, none of those which were clearly criminal acts were ever reported to the police. This cover-up mentality protects the college from public embarrassment, but also

---

3.   John M. Johnson, 'Church Response to Domestic Violence', in Carol J. Adams and Marie M. Fortune (eds.), *Violence Against Women and Children: A Christian Theological Sourcebook*, (Lexington, NY: Continuum, 1995), p. 414.

4.   Johnson, 'Church Response', p. 414.

5.   Mandatory reporting and enforcement of confidentiality by clergy are not even yet recognized in most legal systems in Oceania.

lets the perpetrators off the hook such that women can continue to be abused with impunity.

With this general portrayal in mind, it is important that we analyze more deeply the presuppositions and ideological frameworks that undergird various aspects of theological education in the region. We begin with a critique of the conventional theological curriculum.

A Critique of Patri-Kyriarchal Curriculum

The curriculum offered by the theological schools in Oceania emanates directly from the complementary ideologies of patriarchy ('the reign of the father') and kyriarchy ('the reign of the lord or master') collectively known as *patri-kyriarchy*.[6] This is simply a more nuanced way of describing the patriarchal ideology to which we have referred throughout this work. We employ this broader term here because it has been used effectively to characterize the conventional theological education paradigm. Theological education in Oceania can accurately be said to be *patri-kyriarchal* in content and context.

What is this patri-kyriarchal paradigm, and how does it function in theological education? According to Elisabeth Schüssler Fiorenza, it is not only 'heterosexist patriarchy' that is responsible for much of the suffering of women, but the affiliated kyriarchal power associated with colonialism and imperialism.[7] Kyriarchal oppression 'is sustained by multiplicative structures of control, exploitation and dehumanization: the oppressive powers of hetero-sexism are multiplied by racism, poverty, cultural imperialism, war, militarism, colonialism, homophobia and religious fundamentalism.'[8]

Patri-kyriarchy is also deeply rooted in what Vivian Fox has called the three foundational bodies of Western thought: 'Judeo-Christian religious ideas, Greek philosophy, and the common law legal code.'[9]

---

6. Elisabeth Schüssler Fiorenza provides an excellent discussion of the distinction between patriarchy and kyriarchy in *Discipleship of Equals: A Feminist Ekklesialogy of Liberation* (New York and London: SCM Press, 1993), and *But She Said: Feminist Practices of Interpretation* (Boston: Beacon Press, 1992). Issues such as violence against women are complicated by the interweaving of patriarchy and kyriarchy.

7. Elisabeth Schüssler Fiorenza, 'Editorial — Violence Against Women', *Concilium* 1 (1994): p. vii.

8. Schüssler Fiorenza, 'Editorial', p. vii.

9. Vivian C. Fox, 'Historical Perspectives on Violence against Women', *Journal of International Women's Studies* 4:1 (November 2002): p. 15.

This collective tradition, she argues, has had an extremely negative impact on the view and treatment of women. It has in fact taken for granted certain assumptions about human relationality that have permitted violence against women to be considered as 'a natural expression of male dominance.'[10] Why is this the case? Because this tradition has always 'tended to protect the authority, omnipotence, and omniscience of the father' (or 'ruler').[11] Lamentably, it has also been the bedrock of both Western theological education and the theological education model imported to non-Western contexts, with a few notable exceptions.[12]

The influence of this patri-kyriarchal tradition is clearly evident in the way in which theological education has been shaped in Oceania. Our theological schools were founded under the tutelage of Europeans and, particularly in the case of the only regional and ecumenical theological institution, Pacific Theological College, there has long been a concerted effort to prove to the world that Oceanians can succeed at this model of theological education just as well as Caucasians. (We have heard Oceanian theological educators at Pacific Theological College proudly refer to the college as 'the Harvard of the Pacific' or 'the Oxford of the Pacific.')

Yet it is precisely the deep rootedness of our theological education curriculum in the patri-kyriarchal tradition that must be critiqued as a contributor to the problem of violence against women in Oceanian Christian communities. To support this claim, it will be

10. Fox, 'Historical Perspectives', p. 15.

11. Rita Nakashima Brock, 'And a Little Child Will Lead Us: Christology and Child Abuse', in Joanne Carlson Brown and Carol R. Bohn (eds.), *Christianity, Patriarchy and Abuse: A Feminist Critique*, (Cleveland, OH: The Pilgrim Press), p. 52.

12. There are a few theological institutions in the non-Western world which have embarked upon bold experiments in transformative models of theological education which turn the Western paradigm on its head. Significant strides in grassroots theological education have been made in some of the Latin American and African churches which have been heavily influenced by liberation theology, and in institutions such as the United Theological College in Bangalore, India, and the Latin American Biblical Seminary in Costa Rica. However, while these few theological institutions have dismantled the hegemony of Western theology in certain respects, it is not clear to what extent patriarchal assumptions have been deconstructed. One would need to examine issues such as the leadership role of women in these institutions (and whether or not women's leadership models are taken seriously), and the degree to which female scholars are incorporated into the curriculum. In Oceania, even at Pacific Theological College, which espouses the importance of contextualization, that has consisted mainly of lifting up certain Oceanian imagery and cultural values, but not in challenging the Western patriarchal foundations upon which traditional theological education rests.

helpful to provide several illustrations of the kinds of patri-kyriarchal theological paradigms that are still standard fare in the region's theological school curricula.

Patri-Kyriarchal Teaching about Christ: Rosemary Radford Ruether is one of a number of feminist theologians who have pointed out the roots of the classical Christology still taught in most theological institutions in the establishment of Christianity as the imperial religion of the Roman Empire. The movement from Christianity as a subversive counter-culture to the Christendom era of empire-sanctioned state religion led to the assumption that '[j]ust as the *Logos* of God governs the cosmos, so the Christian Roman Emperor, together with the Christian Church, governs the political universe; masters govern slaves; and men govern women.'[13] In the Christendom model Christ becomes patriarch and kyriarch.

As an alternative to this patri-kyriarchal Christology, Ruether proposes a feminist Christology that allows for a fresh encounter with the historical Jesus: 'Once the mythology about Jesus as Messiah or divine *Logos*, with its traditional masculine imagery, is stripped off,' she asserts, 'the Jesus of the synoptic Gospels can be recognized as a figure remarkably compatible with feminism.'[14] This Jesus is the One who welcomes the witness of women, who seeks out and sides with 'the last and the least' — not only women but all who are marginalized and powerless. This Christ is the antithesis of patriarch and kyriarch.

Rita Nakashima Brock similarly laments the fact that 'the patriarchal family has been and continues to be a cornerstone for the Christological doctrines taught in theological schools, especially in their father-son imagery and in the unquestioned acceptance of benign paternalism as the norm for divine power.'[15] Only when such patri-kyriarchal Christologies are held up for scrutiny and critiqued in our theological institutions can students envision a new Christ who is the friend, empowerer and healer of all — particularly those who are the least powerful in the world's eyes, including women.

13. Rosemary Radford Ruether, *Sexism and God-Talk: Towards a Feminist Theology* (Boston: Beacon Press, 1983), p. 125.
14. Ruether, *Sexism and God-Talk*, p. 135.
15. Brock, 'And a Little Child will Lead Us', p. 42.

To date this has not happened to any significant extent in the teaching of Christology in the theological schools of Oceania. While a few efforts are being made to contextualize Christology, the Oceanian Christ who emerges is still firmly embedded in a patri-kyriarchal framework. He may wear a sulu or lavalava (traditional islander men's wear), and he may appear as a sailor rather than a shepherd, but his patriarchal 'rule' has not been questioned. Indeed, in some attempts at an Oceanian Christology, Jesus is posited as a traditional Oceanian 'high chief' — the epitome of patri-kyriarchy.

This way of appropriating and teaching Christology may make Oceanian theological students feel proud to have freed Christ from his European guise, but it does nothing to provoke the kind of Christ imagery and essence that could free ministers-in-training from the patriarchal theology which they pass on to their parishioners — and which, in turn, perpetuates the mindset that condones discrimination and violence against women.

Patri-Kyriarchal Teaching about God: Another example of the patri-kyriarchal paradigm in theological education in Oceania is the approach generally taken to teaching about God. Any credible model or metaphor for God, according to theologians such as Sallie McFague, Elizabeth Johnson, Denise Carmody, Carol Christ, Marianne Katoppo and others, must be consistent with people's actual limitless experience of God — including women's experience.[16] Images of God such as conqueror, warrior, father, judge, king, and lord are metaphors that serve the patri-kyriarchal agenda well.[17] But they are not liberating or adequate metaphors for God, certainly not for women — who, after all, have been told in Genesis that they are made equally in God's image, yet will never be like any of the above patri-kyriarchal images.

There is an urgent need for theological educators in Oceania to introduce more inclusive and organic metaphors for God that are life-affirming for all, and that do not contribute to the culture of male dominance.[18] This means, in part, recovering rich and

16. See Sallie McFague, *Metaphorical Theology: Models of God in Religious Language* (Philadelphia: Fortress Press, 1982), p. 3, 117.

17. McFague provides a thorough discussion of mechanical versus organic metaphors in *Metaphorical Theology*.

18. For a discussion of the relationship between masculine God imagery and male violence, see, for example, Kathleen Fischer, 'An Image of God Beyond Violence', *National Catholic Reporter* 36 (3 December 1999): pp. 37–41.

appropriate divine metaphors that are closer to the experience of Oceanian people. Pre-Christian indigenous religions in Oceania embraced conceptions of God that were virtually inexpressible. God was creator of life, and in all of life. In most Oceanian languages God was neither male nor female, not confined to any anthropomorphic description. This cultural heritage has great potential to liberate the patriarchal God inherited from Western theology, who is still propounded in Oceanian theological teaching — again, despite recent efforts at contextualization.

Recovering a non-patri-kyriarchal God will necessitate deconstructing the ways in which students have traditionally been taught the entire doctrine of the Trinity, so that the Godhead recovers its complementarity and inclusivity and becomes more than 'two men and a bird.'[19] The standard patri-kyriarchal teaching about the Godhead in Oceania's theological schools at present reveals more about human assumptions about themselves ('it's a man's world') than about the illimitable, all-embracing nature of God. And, as we saw in our theological reflection in Chapter Four, how we think and speak of God has a profound effect on how we do ministry and how we relate to others — including the way we view and treat women.

Patri-Kyriarchal Teaching and Practice of Liturgy: The need for release from captivity to patri-kyriarchal theology extends also to the teaching and practice of liturgy in Oceania's theological institutions. It should go without saying that the language of liturgy 'expresses what we believe and who we believe we are, in word and song and gesture. At the same time, it shapes our identity and self-understanding in relation to God and to the world, both by what is said and done, and by what is omitted.'[20] Since the liturgy of the church is shaped by its theology, the problems with the way theology continues to be taught in Oceania (highlighted above) have become enfleshed in the worship life of our churches and theological schools.

There is, for example, scant recognition in most Oceanian theological schools that the teaching about and celebration of the Eucharist is tormenting for many women who are victims of

19. This phrase is borrowed from the excellent feminist critique of traditional Trinitarian teaching by Sandra Schneiders, 'God is More than Two Men and a Bird', *U.S. Catholic* (May 1990): pp. 20–27.

20. Procter-Smith, 'The Whole Loaf', p. 430.

violence. Traditional interpretations and practices of the Eucharist encourage a theology of dogged endurance, instill a self-fulfilling prophecy of deserved suffering, and shame victims for failing to be more Christ-like. (Refer again to our discussion in Chapter Four of the problems with the Theology of Sacrifice.) Abused women find no spiritual fulfillment or healing in such worship, only a reminder of their worthlessness as believers and persons. One poet has shifted the eucharistic words of institution to the voice of an abused woman, with this reality in mind: 'This is my body which I have given for you / a body full of warmth and life / tortured, raped, cold. / This is my blood which I have shed for you / menstrual blood, blood of childbirth / flowing, dripping, dead.'[21]

According to Marjorie Procter-Smith, this 'lack of spiritual nourishment in the communion meal for survivors of violence stems from three problems in current liturgical practice and theology: issues of authority, issues of sin and guilt, and issues of sacrifice.'[22] The way these issues are dealt with in our theological schools' teaching about the atonement, and their enactment of this teaching in their worship life, are extremely problematic. The end result can be that the very Christian liturgy which we collectively celebrate as theological learning communities 'can disguise and mystify domestic violence and its roots, making the abuse seem not only acceptable, but even divinely sanctioned.'[23]

It is therefore vitally important for our theological schools to become more aware and sensitive regarding the theology of worship they teach and enact, and more intentional about critiquing sexist language, texts and liturgies that are exclusive or demeaning, and highlighting those that are inclusive and affirming for all. Discriminatory texts should not be allowed to remain in the lectionary but should be replaced with texts that affirm the 'discipleship of equals.' The content of the lectionaries currently in use should be critiqued in the classroom with this mandate in mind. This is an urgent task when one considers that 'the two most frequently cited texts in the justification of violence against women—

21. Anon., cited in Hedwig Meyer-Wilmes, 'Excessive Violence against Women in the Name of Religion', p. 61.

22. Anon., cited in Hedwig Meyer-Wilmes, 'Excessive Violence against Women', p. 465.

23. Marjorie Procter-Smith, 'Feminist Interpretation and Liturgical Proclamation', in Elisabeth Schüssler Fiorenza (ed.), *Searching the Scriptures: A Feminist Introduction* (New York: Crossroad, 2001), p. 430.

Genesis 1–2 and the household codes—are part of the three-year
... cycle' (of standard lectionary readings).[24]

Patri-Kyriarchal Teaching of Biblical Studies: Following from the above-
mentioned concern, there is an urgent need for a significant shift in
the way the Bible is taught in the region's theological institutions.
Biblical texts that are oppressive to women must be consistently
exposed and critiqued. Female biblical scholars' perspectives must
be incorporated as a matter of course, alongside those of male
scholars. Women's methods of approaching and exegeting biblical
texts must be taken seriously.

In this regard, the feminist approaches to biblical hermeneutics
that informed the critique of selected Old Testament and New
Testament passages in Chapter Four (which, as we saw, have been
used routinely to justify violence against women) are very much
needed in the Biblical Studies classrooms of Oceanian theological
institutions. At present, if they are incorporated into the Biblical
Studies curriculum at all, it is usually only as a deviation from what
is presented as normative. Until women's 'reading' of the Bible
becomes fully integrated into theological education, the patri-
kyriarchal tradition can never be deconstructed.

Yet it is difficult to see how this can happen as long as the
overwhelming majority (if not all) of the Biblical Studies teachers
in the region's theological schools are men. To our knowledge, there
has only been one female biblical scholar hired as a faculty member
in an Oceanian theological school, and then only for a brief period.
This same imbalance is echoed in the other disciplines as well, and
should be remedied as a matter of urgent affirmative action policy.

These have been just a few examples of patri-kyriarchal
approaches to content and pedagogy in the curriculum of Oceanian
theological schools. But if a transformation of curriculum is to
become a realistic possibility, there is also a need for a radical
overhaul of the entire institutional framework of theological education in the region, an issue to which we now direct our attention.

A Critique of Institutional Polity and Policy

As the last sentence suggests, it is not simply the teaching of bad
theology which undermines our theological school graduates' ability

24. Procter-Smith, 'Feminist Interpretation', p. 431.

to liberate their churches from theological assumptions that undergird or tolerate evils such as violence against women. It is the very institutional models upon which these schools operate, the patri-kyriarchal system that guides the daily life of these centers of ministry formation.

When the fundamental underlying principle of the theological institution is that of patri-kyriarchy, all aspects of its operations will be guided by a 'power-over' mentality which sends a constant message to its students about what constitutes acceptable relational behavior. The 'power-over' relationality modeled during students' theological training by their mentors will continue to be modeled by the students themselves after they have graduated and are engaged in ministry. This model can be characterized as one of authoritarianism, and the following sections will offer several examples of how it functions in the Oceanian theological school context.

Authoritarian Control over Theological Students: Authoritarian control in the theological education context begins with the admissions process. The island churches in Oceania have varying systems of admission for their theological students, but in most cases the requirements are fairly stringent and entail high levels of scrutiny, supervision and control by church authorities.[25] In some denominations theological students are expected to have married prior to commencing their theological studies.[26] They also are

25. In terms of admissions requirements, some theological schools prescribe a term of internship under the supervision of a parish minister prior to recommendation for entrance into the theological school. Others require applicants to submit a completed application with references from church leaders, academic records, etc. In some churches, men seeking entrance to the church's theological schools must (1) be an active confirmed member of the church with proven leadership qualities; (2) have the endorsement of the local minister; (3) gain approval from the district synod to sit an entrance examination; (4) sit and pass the entrance examination; (5) if successful, pass an oral examination with the Board of Church Elders; and, finally, (6) be admitted as a theological student.

26. The need for theological students to be married is related to the requirement of many Oceanian churches that only married men may be parish ministers. In some island churches, if a minister's wife dies, he cannot serve further in parish ministry until he remarries. Parish ministry is *couple ministry*, where the spouse works closely with the husband in all areas of ministry, except for conducting Sunday services and administering sacraments. This system raises serious questions regarding the inclusion of single persons in ministry.

expected to come with rudimentary theological knowledge and biases inculcated from Sunday School, Bible Study and youth groups, and from their affiliations with parish clergy couples.

The point to be made is that, even before the students begin their journey as theological students, they have already had to conform in many ways to the established values, norms and teachings of their respective churches. These values, as clarified previously, are the patri-kyriarchal foundations of church and society, whose leaders are the male heads of families, churches, government, and all professions. Those who have not demonstrated their conformity to these values to the satisfaction of their church authorities will not make it through the front door of the theological school.

These church authorities will then retain firm control over theological students throughout the duration of their theological studies, as they (and their wives, if they are married) are expected to demonstrate at all times that they are upholding the values they were taught at home, in their churches, and in their communities. It is conformity that is rewarded, not prophetic vision or 'boat-rocking' questioning.

This authoritarian control naturally extends to the leadership style practised by many principals, administrators and faculty members in the theological schools themselves. Although Oceanian theological students are adults, some at times even approaching middle age, they are in many respects treated as children by those in authority in the theological school context. This may breed either docile servitude or unexpressed resentment amongst the students, but it does not breed authentic maturity. It does not prepare graduates of theological schools for responsible leadership in the future. It stifles creativity and critical thinking, and encourages theological students to accept unquestioningly the 'standard line' they are taught while students, and to imitate the authoritarian leadership style of their mentors once they leave the theological school.

When this authoritarianism involves 'lording it over' inferiors (all underlings in the pecking order, including women), those in charge in our theological institutions are transmitting to their students the worst possible message. It is a message that can lead to the turning of a blind eye in situations of discrimination against women or, at times, even perpetrating it.

The Treatment of Women in Theological Institutions: Our analysis thus far has focused attention on the negative ramifications of the patri-kyriarchal institutional framework for male theological students and graduates in Oceania. Clearly this institutional paradigm has also had a profound effect on the women who find themselves in the theological education community. We begin with those most at the periphery, and by far the largest contingent of women in our theological schools: the student wives.

As a part of the inculcation of cultural values, student wives typically have their own separate program in the theological school for several hours each week, a program of domestication that prepares them for perfection in their roles as mothers (sewing, handicrafts), wives (cooking, home management) and future ministers' wives (women's fellowship leadership, for which role they are given basic introductory Bible classes).[27]

These women's daily routine in the theological school revolves around child care, preparing meals for the family, washing, cleaning and all other domestic responsibilities. In other words, student wives are largely confined to the domestic arena, and see their role as serving their husbands' needs, providing a tranquil, well-managed home environment within which the husbands will be free to concentrate on their studies with minimal interruption.

In this regard, the story of one student wife at Pacific Theological College is instructive: After being identified by the Coordinator of the Women's Programme as an exceptionally intelligent person with great academic promise, she was given the option of enrolling in the Bachelor of Divinity program. When she did not register for any courses, one of us invited her into our office to find out why she had not enrolled. Tears rolled down her cheeks as she explained, 'my husband will not let me study; he says I am only here to make sure that his studies go smoothly, and he doesn't want to see me reading a book!'

Women in many parts of Oceania continue to be excluded from entering theological education at all because of church policies

---

27. The Women's Programme at Pacific Theological College does make an effort to also provide some classes which are more theologically stimulating. Academically promising student wives may be encouraged to enroll for the Diploma course of study, through the college's distance learning programme (by correspondence) or, in rare cases, to upgrade from diploma level to Bachelor of Divinity level studies. This option is not the norm in the region, however.

forbidding women's ordination. The few women who are full-time students face their own formidable challenges. Although the situation for women students at Pacific Theological College has gradually improved somewhat over the years, they are still a small minority and face many challenges which male students do not face. Because they generally suffer in silence, staff members may not even be aware of these women's realities, such as the classroom scenario presented in our case study in Chapter Six (see p. 136).

That scenario described subtle harassment in the classroom setting, but female students fight an uphill battle not only in the academic arena but in the personal arena. This is especially true for the single women students, who have to contend with routine jokes from their male counterparts about why they are not married, and various forms of subtle or not-so-subtle harassment in the single student quarters and around campus.

Even in the few theological institutions in the region where women study alongside their husbands, patri-kyriarchal values still determine the ultimate valuing of such study. In one theological school in Oceania which accepts only married couples as students, some of these wives have expressed the view that they feel forced to do something which they may not see as their calling. In certain cases a husband and wife may find themselves in competition with each other, which creates resentment in the husbands, especially if the wives surpass them in academic achievement. If the husband fails, both are required to leave the college, even if the wife is doing well. If the husband is not performing well academically, the marks of his wife may be lowered to avoid shame for the husband. Upon graduation, it is the husband who is ordained as a minister and given a parish, while his wife remains only a 'minister's wife,' even though she has equivalent theological training. This unequal treatment reinforces the view that only men are capable of handling the responsibilities of ministry.

The few women in the region who have completed formal theological education often find themselves not utilized at all or under-utilized by their churches. Even those from the churches which nominally allow women's ordination are usually not placed in parishes like their male counterparts after ordination, and almost never on the faculties of their churches' theological schools. One notable exception is in Micronesia, where the Kiribati Protestant

Church, as noted earlier, has ordained significant numbers of women and placed them in responsible pastoral or administrative ministries.

Instead, if these ordained or theologically trained women are employed by the church at all, they are often placed in church work that is deemed to be 'feminine': That is, they are put in charge of the department of women's work, made to teach at church primary schools, or placed as care-givers in church hostels or orphanages. Those married to pastors carry on the responsibilities of a clergy wife. A significant number of the women who have been ordained in Oceanian churches are single women who, if they are placed in a parish, are often sent to a remote or unsavory location where male clergy do not want to go.

Until women are accepted as equal partners in the region's theological institutions—both as students and as faculty members—and utilized by their churches upon graduation in a way that is commensurate with men, the churches of Oceania will never begin to challenge the patri-kyriarchal foundations upon which their church structures, theologies, and approaches to ministry rest. It is only when this challenging finally occurs that problems such as violence against women can be confronted openly and honestly.

Against the backdrop of this realistic portrayal of the patri-kyriarchal foundations and practices of Oceanian theological institutions, we move now to further concretize the interrelationship between the problem of violence against women and its location in theological education by analyzing the findings of a survey conducted with a sampling of theological students.

Listening to Theological Students: Making Connections with Violence Against Women

In order to ascertain how the theological formation of Oceanian theological students has impacted on their views of women (which has implications for their response to violence against women), a qualitative research questionnaire was designed and distributed to two different groups of theological students.[28] For purposes of comparison, a group consisting of international (primarily Caucasian)

---

28. The questionnaire is included as Appendix A to this work. It was designed in conjunction with Joan Filemoni-Tofaeono's research for her D.Min. thesis at San Francisco Theological Seminary.

doctoral candidates at San Francisco Theological School was included in the study. (This group is cited as Group A.) The other group consisted of Oceanian theological students at Pacific Theological College. (This group will be referred to as Group B.)

The majority of respondents in both groups were already ordained clergy. There were equal numbers of respondents in the two groups, and nearly equal percentages of men and women.[29] Although the sampling is relatively small, it provides a representative snapshot of the 'end products' of theological education, from a broad cross-section of denominational backgrounds. The qualitative research design allowed for open-ended elaboration of responses, which was extremely valuable in disclosing underlying premises and influences.

The Responses

A key purpose of the questionnaire was to determine if and how students' theological and cultural backgrounds influence the way they respond to theological questions that have a bearing on violence against women. Our hypothesis was that the understanding of scripture, theology, church teachings and practices inculcated through theological education formation has a significant bearing on how theological students view both the role of women and, indirectly, issues related to violence against women. What follows is a summary of the questionnaire responses.

Question 1 asked how husbands and wives are viewed in the respondents' churches' traditional wedding ceremony. All of the respondents in Group A stated that the wedding liturgy in their churches has been modified somewhat to allow for greater inclusivity of language, greater flexibility to cater for couples' preferences, and greater creativity to allow the couple to design their own vows.

In contrast, the common denominator in Group B was a carefully nuanced defence of their island churches' existing marriage rites.

---

29. The six respondents in Group A (three men and three women) represented five different denominations. Five of the six were North Americans of European origin and one was an Asian student. Group B, the students from Pacific Theological College, consisted of four men (all ordained clergy) and two women (one a clergy spouse studying theology and the other a woman with some background in religious studies). The ages in both groups ranged from early thirties to early fifties.

While the consensus was that the wedding liturgy used in island churches affirmed that women and men are not complete without each other, it was also agreed that it is cultural roles that determine what women do and who they are in society. Women are expected to submit to their husbands in all respects, and will 'get what they deserve' if they do not honor their husbands. The Christian marriage rite upholds this cultural view, in that it admonishes wives to obey their husbands but not vice versa.

Question 2 asked how the church's marriage vows influence what is defined as 'acceptable behavior' between marriage partners. The majority from Group A concurred that the 'oneness' idealized in the vows has often been ignored and the 'obedience' clause in the more traditional vows has sometimes been used to justify male dominance, even in the Western churches.

Only half of Group B responded to this question. The gist of their responses was that Christian marriage vows can never be broken, regardless of what may later occur in the couple's relationship, and that the vows clearly mandate that the wife's role is to submit quietly to her husband's authority.

Question 3 asked about the church's traditional teaching regarding the status and duties of husbands and wives. The men in Group A stated clearly that the church teaches 'mutual submission' of husbands and wives, but that the traditional stance (now shifting in many of their churches) is that the husband takes a leadership role. The female respondents asserted that, while the church has traditionally focused on the husband as dominant, changes in secular society are pushing the church toward a more egalitarian view of marriage.

All of the respondents in Group B stressed the church's teaching that men and women have pre-ordained responsibilities, according to their status in family and society. While the husband is not 'above' the wife in a theological sense, he is the head of the family because of his role to protect and guide. A female respondent stated that, while traditional church teachings have supported the notion that men hold higher status, it is women who work the hardest for family and community.

Question 4 asked what scriptural and theological arguments are used to back up church teachings on men's and women's status and roles. All of those in Group A mentioned various Pauline writings (e.g., I Corinthians 13, Eph. 5: 21–31, Gal. 3: 28), with one noting that it is unfortunate that many ministers still stress women's submissiveness in Pauline texts rather than the oneness of all in Christ.

The texts cited by Group B confirmed the view that the man is the head of the family. Gen. 2: 23 was mentioned by several to support the view that men have the right to control women since the woman was taken out of the man. One interpretation of the meaning of Gal. 3: 28 was that, since both men and women are equal 'in Christ,' but since woman is taken from man, the man who is harsh to a woman is being harsh toward himself. Another respondent, referring to Gomer's unfaithfulness to her husband Hosea, commented that such unfaithfulness can justifiably provoke men to violence.

Question 5 asked what respondents would like to change, if anything, in their churches' existing marriage liturgy and teaching. While half of Group A said 'nothing,' the remainder called for a more specific reference to mutual respect in the wedding vows, and a greater focus on equality in the family.

All respondents in Group B stated that they were satisfied with their churches' present marriage sacrament and teaching on marriage, although there was some acknowledgement that the church needs to better prepare couples for the commitment they will make as marriage partners. The women in Group B did not specifically say 'no change is needed' but they were not forthcoming about what changes might be needed.

Question 6 queried the participants about their personal interpretation of Adam's statement in Gen. 2: 23, 'This at last is bone of my bone and flesh of my flesh … this one shall be called Woman, for out of man this one is taken.' The responses of Group A reflected a diversity of opinions, ranging from the need of males and females for relationship, the purposefulness of men and women, and the divine origins of the marriage covenant.

In contrast, the responses from Group B were much more uniform, basically reaffirming that the passage portrays the patriarchal ancient Hebrew community where women were viewed as secondary and derivative. It was also pointed out that, since the rib was taken from the place close to Adam's heart, men and women cannot be all that God intended them to be until they are bound together in marriage.

Question 7 asked how the church has traditionally interpreted Gen. 2: 23 with regard to the portrayal of women as derivative of men. Group A tended to replace 'church teachings' with their own fairly positive readings of the text—namely, that 'woman from man' need not demean women, that Eve was as human as Adam, and that woman came from man because of God's willingness to support men's need for women.

In Group B, the male respondents tended to stress the fact that, although the church affirms the view that women are derived from men, women are the 'rib bone,' upholding family and culture, and that the church calls on men to care for and respect women as part of themselves. The female respondents cited numerous examples of how church interpretations of Gen. 2: 23 uphold women's subservience to men.

Question 8 asked specifically about the relationship between the church's traditional view of women and violence against women. All of Group A responded that there *is* a connection between a theological understanding of women as derivative and the sanctioning of violence against women, and cited specific examples.

The responses to this question from Group B reflected, for the first time, views that can be clearly generalized as gender-specific. The men responded neither 'yes' nor 'no' to the question, but gave long explanations for why women *should* obey men (and thereby avoid punishment). The women in Group B, on the other hand, firmly indicated a clear 'yes'—that there is a definite connection between the church's derivative view of women and a justification for using violence to put women in their place. But while they 'made the connection' without equivocation, they did not espouse an alternative theological position or interpretation.

Finally, *Question 9* asked the respondents to describe any changes they felt were needed in their churches' teachings and practices regarding the status of women. The comments in Group A suggested that, while the church teaches that men and women are equal, this teaching is not applied consistently around the world, and that, in reality, specific cultures dictate women's status in family and church. It was suggested that churches should better contextualize their theology of marriage and male-female relationships, while ensuring that they critique traditions in any given culture that are oppressive, so that both men and women can have 'full citizenship' in the church.

Group B, again, responded in greater detail than Group A, alternating between defending their churches' positions vis-à-vis women, and making tentative suggestions for change. Males argued that women are not 'second-class citizens' in the church because they lead through participation, service and hard work. One male commented that although, without women, the church would fall apart, they must still come under the umbrella of men's authority.

An Analysis of the Responses

One significant aspect of qualitative research is the investigation of how the collective ethos of a group may shape or influence the way people think and respond, especially to sensitive or provocative issues. In communally oriented cultures such as those in Oceania, many individuals do not freely give their own personal opinions; rather, they respond in a way that takes into account and promotes the harmony and accepted values of the larger community. This was obvious in the way the Oceanians in Group B, especially the men, tended to respond as members of their particular ethnic group, defending the communal value system.

The pivotal role of cultural identity, then, helps to explain the rather stark differences in the way in which the two groups responded to the questions. The mostly Caucasian members of Group A were specific, direct and brief in their responses, which also exhibited quite strongly their personal experiences and opinions. The value placed on individual freedom in their American theological education also allowed them to relativize or minimize aspects of their church teachings with which they personally disagreed, such as traditional teachings that condoned women's subordination.

Group B's responses, in typical Oceanian fashion, were more expansive yet indirect, providing not so much answers as lengthy explanations that were careful not to offend their churches' positions or cultural values. In general, while the two groups were equally articulate in their theologizing, the members of Group A were more openly critical of their churches' teachings than Group B.

Several gender-specific generalizations and differences can be noted. While the Caucasian men from Group A saw violence against women as a generational and cultural problem, the Oceanian men in Group B routinely shifted the focus away from violence against women as a problem to the importance of the social responsibilities of men and women in the community.

While the women from both groups held fairly similar views on the connections between violence against women and traditional church teachings, the Caucasian women in Group A were much more direct and emphatic in pointing out how wrong it is that church teachings have been used to justify violence against women, and how this must change. The Oceanian women were more cautious and less able to directly criticize their churches.

Despite certain limitations,[30] the questionnaire did confirm what our prior analysis of other sources has already suggested: namely, that the normative theology, teaching and practices of our churches have upheld the superiority and headship of men over women. The responses from Group B in particular highlight the centrality of patriarchal values in determining interpretations of Christian theology. Their theological training, even in an ostensibly progressive institution like Pacific Theological College, has done very little to challenge this stranglehold of patriarchal theology and culture. On the contrary, their theological education has only given them sharper skills in theological argumentation to back up their culturally sanctioned misogyny. Their theological training has thus failed them, in the sense of equipping them with the theological tools to undo the damage inflicted upon women by patriarchy.

Although the tendency of the Oceanians in Group B to speak with a 'communal voice' has been noted, it is interesting that in the final question (about the changes needed in the church in relation to women), their personal views became pronounced for the first

---

30. We are aware that the way the questions were structured could contribute to the outcome of the responses. An example is the one question where half of Group B did not give an answer. This may have been related to a lack of clarity, or to the fact that the respondents did not feel free to express their thoughts as individuals. For an issue such as violence against women that is still so sensitive, questionnaires may not be the best way of gathering detailed information, as there is no possibility of asking for clarification of meanings. Providing a questionnaire in English may also have been problematic for some of the participants in Group B. Yet a questionnaire was deemed the only viable research tool for this study, precisely because the topic is too sensitive (in Oceania) to be discussed openly using an interview format.

time. This opening hopefully evidences a growing willingness of theologically trained Oceanians to point out, albeit with hesitation and perhaps pain, that there are flaws in the church (and culture) they love so dearly. This tentative acknowledgement is perhaps the beginning of conscientization[31]—the necessary prerequisite to the reweaving of the relational mat.

To conclude, our analysis of the questionnaire responses confirms our earlier assertion that patri-kyriarchal theology has, in Vivian Fox's words, 'predominated for two thousand years, reinforcing the subordinate position of women.'[32] Although positive changes can be seen in some churches' perceptions of women (particularly in the churches represented in Group A), few changes have occurred in the theology and praxis of Oceanian churches, despite some rhetoric to the contrary. Most Oceanian Christians, even the theologically trained who participated in this research, are still captive to cultural and theological presuppositions that permit women to remain under the control of men.

The questionnaire findings thus reinforce our critique that theological education in Oceania has not yet liberated most of its students, or their churches, from their captivity to the patri-kyriarchal ideology that sustains violence against women. This judgment points up once again the need for a radical transformation of theological education in Oceania—from its curriculum to its administrative and leadership styles.

*   *   *

In this chapter we have attempted to examine in some depth the correlation between the problem of violence against women in Oceania and the context of theological formation in the region's theological institutions. This has entailed an unraveling of the strand of patri-kyriarchy which undergirds theological education in Oceania. This unraveling has made it clear that the theologies that flow from the patri-kyriarchal paradigm have contributed to a

---

31. The term *conscientization* (consciousness-raising stemming from critical reflection on praxis) first gained prominence in liberationist educational and theological circles after its appropriation by Paulo Freire. It has since been further elaborated by a number of liberation theologians. For an extended definition, see Dennis P. McCann, 'Conscientization', in James F. Childress and John Macquarrie (eds.), *The Westminster Dictionary of Christian Ethics* (Philadelphia: Westminster Press, 1986), p. 120.

32. Fox, 'Historical Perspectives on Violence Against Women', p. 17.

theological formation climate that condones the second-class status of women and thus, indirectly, violence against women. This was evidenced in our critique of curriculum, polity and authoritarian leadership, and confirmed in the findings of our questionnaire given to theological students.

It was pointed out earlier in this work that a subtle but equally threatening form of abuse for women is that of men who claim to be in solidarity with women in their struggle when, in reality, they are still seeking power, even while using the rhetoric of liberation. These men 'speak out against patriarchy in the public order, but in their more private relations with their spouses, female friends, or colleagues, they continue to exert subtle and not so subtle control over women.'[33] Regrettably, such men are presently in leading positions of authority in some of Oceania's theological institutions.

These men are asked to seriously consider the authenticity of the theology they proclaim, for the sake of the formation of future leaders in the church. If Oceanian church leaders and theological educators are genuinely concerned with 'stopping physical and sexual abuse, … [they] need to join social workers, … lawyers, psychologists, and judges in educating the public and developing systems of accountability.'[34] They need to draw on the wisdom of those with long experience of caring for, liberating, and being an advocate for female victim-survivors.

Above all else, Oceania's theological educators are called to repentance. They are called to confront the truth that some among their fraternity have exploited and damaged women. At the same time, they are called to a reaffirmation that, as a faith community, in concert with the wider community, we have the resources to 'confront this evil with justice and bring genuine healing in its wake.'[35]

This chapter concludes with an affirmation that the theological institutions of Oceania have a vital role to play in breaking the vicious cycle of violence against women. They can only do so by 'refusing to endure evil and by seeking to transform suffering, [because] we are about God's work of making justice and healing brokenness.'[36]

33. Karen L. Bloomquist, 'Sexual Violence: Patriarchy's Offense and Defense', in Joanne Carlson Brown and Carol R. Bohn (eds.), *Christianity, Patriarchy and Abuse: A Feminist Critique* (Cleveland, OH: The Pilgrim Press, 1989), p. 65.

34. Fortune and Poling, 'Calling to Accountability', p. 453.

35. Fortune and Poling, 'Calling to Accountability', p. 458.

36. Fortune, 'Transformation of Suffering', p. 147.

With this affirmation in mind, we shift attention in our final chapter to practical proposals to combat violence against women in Oceania, situating these proposals for transformation in the milieu of theological education. These proposals are modest contributions to the reweaving of the relational mat, and are intended as a stimulus to fellow Christians in Oceania and elsewhere to search for other strong, liberative fibers with which to design new strands to make a mat of equality and freedom for all in Christ.

Chapter Eight

REWEAVING THE RELATIONAL MAT

This work has entailed the arduous task of unraveling the many strands of patriarchy which have created a relational fabric whose most prominent feature is a 'power-over' way of relating that grants men permission to exert control over women in a multitude of ways. It has been necessary to unravel the entire relational mat of patriarchy, to hold it up for scrutiny, so that it can be discarded and a new relational mat can be woven.

This new mat has essentially one overarching design for all followers of Christ, all over the world. However, in each culture the Christ-centred relational mat will have distinctive colors and weaving patterns, so that it can be easily recognized and affirmed as 'ours' by a given people. In other words, the Christ-centred relational mat is both universal and particular, with features both common and distinctive. In order to begin to reweave the relational mat, then, we must include in our theological re-envisioning a broad and rich mosaic of contributions.

Theological Re-envisioning in the Global Church

This process of theological re-envisioning, the necessary prerequisite to a reweaving of the relational mat, must begin with an unequivocal acknowledgement that patriarchy is a sin. It is a 'spiritual assault because it erodes and attacks the dignity, identity and worth'[1] of the female half of the human species. The World Council of Churches has described the particular form of this evil which manifests itself as violence against women as 'an intolerable manifestation of unequal power relations between women and men; when this human

1. ELCA Commission for Women, 'Sexual Harassment and Abuse', pamphlet on the 1989 Lutheran Churchwide Assembly resolution condemning gender abuse (Chicago: ELCA, 1990).

sin breaks the trust in the community [of the church], Christians are called to … be Christ present for those [the victims] who struggle for their dignity and rights.'[2]

How can Christians express their remorse at their churches' historical captivity to patriarchal relationality? They can remind themselves that, as the African-American theologian Delores Williams has pointed out,

> The church is called to bear witness to a world that is built upon a tradition of dedicated male and female disciples supporting each other in … hastening the Kingdom of God on earth—the Kingdom mandated by God to serve all humanity with justice, care, peace and love.[3]

A number of serious theological efforts have been made in recent years to re-envision the relational mat in ways that highlight the strands of Jesus' inclusive, empowering love for all. At the heart of this task has been the deconstruction of our concepts of the Godhead, a task we have already highlighted earlier in this work. Far from being characterized by the 'power-over' model of relationality which is inherent in patriarchy, God, Jesus and the Holy Spirit must be re-envisioned as 'standing with the vulnerable and powerless and judging the powerful.'[4]

This reformulation of the Godhead, in turn, leads to a reconfiguration of the entire relational web within which we as human beings exist. In this new relational paradigm, the 'other' whom we as followers of Jesus Christ are called to love (as we love ourselves) must always be an equal subject, never an object to be controlled or used for our own ends.

A number of theologians have engaged in theological re-envisioning by proposing alternatives to 'power-over' relationality. Some of these alternatives have included the following: *power-within* relationality, which focuses on the Spirit of God that is alive within every human being;[5] *power-with* relationality, which accentuates the

2. World Council of Churches, *When Christian Solidarity is Broken: Guidelines for Use at Ecumenical Gatherings* (Geneva: WCC, 1991).

3. Delores Williams, address, World Council of Churches' Central Committee, Ecclesiology and Ethics Consultation, Geneva, Switzerland, September 1996, cited in Gnanadason, *No Longer a Secret*, pp. 78–79.

4. Fortune, 'Religious Issues and Violence Against Women', p. 378.

5. Although now embraced by a number of female theologians, the 'power-within' concept was first elucidated by Matthew Fox in his *Original Blessing* (Santa Fe, NM: Bear & Co., 1983).

mutuality of all human relationships, given that we are all 'one in Christ';[6] *power-for* relationality, which highlights our calling as Christians to practice empathy with and compassion for all with whom we are in relationship;[7] and *nutrient power*, a similar construct which advocates the positive use of power to enhance the well-being of all partners in relationship.[8]

Pamela Cooper-White has proposed an even more expansive way for Christians to re-envision the relational mat: as *I-Thou-We*. Building on previous attempts of liberationists such as Paulo Freire to de-objectify human relations by replacing 'I-It' ways of relating with 'I-Thou' ways of relating, Cooper-White adds to the relational web a 'We': the faith community. The church, as the organic and interconnected Body of Christ, becomes the third party in all Christian relationships — the 'safeguard of mutual care and justice..., providing a loving frame for both encouragement and healthy limits.'[9] And it is the non-patriarchal Godhead — Loving Creator, Liberating Savior and Empowering Spirit — which interpenetrates and surrounds this whole I-Thou-We matrix.

In this reconfigured matrix, power becomes the power *to be able*. This is not the power of aggression, domination and manipulation, but quite simply the *power to be* that belongs equally to every human being.[10] Since all Christians are called to affirm and embody this *power to be* in themselves and in every other human being, there can be no cause for or tolerance of any objectifying treatment of women by men.

But how can the dialectic of deconstruction and reconstruction come about in churches and cultures which are infused with patriarchal 'power-over' relationality? A number of feminist theologians have asserted that change can only happen if Christians

6.   The 'power-with' paradigm was first articulated by Starhawk, in *Truth or Dare: Encounter with Power, Authority and Mystery* (San Francisco: Harper & Row, 1987).

7.   The 'power-for' construct has been advanced by Martha Ellen Stortz, in *PastorPower* (Nashville, TN: Abingdon Press, 1993); and, in a similar way, by Karen Lebacqz, in *Professional Ethics: Power and Paradox* (Nashville, TN: Abingdon Press, 1991).

8.   The term 'nutrient power' was first coined by Rollo May, in *Power and Innocence: A Search for the Sources of Violence* (New York: W.W. Norton, 1972), but has since been embraced by some feminist theologians.

9.   Cooper-White, *The Cry of Tamar*, p. 29.

10.   Cooper-White, *The Cry of Tamar*, p. 30.

embrace a *redemption of power* that is facilitated by a *theology of resistance*. Ellen Wandra has defined this project in this way:

> The term *resistance* ... thematizes the particular form of authentic human existence which emerges from reflection on the historical and religious experience of victims of ... domination. Resistance is to be understood as the maintenance by the victims of any shred of humanity in situations of ... dehumanization.[11]

In theological terms, we can liken this posture of resistance to that of Jesus' resistance to the 'power and principalities' in his day. It is a theological stance assumed by all liberation theologians, who remind Christians of their mandate from Jesus to 'take sides' on behalf of and in solidarity with the powerless.

Indeed, when we examine Jesus' own relational paradigm, we see that it hinged on resistance to 'power-over' ways of relating. He scolded the disciples for trying to enhance their own power and prestige (Mt. 19: 23–30; Lk. 18: 9–14). He offered mercy to the woman caught in adultery despite the blame heaped upon her by men (Jn 8: 3–11). He confronted the religious leaders with their own greed for power (Mt. 23: 13–36; Lk. 20: 45–47). He called on leaders to be servants of all, and for the first to be last (Lk. 22: 26). He turned the patriarchal power imbalance on its head by breaking cultural taboos in order to empower women—women such as the Samaritan woman at the well (Jn 4: 5–41), Mary Magdalene (Lk. 8: 1–3), the 'sinful' woman who anointed Jesus' feet (Lk. 7: 36–50), the 'unclean' bleeding woman (Mt. 9: 18–22; Mk. 5: 21–43; Lk. 8: 40–56), the 'pagan' Syro-Phoenician woman (Mk. 7: 24–30; Mt. 15: 21–28), and the sisters Martha and Mary (Lk. 10: 38–42).

The theological re-envisioning task that confronts the worldwide church, then, is nothing less than a turning upside down of the conventional wisdom that has permeated patriarchal theology for many centuries. It requires a radical re-interpretation of scripture and a critique of inherited theology which will be bold enough to denounce the patriarchal assumptions handed down by our many 'church fathers' throughout church history. Growing numbers of Christian women around the globe have embraced this challenge.

Only as this task is undertaken across the board—from dismantling and replacing patriarchal God imagery and Christology, to revolutionizing liturgical language and practice, to liberating our

11. Ellen Wandra, 'The Dialogue Which We Are', unpublished essay, p. 4, cited in Poling, *The Abuse of Power*, p. 32.

ecclesial leadership models and ways of inculcating faith in our children—will we begin to see a fundamental shift in how our churches deal with evils such as violence against women.

But how should the global effort to theologically re-envision the relational mat be understood and contextualized in the churches and theological institutions of Oceania? If, as we have noted, each cultural community should be free to design a Christ-centred relational mat in such a way that it has affinities with its own context, then Oceania is no exception. In the following section we attempt to frame the theological re-envisioning task in a way that resonates with the shared experience of Oceanians.

Theological Re-envisioning in Oceania

The Context in Which we Begin

In Oceania, as in so many other parts of the world, the task of theological re-envisioning, the necessary prerequisite to the reweaving of the relational mat, is a challenge of epic proportions. As our analysis has shown, the churches and theological institutions of the region are still dominated by male theologies and leadership, despite the fact that some theological schools now admit women students and some churches even ordain women to ministry. Regional gatherings of church leaders and principals of theological schools still remain almost exclusively meetings of men. What has 'counted' as theology in the region has been, until very recently, an exclusively male domain.

While male Oceanian theologians have made a significant contribution to contextual theological discourse by highlighting themes and symbols that resonate with the experience of Pacific Islanders,[12] most of these theologians have not, to date, grappled

12. For example, there have been significant advances in the development of an Oceanian eco-theology, by young contextual theologians such as Ama'amalele Tofaeono (Samoa), Cliff Bird (Solomon Islands) and Rumaroti Tenten (Kiribati). The theological contributions of their mentor generation, in relation to communitarian themes such as reciprocity, sharing, and the sacredness of land and sea, are also noteworthy, especially the work of Sevati Tuwere (Fiji) and Jione Havea (Tonga). We are not suggesting that the work of these and other male Pacific Islander theologians is intentionally patriarchal, but only that male Oceanian theology has not yet explicitly or systematically critiqued the patriarchal foundations which undergird both church and culture in Oceania.

in a self-critical way with the theological and cultural manifestations of patriarchy that provide the foundation upon which the church's complicity in evils such as violence against women rests.

There is a danger inherent in every contextual theology—namely, that it will end up in an uncritical embrace of culture for culture's sake. Every culture does this, not just Oceanian cultures. Every theology is in fact a contextual (culturally limited) theology, including the Eurocentric theology which has been predominant in the Oceanian churches. In pointing up the dangers of contextual theologizing, we are in no way seeking to detract from the importance of the efforts of Oceanian theologians to free their theologies from the stranglehold of Eurocentric hegemony. What we are saying is that any contextual theologizing in Oceania must include a critique of the culture's captivity to patriarchy.

All too often we have heard Oceanian women's efforts to question aspects of cultural and theological patriarchy, in the supposedly safe haven of the theological school, brushed off by their male counterparts' standard reply: 'But that's our culture!' The clear message in this retort is that, since culture is sacred, it cannot be challenged. However, for Christians the Gospel must always take precedence over culture. Just as Jesus challenged his own and surrounding cultures—particularly through his revolutionary and scandalous (to the culture) relationships with women—so we who are Jesus' followers today must subordinate our loyalty to culture to a deeper loyalty to the transforming Good News of the Gospel.

Bearing in mind this critical approach to contextualization, we can now ask, 'What might be the most fitting way to engage in the theological re-envisioning task in the Oceanian context?' Re-envisioning contributions from elsewhere, such as those outlined in the previous section (*power-within, power with, power for, nutrient power, power-to-be, I-Thou-We*), certainly all have merit. But we need to bring such concepts closer to home. Theological re-envisioning in Oceania needs to be framed in imagery which resonates with the lived experience of Pacific Islanders.

Oceanian women have already made a beginning in this undertaking. A number of original, creative appropriations of Oceanian generative themes and values have been espoused by Oceanian Christian women in recent years. At various times in this work we have referred to the first major collection of Oceanian women's theological reflections, published in 2003, *Weavings: Women*

Doing Theology in Oceania. Several contributions to that work posit new and liberating Oceanian ways of envisioning God, Jesus and ministry.

For example, Michiko Ete-Lima (Samoa) has articulated an androgynous conceptualization of God patterned after the sacred covenant between sister and brother in Samoan culture.[13] Valamotu Palu (Tonga) has described God as being like the maternal care-givers and gifted artisans personified by the Tongan women who are tapa-makers.[14] Judith Vusi (Vanuatu) has proposed a Melanesian Christology centred around the affinities of Jesus with a legendary dwarf figure in her culture who is scorned by the powerful but defies the 'insignificance' imposed by society to engage in redemptive acts on behalf of the community.[15] Tamara Wete (Kanaky/New Caledonia) has posited a new model of ministry grounded in 'mothering' imagery and values in her culture, which has parallels with Jesus' 'mothering' ministry in the Gospels.[16]

All of these efforts at re-envisioning theology by Oceanian women are helpful contributions which can become valuable resources — rich fibres — to be used in reweaving the relational mat. We seek to add our own contribution to this effort by returning to the Oceanian-wide metaphor of weaving itself. It is a metaphor which is fundamental to and understood by all Pacific Islanders. Although the act of weaving is primarily the domain of women, it also has potential to be an inclusive symbol, because both men and children are included in various aspects of the weaving process, such as collecting the raw materials to be woven, or dying certain strands to produce the colourful designs in the mat. The mat is also the archetypal symbol of Oceanian sociality, for it is on the mat that families, friends and communities traditionally sit together, eating,

13. See Michiko Ete-Lima, 'A Theology of the *Feagaiga*: A Samoan Theology of God', in Johnson and Filemoni-Tofaoeno (eds.), *Weavings*, pp. 24–31.

14. Tapa is a paper-like material made from the bark of the mulberry tree, upon which complex designs are woven. It is presented, particularly in Tonga and Fiji, at ceremonial occasions and as gifts. See Valamotu Palu, 'Tapa Making in Tonga: A Metaphor for God's Care', in Johnson and Filemoni-Tofaoeno (eds.), *Weavings*, pp. 62–71.

15. See Judith Vusi, 'Lord of the Insignificant: A Christ for Ni-Vanuatu Women', in Johnson and Filemoni-Tofaoeno (eds.), *Weavings*, pp. 58–61.

16. See Tamara Wete, 'Woman as "Life-Giver": Toward a Renewed Understanding of Women's Ministry and Leadership in the Evangelical Church of New Caledonia and the Loyalty Islands', M.Th. thesis, Pacific Theological College, 2003.

discussing, socializing, and enacting all important cultural rituals. There is no more holistic communal activity in Oceania than weaving and using the mat.

Weaving the Egalitarian Jesus Mat

We begin our weaving by contrasting the old patriarchal relational mat with a new egalitarian relational mat. In the patriarchal mat, it is only males who select the fibers which are woven together, reinforcing the only design allowed: a pattern of 'power-over' relationships. The fibers chosen, the 'raw materials' of this way of relating, are toxic for women. The entire design is one-dimensional and imbalanced. The 'power-over' pattern is dark, jagged and hideous to behold. Only male 'power-over' strands predominate; the female strands are inferior, small and buried in insignificance. They are utterly dependent upon the dominant male strands.

In contrast, in the egalitarian mat, males are not the designers. Neither are females. Rather, the designer is the Godhead. But this is no patriarchal construction of the Godhead. God is beyond anthropomorphism, beyond male and female. God is the Creator who loves everything that God has created. God loves creation so much that God becomes incarnate, takes on human form, in the person of Jesus. But this Jesus is no patriarch either. Jesus is not modeled after worldly lords or kings, but turns the worldly order upside down.

In this new world order, first characterized by Jesus' mother in the *Magnificat*, the mighty are brought low and the lowly lifted up until there is a new level relational playing field. What counts now in relationality is *agape*—love that is not self-absorbed but other-oriented. What counts is loving the other as one desires to be loved. What counts is empowering the powerless, setting free the captive, lifting up the downtrodden.

How does this happen? Through the liberating power of the Holy Spirit. The Holy Spirit infuses all of life, including human life, with every kind of power except for 'power-over'—power-within, power-with, power-for, power-to-be. This empowering Spirit nourishes, comforts, encourages, guides, challenges and cajoles like a mother. She gives us the energy and motivation to get up, gather our materials, and start weaving a new relational mat.

Unlike the old patriarchal mat, the new egalitarian Jesus mat has a beautiful design. No one strand predominates. There are differing male and female strands, to be sure, of varying colors and distinctive patterns. But one is not more pronounced than the other. The female strand is not inferior to, smaller than, or dependent upon the male strand. Rather, the male and female strands are equal if distinct. They are of the same weight and strength. When they are interwoven each strand makes a unique contribution to the overall design, and that design becomes more striking, powerful and exquisite as a result of the interweaving.

Because the mat belongs to its divine Creator-Saviour-Spirit, it can never be claimed as a possession of either the male or female strands. Men and women exist to make the relational mat strong, durable and glorifying to its Creator. They do that by relating to each other as equals. They express their *agape* love, learned from their engagement with Jesus, in all of their relationships, not only with humans but with God's created world. They honor the whole tapestry of life. All of their human relationships are guided by the principle of mutual respect.

This means that both males and females constantly seek to call forth what is best in the other, whether the other is a spouse, parent, child or friend. There are no strangers in the relational matrix, because in Christ strangers become friends. Since no one has power over the other (although adults have special responsibility for children, the infirm and the differently abled), and since no one could possibly own the other (since we all belong to God), violence, abuse, and controlling behavior of any kind is an impossibility.

The egalitarian relational mat, then, exists for the purpose of calling forth the full personhood of all. The mat provides refuge and protection for all. It encourages, even insists on, the fulfillment of each person's human potential. It refuses to construct obstacles or barriers to the fulfillment of this potential. This means that males and females cannot place limits on one another's potentiality, because their relationality is claimed, owned and guided by the limitless Creator of the relational mat.

The place where this relationality is molded, nurtured, developed, challenged, and protected is the church. The church holds stewardship over the mat. Its members gather regularly to work on the mat, weaving new designs together under the Creator's guidance, and mending places that have become torn or frayed through our inevitable sinfulness. Leadership around the weaving circle that is the church follows the same pattern as the design of the mat itself. No one lords it over anyone else in the church. No one has power over anyone else. Like leadership in the early church, each member of the Body of Christ is given gifts by the Spirit, and is expected and encouraged by the church to exercise those gifts. That is how the mat stays woven.

This has been a theological re-envisioning of the relational mat which has drawn on the rich possibilities of the Oceanian metaphor of weaving. But what might this new egalitarian relational mat mean in concrete terms? What is the praxis of our theological re-envisioning? In the following section we sketch some of the practical implications of a rewoven Oceanian relational mat, with a particular focus on ways to unweave and reweave one of the ugliest blots on the old patriarchal mat: the unsightly scar of violence against women.

Reweaving Challenges to the Churches of Oceania

If the churches of Oceania were to begin the process of reweaving an egalitarian relational mat, what might some of the implications be in terms of their policies and practices regarding women? These would obviously have to be worked out by both men and women working together, in ways that are at once authentically Oceanian and, at the same time, true to the universal mandates of the Gospel. Some tentative suggestions are offered at this point, as a stimulus for this process.

Clearly the churches of Oceania should begin their reweaving by abandoning all theological justifications for the denial of any form of ministry or leadership to women. The only justification for the present gender imbalance in Oceanian churches is by reference to 'power-over' patriarchy which has no place in the Body of Christ. But the churches need to go much further: They need to re-examine their cherished notions about the very nature of male-female relationships. This will have profound implications for many church policies, including those relating to leadership, but we call attention firstly to the need for zero-tolerance policies regarding all forms of violence against women, from overt abuse to covert harassment.

In this regard, the churches of Oceania could benefit from studying the processes by which other churches around the world have established such policies. This should be an effort undertaken not just by male church leaders but by church members across the board, from women's fellowships and men's fellowships to youth groups. We are not suggesting that Oceanian churches should adopt wholesale the anti-discrimination policies designed in other cultural contexts, but there are certain universal principles which need to be taken into account.

Pamela Cooper-White's study of such church policies concludes that any adequate church anti-gender discrimination policy must, at the very least, do the following:

- State that gender discrimination is a sin, and why.
- Affirm that the church and all its institutions must be a 'safe place' for everyone, especially the most vulnerable (women and children).
- Define gender discrimination and harassment clearly and broadly, providing examples of its constituent elements.
- Outline clear procedures for dealing with incidents of abuse and harassment, including measures to protect female complainants from further suffering if they report such abuse or harassment, and clear disciplinary measures for abusers and harassers.
- Articulate and implement the church's visions and goals regarding the education of its members about the sin of gender discrimination, abuse and harassment.[17]

A similar starting point for the Oceanian churches might also be an adaptation of the following Guiding Principles, which have been suggested as a blueprint for 'good practice' amongst church leaders:

- The church's first priority must be the safety of and pastoral care for all victims of abuse.
- In order to stop abusers, church leaders must use wider community structures of accountability.
- Church leaders must be able to combat the secrecy and deception that abusers use to hide their crimes.
- The church must not allow a misuse of confidentiality to prevent it from acting to intervene in situations of abuse.
- In order to stop abusers church leaders must work cooperatively with other professionals.
- Churches must institute effective structures of accountability and consequences for leaders who abuse their power.[18]

17. Cooper-White, *The Cry of Tamar*, p. 76.
18. Fortune and Poling, 'Calling to Accountability', pp. 458–61.

Closer to home, Fr. Seluini Akau'ola of Pacific Regional Seminary in Fiji has suggested that Oceanian churches should embrace the 1992 Pastoral Statement of the New Zealand Roman Catholic bishops condemning violence against women and children. It calls upon all who have 'pastoral responsibility' in the churches to commit themselves to do the following:

- Take seriously the woman or child who discloses abuse.
- Avoid simplistic solutions and a false spiritualizing of the problem.
- Avoid the misuse of Scripture in any way that would appear to justify male domination.
- Be informed as to available community resources (medical, legal, shelter, counseling and educational) and know when and how to refer (victims) to others for specialized help.
- Be ready to deal with the profound spiritual questions that arise concerning the woman's relationship with God and her worth and dignity as a person.
- Create a parish atmosphere where people and church leaders can discuss the question of violence against women and children openly and sensitively.[19]

In order to break the taboos of silence, cover-up and complicity, the churches of Oceania must also, as a matter of urgency, train pastoral counselors who will know how to work, in culturally sensitive but proactive ways, with both victims and perpetrators of gender abuse and harassment. Such counselors must know how to be catalysts for liberation for female victims so that they can understand and articulate their experience of abuse. They must also know how to help perpetrators understand why their 'power-over' behaviour is a sin, and that repentance is a prerequisite for forgiveness. They must be skilled in assisting both abusers and church communities in providing restitution for victims. (Although we include this recommendation here as a priority for churches, it will be revisited in the following section on challenges for theological education, since it is theological institutions which must assume the responsibility to train this new breed of pastoral counselors.)

19. Akau'ola, 'Violence Against Women and Children', pp. 51–52.

The churches of Oceania can also benefit from other initiatives currently being undertaken ecumenically by the world church to combat patriarchal ways of relating to women. A number of important such initiatives were birthed by the Festival to mark the end of the World Council of Churches' Ecumenical Decade of Churches in Solidarity with Women, held in 1998 just prior to the WCC Eighth Assembly in Harare, Zimbabwe. At this Festival the stories of women who had experienced gender violence, harassment and abuse in their churches, often by or with the collusion of clergy and church leaders, were heard loudly and clearly.

As a result, the WCC Eighth Assembly responded by, first, acknowledging publicly that all forms of violence against women are sinful and, second, 'encouraging all churches, their networks and movements, to engage in constructive efforts to overcome such violence in all its manifestations in both church and society.'[20] In addition, the WCC Task Force on Violence Against Women has ensured that, in terms of the WCC's own staffing policies, all forms of gender abuse and harassment 'will not be tolerated or condoned, and offenders will be held responsible for their behaviors.'[21]

As one means of assisting churches to fulfill the above mandate of the Eighth Assembly, the WCC's Women's Advisory Group has established a global project 'to work specifically on resisting and overcoming the causes and consequences of violence against women.'[22] This project is well underway, and is producing resources for use by churches and church organizations in their 'education for transformation' initiatives.

This project has produced a *dossier of good practice* for adoption by the world church. It will include 'a range of materials, emanating from different church traditions and denominations, and from various cultural backgrounds, all of which have proved their worth as important policy statements, useful strategies, significant examples, meaningful liturgies, and so on, in the ongoing task of overcoming violence against women.'[23]

20. 'Response to the Plenary on the Ecumenical Decade of Churches in Solidarity with Women', in Diane Kessler (ed.), *Together on the Way: Official Report of the Eighth Assembly of the Wold Council of Churches* (Geneva: WCC Publications, 1999), p. 249.

21. *World Council of Churches Staff Rules and Regulations* (Geneva: WCC Publications, 1992), Chapter VI.

22. Hood, 'Speaking Out and Doing Justice', p. 218.

23. Hood, 'Speaking Out and Doing Justice', p. 219.

Churches and church organizations in Oceania should be encouraged to be proactive in taking full advantage of this 'range of materials' and resources. In addition, regional ecumenical church bodies such as the Pacific Conference of Churches should offer the services of qualified Oceanian church women to contribute to the development of the 'dossier of good practice.' Since another aim of this WCC project is to establish a network of theological educators worldwide who are engaged in research, curriculum development and teaching ventures that address the problem of violence against women, the churches of Oceania should make every effort to join in this network. A first step would be to support women who are willing to undertake research and to develop resources on issues of gender relationships, including violence against women, that can be used by the churches.

At the heart of our call to the churches of Oceania to evidence their commitment to reweaving the relational mat, by taking concrete steps to overcome the legacy of patriarchy, is the moral imperative to bring an end to destructive practices of gender abuse and to the churches' collusion in this evil. This is a prophetic, pastoral and educational challenge that must stretch from earliest childhood through adulthood, embracing boys, girls, women and men.

All of the issues that have arisen from our critique of patriarchal culture and theology, and that overflow into every aspect of gendered relationality, must be addressed by the church—in the pulpit, in the Sunday Schools, in youth groups, in women's and men's organizations—and, as a matter of utmost urgency, in the classrooms and living spaces of our theological schools. As we continue to reweave the relational mat, we turn once again to the arena of theological education, this time with concrete proposals for transformation.

Theological Praxis: Reweaving the Relational Mat
in Oceanian Theological Education

We previously made the case that theological institutions are one of the most critically important arenas in which relational attitudes and actions are fostered, and in which the churches' patriarchal attitudes and actions can be transformed. It is there that our future pastors, priests and church leaders must be equipped to become prophetic spokespersons for visionary change in their churches and in their own gendered relationships. The theological school is better positioned than any other ecclesial institution to be on the front line and on the cutting edge of initiatives to reweave the relational mat.

There are many complementary tasks involved in this reweaving. The critical analysis entailed in undertaking this study has pointed up the need for a radical and comprehensive overhaul of Oceania's theological institutions—a need which both encompasses and goes beyond the ethical imperative to combat violence against women. As we have seen, 'power-over' relationality infuses the entire fabric of theological education, from its authoritarian administrative and leadership structure to its patriarchy-laden curriculum to its praxis of interpersonal and communal relationships. If Christ-centered egalitarian relationality is to be taken seriously by the theological education community, *all* aspects of the life of this community will come under scrutiny and demand transformation.

There is not space here to offer specific reweaving recommendations regarding all of these aspects of theological education. We would like to return to one recommendation mentioned in the previous section, before moving on to a specific proposal related to the transformation of curriculum. This concerns our plea for the urgent training of pastoral care-givers and counselors who have an informed, liberative consciousness of the egalitarian basis of Christ-centred relationality.

The Transformation of Pastoral Care Training

The above plea clearly has implications for new programs of study in our theological schools (most likely beginning with higher degree-level institutions such as Pacific Theological College, which have greater resources to develop new programs). This would require a commitment to search the world over for the most appropriate staff with the requisite skills to develop this new niche area of liberative pastoral care training.

But it would also necessitate a prior shift in understanding amongst our theological educators about the relative value of pastoral/practical theology in theological education. The tradition, certainly at Pacific Theological College, has been to elevate the so-called 'more academic' disciplines of systematic theology and biblical studies, and to view the department of ministry/practical theology/pastoral theology as the academically weaker, more peripheral field of study.

The brightest students are steered away from these more praxis-oriented disciplines and, although Pacific Theological College has had a faculty development scheme for over fifteen years, it has never once selected a promising student to be the recipient of higher-level overseas training in a practical theology field such as pastoral care and counseling. This is further evidence of the lack of attention given to praxis in Oceanian theological education, which has had such dire consequences in terms of the failure to equip theological students to meet the critical needs of their peoples and societies.

But the need for a transformation of attitude, commitment and training in critically important fields such as pastoral care and counseling goes beyond what might be offered for students. Almost all of our case studies in Chapter Six pointed up an institutional failure. In so many of these crises of violence against women, the men in positions of authority in the theological school were unable or unwilling to help either the victim or the perpetrator. In some cases those in authority had very good intentions, and a caring heart; but they were not trained nor were there institutional policies to provide justice and assistance for victims, accountability for perpetrators, and enforcement mechanisms to prevent further occurrences of violence and discrimination. In the worst cases, the men to whom victims went for help actually compounded their suffering. Some of these men were guilty of abuse themselves.

What this situation means is that not only theological *students* but theological *educators* urgently need training in pastoral care and counseling. Some of them have been, wittingly or unwittingly, part of the relational problems on campus rather than part of the solution. For that reason, any new reweaving initiatives in the area of pastoral care and counseling should include consciousness-raising and skills training for the staff of our theological schools. They must personally become part of the process of transformation, cultivating an attitude of humility and openness to new learning which may challenge some of their most taken-for-granted ways of relating.

The Transformation of Curriculum

As another key step in the process of transformation, our theological schools must re-envision their curriculum, so that it can more adequately critique patriarchal theology and church teachings. What follows is an outline of one such attempt at curricular re-envisioning: a new three-pronged praxis-oriented course that re-examines biblical and church teachings which have been stumbling-blocks to the churches' capacity to combat the scourge of violence against women.

A central aim of this course is to equip Oceanian theological students to be more intentional and effective in developing pastoral/ prophetic responses to discrimination and violence against women in their own churches and communities. A larger intention of the proposed course is that it can be a stimulus for the theological schools in Oceania to develop a Peace Culture through a re-envisioning of their entire curriculum. In addition, our hope is that the wider readership of this book will stimulate adaptations of this course for other theological education contexts, in a variety of cultures around the world.

It is suggested that this particular course be trialled initially at Pacific Theological College, since its students represent all major denominations and Oceanian communities. Although the course is designed for Bachelor of Theology or Bachelor/Masters of Divinity level, it could also easily be adapted for Diploma level and offered at any of the other Oceanian theological schools which do not go beyond the Diploma. It is further proposed that the course be a mandatory requirement for graduation for all students and their spouses.[24]

The majority of final-year theological students will be working in parishes upon graduation, yet most have not grappled in any serious way in their theological study with pastoral/prophetic responses to social problems. To counteract this dearth of praxis-oriented theological curriculum, this course is conceived somewhat differently from conventional academic courses in our theological schools. First, it is a year-long endeavor, covering all three terms of the typical trimester system adopted by most Oceanian schools; it is also situated both on and off campus, entailing a significant field education component; and it demands a high degree of student interaction and input.

---

24. As we have noted previously, student wives in the theological colleges will possibly enroll in Women's Program courses (which are neither accredited nor formally recognized), and occasionally in college courses. Because these spouses will be directly involved in issues of violence as clergy wives, we recommend that this course be made mandatory for all spouses as well as students.

Phase One: The Practical Component: In the first term, students would be assigned to a field placement for ten weekends in two different contexts (five weekends in a rural setting, five in an urban setting). They would be placed as participant-observers, living with parish families. The intention is for students to become immersed in the daily lives of parishioners and communities, so that they can become more sensitive to the causes and manifestations of conflicts and other situations that could lead to violence.

During the first week of the term, students would be introduced, in a one-week intensive block, to the theology and practice of field work in theological education.[25] They would be given skills-training in participant-observation, praxis analysis, journal writing and verbatim reporting. The following ten weeks of field placement would then be punctuated by once-weekly class meetings, in which students would share reflections emanating from their verbatim reports, attend colloquia, submit journals periodically, and engage in mutual evaluation and feedback. During the colloquia, each student would lead a class presentation on an issue or incident arising from the field placement experience.

Phase Two: The Academic Component: In the second term, students would enroll for the course, 'Promoting a Culture of Peace: Theology and Praxis.' It would focus particularly on a theological response to the problem of violence against women. It would seek to create, in the first instance, a safe place for learning and a safe space for sharing on an issue that is presently a controversial or taboo subject. The course is designed in eleven modules, in accordance with the trimester system. Below is a suggested outline of the course structure:

Module 1: Un-tabooing the Taboo

- General Discussion on Course Expectations and Aims.
- Global and Local Contexts of Violence.
- Why Violence against Women is a Taboo Topic in Oceania.

25. Field education is virtually non-existent at Pacific Theological College, and is not incorporated in any systemic or serious way into students' theological education. There is a dire need for the college to hire a faculty member who has expertise in the theory and praxis of field education, and for the faculty as a whole to receive in-service training in praxis-centered theological education models.

Module 2: Understanding the Nature and Causes of Violence Against Women

- Insights from Secular Sources.
- Insights from Theological Sources.
- Insights from Local/Cultural Sources (including student input).

Module 3: Situating Violence Against Women in Oceania

- Panel Presentations by guest speakers (lawyer, doctor, counselor, indigenous leader) on violence against women and children in Oceania.
- Small Group Discussion on Panel Presentations.
- Situating Violence Against Women in Oceanian Contexts (group presentations).

Module 4: Case Studies of Violence Against Women in Oceania (I)

- Video Presentations on Violence against Women and Children in Oceania.[26]
- Thematic Group Discussions on Video Presentations.

Module 5: Case Studies of Violence in Oceania (II)

- Analysis of Case Studies from this work.
- Analysis of Case Studies brought by students.

Module 6: Examining Problems with Patriarchal Theology (I)

- Theology of Suffering and Sacrifice.
- Theology of Forgiveness.
- Alternative Theologies.

Module 7: Examining Problems with Patriarchal Theology (II)

- Theology of Marriage.

---

26. A video is being produced on violence against women by *Weavers*, the women's advocacy arm of the South Pacific Association of Theological Schools, which can hopefully be available for this course. There may be other video resources available through the Fiji Women's Crisis Centre, Fiji Women's Rights Movements, or FemLink Pacific.

- Theology of Headship/Submission.
- Alternative Theologies.

Module 8: Critiquing Patriarchal Biblical Interpretations

- Critical Examination of Selected Old Testament Texts.
- Critical Examination of Selected New Testament Texts.
- Alternative Interpretations.

Module 9: Analyzing Problems with the Power of the Clergy

- Sources and Manifestations of Abusive Clergy Power.
- Alternative Constructions of Power.
- Alternative Models of Ministry.

Module 10: Creating a Culture of Peace in the Churches of Oceania

- Embodying a Theology of Peace.
- Restorative Justice.
- Recommendations for Change in Church and Community.

Module 11: Wrapping Up – Critical Analytical Work

- Critical Analysis of Field Placement Experience.
- Critical Analysis of Students' Churches and Cultures.
- Critical Analysis of Course and Recommendations for Change.

Phase 3: Training Workshop and Practicum: During the first week of the final trimester, students and spouses will attend a six-day Intensive Training Workshop on 'Pastoral Care and Counseling in Conflict Situations.' The aim of the workshop is to equip clergy couples to more effectively deal with conflict issues they may confront in their ministries. A proposed timetable for this workshop may be found as Appendix B to this work.

For the remaining ten weeks of the term, students will participate in a Practicum, working with a care-giving NGO for five weeks and a care-giving government agency for the other five weeks, for three hours weekly. They will be asked to write a reflection paper on any of the themes discussed during the eight sessions of the intensive training workshop. In this paper they will (1) identify why they have chosen to write on the chosen theme; (2) analyze a case study (from their Practicum placement) related to this theme; (3) critically evaluate the cultural, social and religious factors contributing to the case; and (4) prepare a concrete action plan to address the problem. (Here the action plans developed during the training workshop can be integrated.)

Students must demonstrate a solid grasp of the information they have gleaned from the intensive training workshop, scholarship and research related to the issue, and their own creative ideas regarding how to deal with a specific situation of violence against women. They also have the option of drafting a Training Program for Parishes on any of the themes highlighted during the training workshop.

A Contextual Critique of the Curriculum

One distinctive feature of the proposed three-phased course is the focus on violence as appropriate subject matter for theological education in Oceania. Moreover, the pedagogical structure differs in key respects from most existing curriculum, since the course is spread across a full academic year and there is much greater scope for a praxis orientation (with field experience, case studies, and ample space for group work). Despite these innovations, however, after re-appraising the course from a cultural perspective our conclusion was that the new curriculum had no particular appreciation of Oceanian approaches to learning.

In order for theological education to be transformational for the peoples and churches of Oceania, theological educators must thoroughly re-examine not only the validity of the content of the curriculum used, but the methodologies and learning approaches employed. In that light, while the above curriculum may be a helpful starting point, the following adaptations are also offered as a possibly more contextually sensitive alternative.

Given the communal orientation of Oceanian cultures, some individual student presentations could be replaced with more small group presentations. In a regional theological school context such as Pacific Theological College, students could at times work in discrete language groups, identifying an issue of violence from their specific context and creating collective presentations around this issue. Otherwise, students could work in thematic groups, based on shared interests.

One other proposal related to presentations is offered for consideration. Rather than having students do presentations for enrolled classmates only, the whole campus community (student and staff spouses and support staff) could be invited to attend and be part of the discussion. The presentation time could be flexible to allow for family members to take part. Built into such an event would be a time for interaction between the class and the visitors. The class could then discuss the presentation later in greater depth.

As an alternative to writing a standard (Western-modeled) research essay, students could again work in groups on a project that is praxis-oriented. This project could be designed for a parish context, a community care-giving context, or for the college community. The aim would be for students not only to design but to implement at least one practical project during their years in the theological school. Ideally, it would be helpful to encourage projects that can be continued when students return to their home islands and parishes.

Groups preparing presentations could also collectively identify scenarios in which violence is typically used as a 'solution.' They could take part in role-playing these scenarios for the class. Time would then be allocated for class discussion to ensure that the class has fully understood the problem. After the class discussion, the members of the group could comment on their individual roles in the presentation.

It is in learning situations such as this that an Oceanian version of Letty Russell's Spiral of Action/Reflection conscientization methodology[27] could be used. In a critical analysis of the identified scenarios, one group member could explore the roots of the problem in the cultural context, another could examine the role of church traditions and teachings. A third could identify sources in the culture, church tradition and society that may help alleviate the problem. A fourth could describe a practical project that might help address

---

27. See Letty Russell, 'Methodology in Liberation/Feminist Theologies: A Theological Spiral of Action/Reflection'. The Spiral was originally presented by Russell at the National Assembly of Women Religious, USA, 1984. It can be found as an Appendix in *Women's Theology: Pacific Perspectives* (Suva, Fiji: SPATS, 1996). In the Spiral, the starting point of learning is not theory but praxis. Lived experience is reflected on by means of critical analysis of the intersections between that experience and 'ideas' (e.g., theological and biblical reflection)—which then leads to a response, in the form of 'action.' This action becomes the new experiential starting point in an ever-widening spiral of action/reflection.

the problem. Each of these strands could then be woven together to produce an integrated, multi-faceted response to the problem.

The above suggestions are contextually relevant means of enhancing theological learning. They emphasize collective ways of doing things over against the Western model of individualism, which stresses competitiveness and individual achievement. But they also happen to be consistent with our Christ-centered egalitarian relational mat. Our cultural critique of our own proposal thus offers a pleasant theological surprise: Working together, as equals, will not only make it easier for Oceanians to learn; it will also better enable them to reweave the egalitarian Jesus mat.

Our pedagogical critique is also offered as a challenge for the region's theological educators to re-examine their curriculum as a whole, in the light of both culturally appropriate pedagogical principles and non-patriarchal theological principles. The old model of one person (usually a male) standing in front of a class, lecturing to students while they passively receive his wisdom, must be challenged on both theological and pedagogical grounds.

In fact, in our new egalitarian Jesus mat, we need a new title to replace the outmoded term 'lecturer' still used to describe faculty members in our theological schools. Educationalists have demonstrated through many scientific studies that listening to a lecturer lecture, in any cultural context, is the worst way to learn. Even in the rare cases when the Oceanian theological lecturer happens to be a female, the model of the all-wise expert 'imparting' knowledge to passive students is a patriarchal model. It is what liberationist Paulo Freire called the 'banking system' of learning, in which teachers 'deposit' knowledge into the 'bank' which is the mind of the 'domesticated' learner.[28] Such passive learners are ill-equipped to become active moral agents of transformation.

If we are to be serious about reweaving the theological/relational mat, then we must liberate the entire way we learn in our theological institutions. We must move from our present authoritarian model to a more egalitarian model that makes students more responsible

28. For a critique of the 'banking system' of learning, see Paulo Freire, *Pedagogy of the Oppressed*, (London: Penguin, 1972); and his later work, *Pedagogy of the Heart* (New York: Continuum, 1998). The banking system has also been critiqued from a theological perspective by Latin American liberation theologian Juan Luis Segundo, in *A Theology for Artisans of a New Humanity, Vol. 4: The Sacraments Today* (Maryknoll, NY: Orbis Books, 1974).

for their own learning, as co-learners with teachers who do not 'lord it over' their students.[29]

The course we have proposed above is designed to be accommodated, with as many modifications as are feasible, within the existing curricular framework of Oceanian theological education, particularly as it exists in the ecumenical environment of Pacific Theological College. In the following section we will summarize a more expansive effort at conscientization and theological reweaving that embraces all of the theological institutions in Oceania.

Reweaving the Relational Mat Beyond the Theological School Classroom

If Oceanian churches are to take seriously the challenge to reweave the relational mat so that discrimination and violence against women will no longer plague our ecclesial and communal life, efforts at conscientization must be broadened beyond the confines of the typical theological school program of academic study. To that end, what follows is a synopsis of a four-year plan of action/reflection which embraces all of Oceania's churches and theological schools. It was designed originally by Joan Tofaeono and was eventually adopted as an action plan by *Weavers*, the women's advocacy wing of the South Pacific Association of Theological Schools.

The major aims of this program of conscientization and action are as follows:

- To raise the awareness of theological students and their families regarding the serious effects of discrimination and violence against women on the lives of Oceanian peoples.

---

29. For an exposition of 'liberating learning models' in non-Western theological education, see Lydia Johnson, 'Liberating Learning: Two Case Studies in Emancipatory Theological Education', in Roswith Gerloff (ed.), *Mission is Crossing Frontiers: Essays in Honour of Bongani Mazibuko* (Pietermaritzburg, SA: Cluster Publications, 2003), pp. 382–413. Seminal scholarly contributions to the field of emancipatory theological education include Paul Bergevin, *A Philosophy of Adult Education* (New York: Seabury Press, 1967); Jack Mezirow, *Fostering Critical Reflection in Adulthood: A Guide to Transformative and Emancipatory Learning* (San Francisco: Jossey-Bass, 1990); J.L. Seymour and D.E. Miller, (eds.), *Theological Approaches to Christian Education* (Nashville, TN: Abingdon Press, 1990); and Gabriel Moran, *Education Toward Adulthood: Religion and Lifelong Learning* (New York: Paulist Press, 1979).

- To provide a platform for theological reflection about the roots of discrimination and violence against women in patriarchy.
- To train future church leaders on how to respond more effectively to social problems such as violence against women, personally, professionally and pastorally.
- To advocate for the inclusion of social issues (not only violence against women, but social problems such as AIDS, regional effects of globalization, civil strife, etc.) in the curriculum of the region's theological schools.
- To encourage Oceanian theological schools to provide mandatory training for theological students and their spouses in crisis pastoral care and counselling.
- To equip Oceanian churches to repudiate patriarchy theologically and by means of concrete changes in policy and practice.

The plan of action consists of the following four phases, spread across a four-year time frame:[30]

Phase 1: Forum and Follow-up Dialogue on 'Violence Against Women: A Theological Challenge'

Phase 1 consists of a broad introduction to the issue of violence against women. It is a consciousness-raising exercise that centers on providing factual information about the realities of violence against women in Oceania. Situating a Forum and follow-up Dialogue event in Suva, Fiji (the hub of Oceania and site of six theological schools), and opening it up to both church and theological communities as well as the public, contributes to the raising of awareness about violence as a region-wide problem that must be addressed by Christians.

Part One: Forum: The forum (first held in Suva in April, 2003) was facilitated by expert panelists from different professional backgrounds who were invited to speak on the topic 'Violence Against Women: A Theological Challenge'. Representatives of civil societies and government (under the Ministry of Women) were among those selected to speak because they have been actively

---

30. Since it began in 2003, several phases have already been implemented. Because theological institutions in other contexts may wish to adapt this plan, we have tried to minimize past-tense descriptions, so as not to limit the ways in which each phase might be structured.

involved in addressing the social, economic and psychological aspects of violence. *Weavers* focused on the theological aspects of the problem, challenging the theological schools and the churches to address the issue as one that is relevant for theological reflection and education. The forum provided much-needed information and raised the awareness of participants that violence against women is a problem that cannot be taken lightly by Christians in Oceania.

Part 2: Follow-up Dialogue: Invitations were sent to Fiji-based theological schools, government agencies and civil societies affiliated with *Weavers*/SPATS, and other interested persons to attend a follow-up discussion on the most critical issues related to violence, particularly violence against women. The meeting was facilitated by a member of *Weavers* and geared towards preparation for the next phase of the action plan.

Part 3: Production of a Video as a Resource for Phase Two: One of the disadvantages of attempting to address controversial social issues in Oceania (especially those which have previously been avoided) is the lack of resources *from* Oceania *for* Oceanian people. It is thus helpful to present Pacific Islanders themselves discussing the issue of violence against women. Footage from the Forum and follow-up Dialogue session, as well as interviews with individual women, is incorporated into the video. Churches and theological schools can hopefully utilize the video as a consciousness-raising tool that will also demonstrate to their constituents that it is not only 'outsiders' who consider violence against women unacceptable, but fellow Pacific Islanders.

Phase 2: Dialoguing on Violence: Talking and Doing Theology

A Workshop on the above topic is designed to assist the theological community to strategize around the issue of how our churches can combat violence against women. Each of the twenty-five Oceanian theological schools is asked to designate two representatives to travel to Suva for the workshop—either a male and female faculty member or, since most member schools have no female faculty, a female faculty spouse or designated *Weavers* representative.

The main aim of the workshop is to conscientize participants regarding the severity of the problem of violence against women, so that they in turn will be able to work as a team to conscientize their colleagues and students in their theological schools. This is a *train-the-trainer* process of conscientization.

Facilitators assist participants in planning a follow-up workshop in their local colleges for the following year. These resource persons include a theologian, lawyer, medical doctor, representative of an NGO working with victims and/or perpetrators of violence against women, and a pastoral counselor. With their help, by the end of the workshop participants should submit a tentative plan for the follow-up workshops.

Phase 3: Being Church in a Context of Violence – Taking a Theological Stance

Phases 1 and 2 should prepare participants to carry out the responsibility given to them to plan and implement a follow-up workshop. These workshops, held at each of the region's theological schools, are designed around the theme, 'A Christian Response to Violence Against Women'. The targeted participants are all enrolled students and their spouses at each college. The workshops are coordinated by the representatives who participated in the previous workshop. The assistance of the members of *Weavers* (theologically trained women) in each country helps to ensure that Phase 3 is carried out successfully.

The principals of the local theological schools are asked for their support in hosting these two-day workshops as part of their academic year. They are also asked to include the theme 'A Christian Response to Violence Against Women' as a topic of theological discussion in their schools. It is suggested that the various academic departments in each school be asked to select a representative to write a paper on the workshop topic, approaching it from the perspective of their respective disciplines.

The objectives of this phase of the action plan are: first, to take up the issue of violence against women as a 'generative theme' in theological discourse, so that students and their spouses can benefit from examining the roots of violence against women; and, second, to prepare future ministers and spouses to address this problem by articulating a concrete 'way forward' for their churches and communities.

Phase Four: Churches and Theological Institutions Joining Together to Combat Violence

No changes can be implemented in Oceanian theological schools without the support of the church leaders and the blessing of the churches. This is why Phase 4 is proposed as a way for church leaders and theological educators to dialogue and take positive steps together on the issue of violence. The ultimate goal is to achieve a public stance from church leaders condemning violence, to gain their endorsement and backing in challenging the churches to overcome violence in their families and communities, and to begin to implement changes in the theological schools that incorporate responses to social problems such as violence against women.

In order to achieve this goal, a Consultation is envisioned that brings together theological educators and church leaders, for the purpose of formulating a public stance against all forms of violence and designing a liberative curriculum that reweaves the relational mat. This consultation will: (1) synthesize learnings from the previous two years of workshops; (2) publish the consultation proceedings and new curriculum as a resource for Oceanian churches and communities; and (3) encourage cooperative, ecumenical networking amongst church bodies and the region's theological institutions in practical efforts to overcome violence, including violence against women, particularly in theological education and church policy.[31]

The targeted group of participants in the consultation will be two representatives (a woman and a man) from each Oceanian church. It is necessary to include church representatives in this consultation as well as theological educators, since it focuses on 'church leaders.' Again, since most theological schools do not have female faculty members, and the churches do not have female church leaders, women who participated in the last two workshops, or churchwomen committed to this project, should be the female representatives. The facilitators should include representatives of churches outside Oceania to gain a balanced presentation of 'insider' and 'outsider' perspectives.

---

31. A copy of the proposed Program for the Consultation is included as Appendix C.

In this chapter we have attempted to move from a critique of the old relational mat of patriarchy to a constructive reweaving of a new, Christ-centered, egalitarian relational mat. We chose the metaphor of weaving both because it resonates with the lived experience of Oceanian peoples and because it provides a fitting way to re-envision God's intended relational ethic. In replacing the unbalanced and unjust patriarchal mat with the egalitarian Jesus mat, we have been able to propose a 'way forward' for the Oceanian churches (and hopefully churches in other contexts as well) regarding the evil of discrimination and violence against women.

Because, in our view, all theology *is* praxis, we have also grounded our re-envisioning in concrete proposals for change in the Oceanian context. Our proposal for a new curriculum, one small strand in the theological reweaving of the relational mat, is intended to spur women, theological educators, students and church leaders in Oceania and elsewhere to repudiate patriarchy and the violence against women which it engenders.

But this has to be a holistic undertaking. As we have seen, it is not enough merely to include new academic theological perspectives in the same old classroom setting. Not only the content but the context of theological education has to change. New egalitarian, liberative methodologies and pedagogies have to emerge. The entire structure of our theological schools must be opened up for scrutiny and critical analysis as we share together, as equals, in the reweaving of the divine mat.

We have also attempted to open up the re-envisioning and reweaving challenge beyond the theological school classroom, to the wider church. The plan of action we have proposed is only one small way of initiating the very important process of encouraging dialogue both among Oceanian Christians and with Christians in other contexts—dialogue between men and women, between the church and the theological school, and across denominational and cultural lines. Once again, this is not merely dialogue for the sake of conversation, which ends with the production of final reports and statements. This is dialogue for the sake of transformation. It is action/reflection, genuine theological praxis. In the liberating Christ-Spirit in whom we live and move and have our being, we humbly offer these challenges to reweave the relational mat, in the islands of Oceania and beyond.

Chapter Nine

Epilogue: Final Reflections

The Terrain We Have Traveled

We have shown in this work how violence against women is both a global and a local problem—that is, it is global in reach and has certain universally shared dimensions and characteristics, while at the same time it is also manifested in particular ways in a given context.[1] Although our particular concern has been the reality of violence against women in Christian contexts in Oceania, we believe that our analysis has implications for other cultural contexts as well.

Our critical reflection has focused on the role of the church and its theological institutions in the perpetuation and escalation of violence against women in Oceania, through its upholding of a patrikyriarchal theology and ecclesial praxis that exerts control over women in every sphere of life.

We began our analysis in Chapter One by disclosing the global context of violence. We identified the interwoven matrix of patriarchal strands which weave a complex web of violence whose manifestations are multiplicative. Connections were made between violence and the capitalist economic world order, colonialism, and militarism. Within this larger fabric of violence we were then able to situate the particular strand of violence which is violence against women, by elaborating the ideology of patriarchy from which it emanates.

In Chapter Two we examined violence against women more closely, by highlighting its many forms and manifestations. This included physical and sexual assault, both within and outside the

1. Robert Schreiter and others have coined the term *glocal* to refer to the interconnection of global and local contexts in social problems. See especially, Robert Schreiter, *Doing Local Theology: A Guide for Artisans of a New Humanity* (Faith and Cultures Series) (Maryknoll, NY: Orbis Books, 2002); and *The New Catholicity: Theology Between the Global and the Local* (Faith and Cultures Series) (Maryknoll, NY: Orbis Books, 1997).

home. We also unraveled the more covert and subtle strand of violence against women which is gender harassment, in its many guises. By tracing the contours of the various strands of violence against women, and accentuating their devastating consequences for women worldwide, we laid the groundwork for a contextualization of violence against women in Oceania.

In Chapter Three, then, we continued our unraveling of the fabric of patriarchy by situating the problem of violence against women in the island communities in Oceania. The roots of violence against women in the region were traced to both the impacts of globalization (the new face of colonialism) and indigenous patriarchal life-ways and traditions (noting how they are reinforced by sacred myths). The scope and severity of violence against women in Oceania were demonstrated through documentary evidence.

Chapter Four unraveled the interwoven strands of religion and violence against women. After highlighting the larger mosaic in which the teachings of various religions have been interpreted by their adherents in such a way as to support violence, attention was focused on the interplay of Christianity and violence against women. We examined Oceanian Christianity's captivity to patriarchal theology (particularly its theologies of headship, marriage, sacrifice and forgiveness) and patriarchal biblical interpretations (by examining several passages which have contributed to the condoning of violence against women).

In Chapter Five we continued our unraveling of the ecclesial strand of violence against women in the Oceanian context by critiquing the region's patriarchal church traditions. We saw how these traditions have become an influential contributor to the perpetuation of violence against women given the central role of the church throughout Oceania. The almost unlimited power of the male clergy in the Oceanian church and culture—and its inevitable spin-off, clergy abuse—were exposed as particularly virulent strands in the patriarchal fabric of violence against women in the region.

Chapter Six shifted the locus of our concern to the arena of theological education, given the fact that Oceania's theological schools are such an important force in 'church-shaping,' through their inculcation of 'power-over' relationality in the clergy—the most revered and influential people in Oceanian societies. This chapter became a pivotal moment in our study, as it enfleshed our analysis of violence against women by allowing Oceanian women's stories of abuse and harassment to speak for themselves. Our re-telling and analysis of these stories grounded our theological unraveling of patriarchal relationality in the praxis of the suffering of women in our most cherished Oceanian Christian institution, the theological school.

Chapter Seven extended our interweaving of the strands of theological patriarchy and violence against women in Oceania by focusing on the patri-kyriarchal social ethos, curriculum, administrative policy and leadership in the theological schools of Oceania. Examples were provided of unsound approaches to the teaching of theology, biblical studies and liturgy which have led to a legitimization of women's second-class status, and thus indirectly to the condoning of violence against them. The results of a qualitative research effort with theological students confirmed our hypothesis that both patriarchal socio-cultural location and theological predispositions have a strong bearing on how women are viewed and treated.

In Chapter Eight we engaged in an exercise of theological re-envisioning in order to 'reweave the relational mat.' In our re-envisioning we drew upon the contributions of female theologians from both beyond and within Oceania. Our own contribution made use of the archetypal Oceanian metaphor of *weaving*, and the sociality associated with the resulting *mat*, to guide our act of reweaving. Replacing the old patriarchal relational mat, we proposed a Christocentric 'egalitarian relational mat' to free women and men from the 'power-over' relational paradigm.

We then incarnated our rewoven relational mat in praxis. Centering our proposals for transformation in the theological education milieu, we highlighted the need for radical institutional change, including a new commitment to across-the-board capacity-building in pastoral care and counseling. We then proposed a new curriculum for Oceanian theological schools that centers a theological critique of patriarchal theology in the praxis of field education and interactive engagement by students in the process of unraveling and reweaving the relational mat. We also broadened our praxis-centered efforts beyond the theological school classroom by proposing a four-year action plan—a program of conscientization aimed at raising the critical awareness of the theological and ecclesial communities of Oceania, and then moving toward the implementation of workable transformative change.

Remaining Challenges to the Churches of Oceania

The Challenge to Church Leaders

As this study has clearly demonstrated, the patriarchal ethos which still defines the churches of Oceania has indoctrinated many of its members, both men and women, not to question the values, customary practices and 'rules' that are normative for their societies. It is deeply ingrained into the psyches of Pacific Islanders not to question the absolutizing hold of culture over their lives. They must not question men's 'power-over' ways of relating to women. Most of all, they must not question the unfettered power of sacred authority (invested in the clergy/Men of God) and the institution they control (the church).

We challenge the church leaders of Oceania to lead the way in freeing themselves and their people from captivity to the patriarchal aspects of their culture by remembering that the church is not the servant of culture. Rather, as Christians our ultimate loyalty is to the liberating Gospel of Jesus Christ. If our Oceanian Christian community is to be the true harbinger of this Good News, it must become a questioning church. It must encourage the questioning of any theology, tradition, institution, custom, value or practice that permits 'power-over' relationality. And in order to become a questioning church, our church leaders must create an environment in which everyone's voice can be heard, in which no one is silenced.

But our guess is that it will not necessarily be the male church authorities but the Christian women of Oceania who will have to take the initiative to nudge their church leaders toward a wholesale repudiation of gender discrimination. (Transformation is more often initiated from below than from above.) This will not be an easy task, for these women know all too well the negative repercussions of challenging the status quo of patriarchy. Yet it is not an impossible task, if women join together in solidarity and appeal boldly to the liberating and transforming power of the Gospel.

The Challenge to Oceanian Women to be Agents of Change

If our hypothesis about women's prophetic mission is to bear fruit, it is important that a challenge be issued directly to the Christian women of Oceania to unravel the patriarchal mat and reweave an egalitarian mat. They can begin this process in their own homes, by teaching their children, both boys and girls, new ways of relating.

They can further crack open the doors of silence about women's oppression as they meet with other women, encouraging one another in the power of the Holy Spirit to 'name' their experiences of exploitation, and empowering one another to move from domination by men to equal partnership with men. Through this networking, they will find the strength to challenge their husbands, brothers, fathers, ministers and church authorities to proclaim and celebrate the equality and oneness of males and females in Jesus Christ.

A point needs to be made here about Oceanian women's agency. Our stark portrayal of the reality of violence against women in Oceania may have indirectly downplayed the ways in which Oceanian women have also been agents of change and not merely victims of violence. Increasing numbers of Oceanian women are indeed becoming agents for liberation from gender discrimination and abuse. A dedicated core of prophetic women is in the forefront of un-tabooing the taboos through their advocacy in revealing the seriousness of the problem of violence in our homes, communities and nations.[2]

There are also traditional 'cultural ways' in which Oceanian women attempt to resist their abuse. In many Oceanian communities, the sister has a central role within her family of origin, even if she marries. This role has been helpful in cases of abuse against sisters-in-law and other women in the extended family. The sisters in many cases stand with their sisters-in-law, condemning the actions of their brothers publicly and even giving the brothers an ultimatum to stop the abuse or else be confronted with the loss of the abused spouse or partner. The women who resist violence in this way risk being ostracized by their community, workplace and church, and their courage is to be commended.

More generally, many abused Oceanian women have developed strong coping mechanisms and survival strategies. This focus on coping should not portray a picture of Oceanian women as weak, because their very survival is a sign of their strength to endure, to 'keep on keeping on' no matter what they have to contend with.

2.   Women's NGOs, such as the Fiji Women's Crisis Center, Fiji Women's Rights Movement, UNIFEM Pacific, FemLink and *Weavers* (all based in Fiji), Mapusaga o Aiga (Samoa), Women's Desk of the South Pacific Communities (New Caledonia/ Kanaky), the Women's Fellowships in the Solomon Islands, Papua New Guinea and Vanuatu, and other women's groups are working tirelessly to assist women to resist acts of violence against them. They have led the way in providing training for both women and men to develop non-violent ways of handling crisis situations.

The time has come, of course, for Oceanian women to shift from 'enduring' to more active 'resisting.' 'Enduring' promotes the Oceanian cultural value of preserving harmony, peace and unity at all costs. This myth of Oceanian peace and harmony needs to be de-mythologized, as it has been more harmful than life-affirming for women. Peace that does not embrace everyone is peace in name only, and makes the standard connotation of the word 'Pacific' a sham.

Our challenge to the Oceanian women who are already struggling to be agents for change is to continue their prophetic calls for non-violence and mutual respect. We acknowledge that, in the Oceanian context, *personal agency* must always also be *community agency*. But the communal ethos which Pacific Islanders so greatly revere, and which is at the core of their cultural identity, can never truly be cohesive and harmonious until all of its members—men, women and children—have equal opportunity for self-development and equal protection against mistreatment in any form.

There is an ancient Samoan saying which states, '*Afai ua sala uta, ia tonu tai. Faamoemoe i le lagi e mama, ta te folau ai*' ('If there is misfortune in the land, let there be fortune in the sea, hoping that in the clarity of the skies we can safely and freely sail on'). Oceanian women who are agents of transformation are re-framing this wisdom saying as follows: If there is any deficiency in the inherited theological, cultural or other traditions that legitimates violence, our focus of vision must be shifted, so that there can be hope for fullness of life for all of God's creation.

The Challenge to Oceanian Theological Educators

We have argued in this work that one of the most critical arenas for the transformation of Oceanian Christian communities, so that the patriarchal relational mat can be discarded and the egalitarian relational mat rewoven, is in our theological schools. Our theological educators have enormous influence over our future church leaders. They have the wherewithal to transform their theology, biblical interpretations, worship, ministry formation, pastoral care, institutional policies and leadership styles, such that women become genuinely equal partners in theological praxis. We challenge them to do so.

They can make a start in that direction by prayerfully studying and embracing the following objectives adopted by the World Council of Churches' Decade to Overcome Violence:

General Principles and Objectives for Churches Seeking to Overcome All Forms of Violence Against Women

1. To reflect on biblical and theological perspectives that impact attitudes and behavior in relationships and church practice.
2. To implement educational strategies which will develop awareness and training in all parts of the church community (local, national, international, and for lay and ordained, where these distinctions are applicable).
3. To commit ourselves, and encourage our churches, to use language that is not violent and does not exclude the experience of anyone.
4. To sustain a safe environment within the faith communities where all will be empowered.
5. To achieve good practice in all church structures for prevention and intervention.
6. To be 'church together,' understanding and affirming diverse theologies, cultures, languages and structures.
7. To effect and develop a network of concerned persons and church bodies which can enable the sharing of resources, understanding and good practice.
8. To work in partnership with the wider community in overcoming violence against women.
9. To ensure funding in order to realize goals.
10. To adopt an agenda which will address all issues that concern violence against women and its consequences for individuals, faith communities and societies.[3]

In order for the theological educators of Oceania to be able to embody these guiding principles, however, they must first be challenged to a new commitment to self-critical reflection. This commitment to what the liberation theologians often call *autocriticality*, or what we have referred to elsewhere in this work as critical analysis, action/reflection, or theological praxis, can be incarnated by taking the following steps:

3. 'General Principles and Objectives for Churches Seeking to Overcome All Forms of Violence Against Women', final statement, WCC-DOV Consultation, Dundee, Scotland, 23–28 August 2001.

First, our theological educators need to identify their own location in the problem of violence against women, and re-examine the ways in which their theology and culture have contributed to this problem. Second, they must provide a safe and encouraging space for the women in their churches and theological communities to tell the untold, hidden, painful stories of domination, exploitation and violence at the hands of men; and they must open their hearts to listen more attentively to these previously unheard women's laments. Finally, they must create a new rhythm for justice in theological education and the church, with the compassionate beat of their hearts and the humble searching of their minds, performed by the actions of their hands, activated and guided by the empowering work of the Spirit.

A Final Challenge

A challenge to the Christian communities of Oceania regarding violence against women has already been issued by a number of leading church women. It is found in the final Declaration of a gathering of women from all parts of Oceania who met at the Pacific-region World Council of Churches' Workshop on Violence Against Women, held in 1996 in Samoa as part of the WCC Decade of Churches in Solidarity with Women.

The women gathered in this consultation listened to women's stories of male violence of all forms, heard and felt the pain of these victim-survivors, struggled to deal with their frustrations, wept for healing and prayed for action. A decade has now passed since these Oceanian Christian women declared in writing their challenge to the churches and communities of Oceania to take a stand to end violence against women. To date no substantive changes have been implemented by the churches of Oceania as a result of their plea.

These women's statement, known as the Apia Declaration, along with the silent cries of abused women around the region and the world, remain a constant challenge for all who believe in Jesus, the peace-bringer and peace-maker. We end our work with the lament of these Oceanian women:

> *A Plea from the Women of Oceania: Tofamamao – No More Violence in Paradise*
>
> *Strengthened and encouraged by each other and the unconditional love of God, we have reached out to each other and shared our painful*

experiences and stories of the violence against women throughout our Pacific Islands.

We have heard of lack of support by governments, churches and the society as a whole for women in violent situations, either at home or at work or in society.

We have wept for the thousands of women who, because of cultural and religious pressures, have suffered violence silently and alone.

We have heard that for thousands of women and girls, home is no longer a safe place, but a place of fear, pain and terror.

We are confronted with the knowledge that our cultures have been used as justification for violence against women.

We acknowledge that the kind of theology taught by the church not only perpetuates violence against women but often condones violence.

We have listened to the stories of the betrayal of women's and children's trust by the clergy through acts of sexual harassment and abuse.

We have discovered the painful reality that we are often victims of these destructive acts of violence.

We mourn the thousands of women and girls who are raped.

We affirm that we are survivors of the violence and committed to struggle until justice is done.

We listened, we heard, we struggled, we wept and we prayed.[4]

How much longer must the weeping and the praying continue before the churches of Oceania respond? How many more victims will there be? When will there be hearts to hear women's cries to end the evil of patriarchy? This is our plea to the Christian communities of Oceania and beyond: Play your part as agents of peace, vessels of hope and doers of justice for all of God's creation. Together, women and men, let us reweave the relational mat as equal partners in God's mission of love.

4.   'Tofamamao: No More Violence in Paradise', Apia Declaration, WCC Decade of Churches in Solidarity with Women Pacific Regional Consultation, Apia, Samoa, 12–15 March 1996.

Appendices

APPENDIX A — QUESTIONNAIRE FOR THEOLOGICAL STUDENTS: THEOLOGICAL TEACHINGS AND ATTITUDES TOWARD WOMEN

[This is an open-ended questionnaire format. Please feel free to expand on any question, and to comment at length if you choose.]

1. In your church's standard wedding ceremony, are husbands and wives viewed exactly the same, or are there any differences — e.g., does the wife promise to 'obey' the husband but not vice-versa; does the liturgy refer to 'man and wife' rather than 'husband and wife'?
2. How have these church customs influenced what has been considered to be the acceptable relationship between husbands and wives?
3. What has been your church's traditional teaching in general regarding the relative status and duties of husbands and wives/ men and women?
4. What scriptural and theological arguments have been used to back up this teaching?
5. What would you like to change, if anything, in your church's existing marriage sacrament? Explain the reasons for your answer.
6. What is your understanding of Adam's statement in Gen. 2: 23 — 'This at last is bone of my bones and flesh of my flesh; this one shall be called Woman, for out of Man this one is taken'?
7. How has your church interpreted the above passage traditionally, in terms of the common portrayal of women as being derived from and therefore inferior to men?
8. Do you see any connections between the traditional view of wives as being derived from and subservient to their husbands and the sanctioning of violence against women? Explain.
9. What overall changes are needed in your church's teaching and practice regarding the status of women?

APPENDIX B – PROGRAM FOR INTENSIVE TRAINING WORKSHOP FOR THEOLOGICAL STUDENTS

Monday	*Tuesday*	*Wednesday*	*Thursday*	*Friday*	*Saturday*
MORNING DEVOTIONS					
Session 1 Counseling Methods; Spiral of Action/ Reflection	*Session 3* Pastoral Care/ Counseling in Crisis Situations	*Session 5* Pastoral Care/ Counseling for Harassment	*Session 7* Pastoral Intervention, Confidentiality, Mandatory Reporting	Action Plan for parishes or other ministries (in small groups)	Small Group Presentations of Action Plans
MORNING BREAK					
Small group discussion on Session 1	Small group discussion on Session 3	Small group discussion on Session 5	Small group discussion on Session 7	Action Planning cont. (small groups)	Small Group Presentations (cont.)
LUNCH					
Session 2 Pastoral Care/ Counseling in Oceanian Perspective	*Session 4* Pastoral Care/ Counseling in Situations of Violence Against Women	*Session 6* Clergy Ethics and Pastoral Relationships	*Session 8* Restorative Justice, Reconciliation and Healing	Concrete Actions and Visions: Small group presentations of Action Plans in Plenary	Small Group Presentations (cont.)
AFTERNOON BREAK					
Group Discussion on Session 2	Group Discussion on Session 4	Group Discussion on Session 6	Group Discussion on Session 8	Action planning continued	Group Evaluation
CLOSING WORSHIP/DINNER					
EVENINGS Plenary Sessions: Follow-up general discussions of group presentations; Guest speakers					

APPENDIX C – PROGRAM FOR THEOLOGICAL EDUCATORS/ CHURCH LEADERS CONSULTATION

Day 1	Day 2	Day 3	Day 4	Day 5	Day 6
THEMES					
The Bible and Violence (O.T.)	The Bible and Violence (N.T.)	Christian Theology and Violence	Church History and Violence	Theological Education and Violence	Clergy Power and Violence
BIBLE STUDY ON THE THEME OF THE DAY					
PANEL DISCUSSIONS OF THE BIBLE STUDY FROM REPRESENTATIVES OF VARIOUS DISCIPLINES					
MORNING TEA BREAK					
PRESENTATIONS ON THE THEME OF THE DAY: ROOTING THE THEME IN THE PRAXIS OF OUR CULTURES AND CHURCHES					
Thematic group work on Presentation	Thematic group work on Presentation	Thematic group work on Presentation	Thematic group work on Presentation	Thematic group work on Presentation	Curriculum Presentations (Interdisciplinary)
LUNCH BREAK					
CREATIVE GROUP PRESENTATIONS AND FOLLOW-UP DISCUSSIONS IN PLENARY SESSION					
Curriculum Development in Discrete Discipline Groups	Curriculum Development in Discrete Discipline Groups	Curriculum Development in Discrete Discipline Groups	Interdisciplinary Group Work on Curriculum Design	Interdisciplinary Group Work on Curriculum Design	Presentation and Discussion of New Curriculum (cont.)
AFTERNOON TEA BREAK					
Group Presentations of Work in Progress in Plenary	Group Presentations of Work in Progress in Plenary	Group Presentations of Work in Progress in Plenary	Group Presentations of Work in Progress in Plenary	Group Presentations of Work in Progress in Plenary	Summary and Evaluation
CLOSING WORSHIP					
CLOSING DINNER					

Bibliography

Adams, Carol
  1994   *Woman-Battering: Creative Pastoral Care and Counseling* (Minneapolis, MN: Fortress Press).

Adams, Carol, and Marie M. Fortune (eds.)
  1995   *Violence Against Women and Children: A Christian Theological Sourcebook* (Lexington, NY: The Continuum Publishing Company).

Afamasaga, Faasili, and Kuiniselani Tago
  2003   'Family Health and Safety Study of Violence Against Women in Oceania'. Paper presented, Pacific Regional Workshop on Strengthening Partnerships for Eliminating Violence Against Women (Pacific Forum Secretariat, Suva, Fiji, 17–19 February).

Aiono, Fana'afi
  1986   'Western Samoa: The Sacred Covenant' in Bolabola *et al.*, 1986a, pp. 96–115.

Akau'ola, Seluini
  2003   'Violence Against Women and Children: A Theological Challenge', *Pacific Journal of Theology* II: 30: pp. 49–53.

Ali, Imran
  2002   'Father Under Probe for Sex Crimes' in *The Fiji Times*, 15 November.

Ali, Shamima
  1996   'Violence Against Women' in *Women's Theology: Pacific Perspectives*, pp. 57–60 (Suva, Fiji: SPATS).

Amnesty International
  1991   'Rape and Sexual Abuse: Torture and Ill-Treatment of Women in Detention' *ACT 77* (November 1991): n.p.

Amoah, Elizabeth
  1996   'Sacrifice/Self-Negation' in Letty Russell and J. Shannon Clarkson (eds.), *Dictionary of Feminist Theologies* (Louisville, KY: Westminster/John Knox Press), p. 254.

Andrews, David
  2002   'What is Globalization, and What is an Ethical Response?' *Witness* (Fall): pp. 15–21.

Ariarajah, S. Wesley
  2002a 'What Difference Does Religious Plurality Make?' *Current Dialogue* 34 (February 2000). http://www.wcc-coe.org/ wcc/what/interreligious/cd34-02.html.
  2002b 'Religion and Violence: A Protestant Christian Perspective', *Current Dialogue* 39 (June 2002). http://www.wcccoe.org/wcc/what/interreligious/ cd39-01.html.

Auckland Technical Institute
  1989 'Policy Statement on Sexual Harassment' in Audrey Colbert (ed.), *Dealing with Sexual Harassment: A New Zealand Handbook* (Wellington, NZ: GP Books).

Azariah, Samuel
  2000 'The Violence of Religious Intolerance', *Echoes* 17. http://www.wcc-coe.org/wcc/what/jpc/echoes/echoes-18-06.html.

Bal, Mieke
  1987 *Lethal Love: Feminist Literary Interpretation of Biblical Love Stories* (Bloomington, IN: Indiana University Press).

Bal, Mieke (ed.)
  1989 *Anti-Covenant: Counter-Reading Women's Lives in the Hebrew Bible* (Sheffield: Sheffield Academic Press).

'Bali Declaration of Asian Women on Violence Against Women'
  1996 WCC Asia Regional Workshop on Violence Against Women (Bali, Indonesia).

Barr, Kevin
  1990 *Poverty in Fiji* (Suva, Fiji: Fiji Forum for Justice, Peace and the Integrity of Creation).

Bassler, Jouette M.
  1988 '1 Corinthians' in Carol A. Newsom and Sharon H. Ringe (eds.), *Women's Bible Commentary* (Louisville, KY: John Knox Press), pp. 411–19.

Beaman, Lori G.
  1999 *Shared Beliefs, Different Lives: Women's Identities in Evangelical Context* (St Louis, MO: Chalice Press).

Belleville, Linda
  2000 *Women Leaders and the Church: Three Crucial Questions* (Grand Rapids, MI: Baker Books).

Bellis, Alice Ogden
  1994 *Helpmates, Harlots, Heroes: Women's Stories in the Hebrew Bible* (Louisville, KY: Westminster/John Knox Press).

Benson, D., and G. Thompson
  1992 'Sexual Harassment on a University Campus: The Confluence of Authority Relations, Sexual Interest, and Gender Stratifications', *Social Problems* 29:3: 236–51.

Bergevin, Paul
 1967   *A Philosophy of Adult Education* (New York: Seabury Press).

Beuken, Wim, and Karl-Josef Kuschel (eds.)
 1997   *Religion as a Source of Violence?* (London: SCM Press; Maryknoll, NY: Orbis, Books).

Bloomquist, Karen L.
 1989   'Sexual Violence: Patriarchy's Offense and Defense' in Joanne Carlson Brown and Carol R. Bohn (eds.), *Christianity, Patriarchy and Abuse: A Feminist Critique* (Cleveland, OH: The Pilgrim Press), pp. 62–69.

Bolabola, Cema *et al.*
 1986a *Land Rights of Pacific Women* (Suva, Fiji: Institute of Pacific Studies/University of the South Pacific).
 1986b 'Fiji Customary Constraints and Legal Progress' in Cema Bolabola *et al.*, *Land Rights of Pacific Women*, pp. 1–15.

Bowker, Lee H.
 1982   'Battered Women and the Clergy: An Evaluation', *Journal of Pastoral Care* 46:4 pp. 226–34.

Boyd, Susan
 2001   Keynote address, Third Regional Meeting of the Pacific Women's Network on Violence Against Women. Fiji Women's Crisis Centre, Korolevu, Suva, Fiji, 19 February–2 March.

Bradley, C.S.
 1985   'Attitudes and Practices Relating to Marital Violence Among the *Tolai* of East New Britain' in PNG Law Reform Commission (ed.), *Domestic Violence in Papua New Guinea* (Goroko, PNG: Law Reform Commission), pp. 32–71.

Brenner, Althalya, (ed.)
 1999   *Judges: A Feminist Companion to the Bible* (Sheffield: Sheffield Academic Press), 2nd edn.

Brock, Rita Nakashima
 1988   *Journeys by Heart: A Christology of Erotic Power* (New York: The Crossroad Publishing Company).
 1989   'And a Little Child Will Lead Us: Christology and Child Abuse' in Joanne Carlson Brown and Carol R. Bohn (eds.), *Christianity, Patriarchy and Abuse: A Feminist Critique* (Cleveland, OH: The Pilgrim Press), pp. 42–61.
 2001   'Dusting the Bible on the Floor: A Hermeneutic of Wisdom' in Elisabeth Schüssler Fiorenza (ed.), *Searching the Scriptures: A Feminist Introduction* (New York: The Crossroad Publishing Company), pp. 64–75.

Brock, Rita Nakashima, and Susan Brooks Thisthethwaite
 1996   *Casting Stones: Prostitution and Liberation in Asia and the United States* (Minneapolis, MN: Fortress Press).

Brock, Rita Nakashima, and Rebecca Ann Parker
 2001   *Proverbs of Ashes: Violence, Redemptive Suffering, and the Search for What Saves Us* (Boston: Beacon Press).

Brown, Joanne Carlson, and Carole Bohn (eds.)
 1989   *Christianity, Patriarchy and Abuse* (New York: Pilgrim Press).

Brown, Joanne Carlson, and Rebecca Ann Parker
 1997   'For God so Loved the World?' in Carol J. Adams and Marie M. Fortune
        (eds.), *Violence Against Women and Children* (Lexington, NY: Continuum),
        pp. 36–59.

Brown, L.
 2001   *Sex Slaves: The Trafficking of Women in Asia* (London: Virago Press).

Brownmiller, Susan
 1993   *Against Our Will: Men, Women and Rape* (New York: Fawcett Columbine).

Brundtland, Gro Harlem
 2002   'Preface' in World Health Organization, *World Report on Violence and Health*
        (Geneva: WHO).

Cahill, Lisa Sowle
 1996   'Marriage' in Letty Russell and Shannon J. Clarkson (eds.), *Dictionary of Femi-
        nist Theologies* (Louisville, KY: Westminster/John Knox Press), pp. 172–73.

Canadian Center for Justice Statistics
 2000   *Family Violence in Canada: A Statistical Profile* (Ottawa: Statistics Canada).

Castelli, Elizabeth (ed.)
 2001   *Women, Gender, Religion: A Reader* (New York: Houndmills; London: Palgrave).

Caucau, Asenaca
 2003   Keynote address, Pacific Regional Workshop on Strengthening Partnerships
        for Eliminating Violence Against Women. Pacific Forum Secretariat, Suva,
        Fiji, 17–19 February.

Clark, Elizabeth
 1983   *Women in the Early Church* (Wilmington, DE: M. Glazier).

Cloke, Gillian
 1995   *This Female Man of God: Women and Spiritual Power in the Patristic Age* (Lon-
        don: Routledge).

Colbert, Audrey
 1989   *Dealing with Sexual Harassment: A New Zealand Handbook* (Wellington, NZ:
        GP Books).

Collins, Sheila
 1974   *A Different Heaven and Earth* (Valley Forge, PA: Judson Press).

Cooper-White, Pamela
 1995   *The Cry of Tamar: Violence Against Women and the Church's Response*
        (Minneapolis, MN: Fortress Press).

Council for World Mission
 2002a *Intimate Partner Violence.* FACTS Action Sheet [Unnumbered] (London:
        CWM).
 2002b *Women and Violence.* FACTS Action Sheet 4 (London: CWM).

2002c *Women, Culture and Equality*. FACTS Action Sheet 6 (London: CWM).

Counts, A. Dorothy
1990 'Domestic Violence in Oceania', *Pacific Studies* 13: pp. 22–27.

Cribb, J., and R. Barnett
1999 'Being Bashed: Western Samoan Women's Responses to Domestic Violence in Western Samoa.' *Western Samoa and New Zealand: Gender, Place and Culture* 6 (January): 49–65.

Crull, P.
1981 'The Stress Effects of Sexual Harassment on the Job', *American Journal of Orthopsychiatry* 52: pp. 539–44.

Daly, Mary
1968 *The Church and the Second Sex* (London: Geoffrey Chapman).
1973 *Beyond God the Father: Toward a Philosophy of Women's Liberation* (Boston: Beacon Press).

Davidson, Terry
1978 *Conjugal Crime: Understanding and Changing the Wife-Beating Pattern* (New York: Hawthorn).

DeCoster, S., S.B. Estes and C.W. Mueller
1999 'Routine Activities and Sexual Harassment in the Workplace', *Work and Occupations* 26:1: 21–43.

Deegalle, Mahinda
2002 'Is Violence Justified in Theravāda Buddhism?' *Current Dialogue* 39 (June). http://www.wcc-coe.org/wcc/what/ interreligious/cd39-01.html.

de Ishtar, Zohl
1994 *Daughters of the Pacific* (Melbourne: Spinifex Press).

de Marinis, Valerie M.
1993 *Critical Caring: A Feminist Model for Pastoral Psychology* (Louisville, KY: Westminster/John Knox Press).

de Vries, Hent
2002 *Religion and Violence: Philosophical Perspectives from Kant to Derrida* (Baltimore, MD: John Hopkins University Press).

Dinan, K.
2000 *Owed Justice: Thai Women Trafficked into Debt Bondage in Japan* (New York: Human Rights Watch).

Dobash, Rebecca E., and Russell P. Dobash
1979 *Violence Against Wives: A Case Against the Patriarchy* (New York: Free Press).
1992 *Women, Violence and Social Change* (New York: Routledge).

Dobash, Rebecca E., and Russell P. Dobash (eds.)
1998a *Rethinking Violence Against Women* (Thousand Oaks, CA: Sage Publications).
1998b 'Cross-Border Encounters: Challenges and Opportunities' in Dobash and Dobash (eds.), 1998a: pp. 9–27.

Douglass, Jane Dempsey
1985   *Women, Freedom and Calvin* (Philadelphia: Westminster Press).

Driver, John
1986   *Understanding the Atonement for the Mission of the Church* (Scottsdale, PA: Herald Press).

Dube, Musa
2000   *Postcolonial Feminist Interpretation of the Bible* (St Louis, MO: Chalice Press).

Eilts, Mitzi
1988   'Saving the Family: When Is the Covenant Broken?' in Anne L. Horton and Judith A. Williamson (eds.), *Abuse and Religion: When Praying Isn't Enough*, n.p. (Lexington, MA: Lexington Books).

ELCA Commission for Women
1990   'Sexual Harassment and Abuse', pamphlet on 1989 Lutheran Church-wide Assembly Resolution on Gender Abuse (Chicago: ELCA).

Emberson, Atu Bain (ed.)
1994   *Sustainable Development or Malignant Growth? Perspectives of Pacific Island Women* (Suva, Fiji: Marama Publications).

Enloe, C.
1994   *The Morning After: Sexual Politics at the End of the Cold War* (Berkeley, CA: University of California Press).

Erickson, Millard
1998   *Christian Theology* (Grand Rapids, MI: Baker Books), 2nd edn.

Erickson, Victoria Lee, Michelle Lim Jones, and Kwang-Sin Si (eds.)
2002   *Surviving Terror: Hope and Justice in a World of Violence* (Grand Rapids, MI: Brazos Press).

Ess, Charles
1995   'Reading Adam and Eve: Re-Visions of the Myth of Woman's Subordination to Man' in Carol J. Adams and Marie M. Fortune (eds.), *Violence Against Women and Children: A Christian Theological Sourcebook* (Lexington, NY: Continuum), pp. 92–120.

Etchegoyan, Aldo M.
2000   'Editorial on Violence', *Echoes: WCC Justice, Peace and Integrity of Creation Newsletter* 17. http://www.wcc-coe.org.wcc/what/jpc/echoes/echoes-18-00.html.

Ete-Lima, Michiko
2003   'A Theology of the *Feagaiga*: A Samoan Theology of God' in Lydia Johnson and Joan A. Filemoni-Tofaeono (eds.), *Weavings: Women Doing Theology in Oceania* (Suva, Fiji: Institute of Pacific Studies/SPATS), pp. 24–31.

Evans, Patricia
1996   *The Verbally Abusive Relationship* (New York: Adams Media Corporation).

Ewudziwa, Amba
    2000   'So Much Violence in the Bible', *Echoes* 17. http://www.wcc-coe.org/wcc/what/jpc/echoes.echoes-18-07.html.

Faatauva'a, Roina
    1992a 'Samoan Women: Caught in Culture Change', *Pacific Journal of Theology* II:7: pp. 15–27.
    1992b 'The Theology of *Feagaiga*', B.D. thesis, Pacific Theological College.

Fabella, Virginia M., and Mercy A. Oduyoye (eds.)
    1988   *With Passion and Compassion: Third World Women Doing Theology* (Maryknoll, NY: Orbis Books).

Fabella, Virginia M., and Sun Ai Lee Park (eds.)
    1990   *We Dare to Dream: Doing Theology as Asian Women* (Maryknoll, NY: Orbis Books).

Farley, Edward
    1983   *Theologia: The Fragmentation and Unity of Theological Education* (Philadelphia: Fortress Press).

Farley, Lin
    1978   *Sexual Shakedown: The Sexual Harassment of Women on the Job* (New York: McGraw-Hill Publishers).

Ferder, Fran, and John Heagle
    1989   *Partnership: Women and Men in Ministry* (Notre Dame, IN: Ave Maria Press).

Fernandez, Eleazar S.
    1994   *Towards a Theology of Struggle* (Maryknoll, NY: Orbis Books).

Ferris, Elizabeth G.
    1996   'Women as Peacemakers' in Aruna Gnanadason, Musimbi Kanyoro and Lucia Ann McSpadden (eds.), *Women, Violence and Non-Violent Change* (Geneva: WCC Publications), pp. 2–28.

Fiji Women's Crisis Centre
    2001   *The Impact of the May 19 Coup on Women in Fiji* (Suva, Fiji: Fiji Women's Crisis Centre).
    2002   'Annual Report' (Suva, Fiji, Women's Crisis Centre).
    n.d.   *The Incidence, Prevalence and Nature of Domestic Violence and Sexual Assault in Fiji* (Suva, Fiji: Fiji Women's Crisis Centre).

Finger, Thomas N.
    1985   *Christian Theology: An Eschatological Approach.* Vol.1. (Nashville, TN: Thomas Nelson Publishers).

Fiorenza, Elisabeth Schüssler
    1983   *In Memory of Her: A Feminist Theological Reconstruction of Christian Origins* (New York: Crossroad).
    1985   'The Will to Choose or Reject: Continuing our Critical Work' in Letty Russell (ed.), *Feminist Interpretation of the Bible* (Philadelphia: Fortress Press), pp. 123–35.

1992   *But She Said: Feminist Practices of Interpretation* (Boston: Beacon Press).
1993   *Discipleship of Equals: A Critical Feminist Ekklesialogy of Liberation* (New York: Crossroad).
1994   'Editorial – Violence Against Women', *Concilium* 1: pp. vii–xxiii.

Fiorenza, Elisabeth Schüssler (ed.)
2001   *Searching the Scriptures: A Feminist Introduction* (New York: Crossroad Publishing).

Fischer, Kathleen
1999   'An Image of God Beyond Violence', *National Catholic Reporter* 36 (3 December): pp. 37–41.

Fitzgerald, L., and M. Hesson-McInnis
1989   'The Dimensions of Sexual Harassment: A Structural Analysis', *Journal of Vocational Behaviour* 35: pp. 309–26.

Forman, Charles W.
1982   *The Island Churches of the South Pacific: Emergence in the Twentieth Century* (Maryknoll, NY: Orbis Books).

Fortune, Marie M.
1980   *Family Violence: A Workshop Manual for Clergy and Other Helpers* (Seattle, WA: Center for the Prevention of Sexual and Domestic Violence).
1983   *Sexual Violence: The Unmentionable Sin* (New York: Pilgrim Press).
1984   'The Church and Domestic Violence', *TSF Bulletin* 4 (November/December): pp. 17–20.
1986   'Confidentiality and Mandatory Reporting: A False Dilemma?', *The Christian Century* 18:25: pp. 582–83.
1987   *Keeping the Faith: Questions and Answers for the Abused Woman* (San Francisco: Harper and Row).
1989a *Is Nothing Sacred? When Sex Invades the Pastoral Relationship* (San Francisco: Harper and Collins Publishers).
1989b 'Transformation of Suffering: A Biblical and Theological Perspective' in Joanne Carlson Brown and Carol R. Bohn (eds.), *Christianity, Patriarchy and Abuse: A Feminist Critique* (Cleveland, OH: The Pilgrim Press), pp. 139–47.
1991a 'Violating the Pastoral Relation'. Review of Karen Lebacqz and Ronald G. Barton, *Sex in the Parish, Christianity and Crisis* 51:16–17 (18 November): pp. 367–68.
1991b *Violence in the Family: A Workshop Curriculum for Clergy and Other Helpers* (Cleveland, OH: The Pilgrim Press).
1992   *Clergy Misconduct: Sexual Abuse in the Ministerial Relationship* (Seattle, WA: Center for the Prevention of Sexual and Domestic Violence).
1995a 'Is Nothing Sacred? The Betrayal of the Ministerial or Teaching Relationship' in Carol J. Adams and Marie M. Fortune (eds.), *Violence Against Women and Children: A Christian Theological Sourcebook*, pp. 351–60.
1995b 'The Transformation of Suffering: A Biblical and Theological Perspective' in Carol J. Adams and Marie M. Fortune (eds.), *Violence Against Women and Children: A Christian Theological Sourcebook*, pp. 85–91.

1995c Fortune, Marie M., and James N. Poling 'Calling to Accountability: The Church's Response to Abusers' in Carol J. Adams and Marie M Fortune (eds.), *Violence Against Women and Children: A Christian Theological Sourcebook*, pp. 451–63.

2000 *A Commentary on Religious Issues in Family Violence* (Seattle, WA: Center for the Prevention of Sexual and Domestic Violence).

2001 'Religious Issues and Violence Against Women' in Claire M. Renzetti, Jeffrey L. Edleson and Raquel K. Bergen (eds.), *Sourcebook on Violence Against Women* (Thousand Oaks, CA: Sage Publications), pp. 370–83.

Fox, Matthew

1983 *Original Blessing* (Santa Fe, NM: Bear & Company).

Fox, Vivian

2002 'Historical Perspectives on Violence Against Women', *Journal of International Women's Studies* 4:1 (November): pp. 15–34.

Frazer, Elizabeth, Jennifer Hornsby and Sabina Lovibond (eds.)

1992 *Ethics: A Feminist Reader* (Cambridge, UK: Blackwell).

Freire, Paulo

1972 *Pegagogy of the Oppressed* (New York: Continuum).

1998 *Pegagogy of the Heart* (New York: Continuum).

Fulton, Rachel

2002 *From Judgment to Passion: Devotion to Christ and the Virgin Mary, 800–1200* (New York: Columbia University Press).

Garrett, John

1992 *Footsteps in the Sea: Christianity in Oceania to World War II* (Suva, Fiji: Institute of Pacific Studies/University of the South Pacific, in association with World Council of Churches).

Gilligan, James

2001 *Preventing Violence* (New York: Thames and Hudson).

Gnanadason, Aruna

1997 *No Longer a Secret: The Church and Violence Against Women* (Geneva: WCC Publications), rev. edn.

Gnanadason, Aruna, and Lucia A. McSpadden (eds.)

1996 'Introduction" in *Women, Violence and Non-Violent Change* (Geneva: WCC Publications), pp. 1–12.

Godobo-Madikizela, Pamela

2000 *A Human Being Died that Night: A South African Woman Confronts the Legacy of Apartheid* (New York: Houghton Mifflin Company).

Goodman, Jill

1978 'Sexual Demands on the Job', *The Civil Liberties Review*: pp. 53–62.

Gopal, Avinesh

2002 'Child Molester Goes to Prison', *The Fiji Times*, 24 April.

Gounder, Sanday
  2002	'A Lautoka Father…Pleads Guilty on Rape and Indecent Assault', *Fiji Sun*,
        12 November.

Grange, John M.
  2002	'Violence is a Major Health Issue', *Overcoming Violence Newsletter* 3 (WCC/
        DOV Newsletter) (3 January): p. 7.

Gray, Elizabeth Dodson
  1982	*Patriarchy as a Conceptual Trap* (Wellesley, MA: Roundtable Press).

Griffen, Vanessa
  1989	*Development and Empowerment: A Pacific Feminist Perspective* (Suva, Fiji:
        Star).

Griffen, Vanessa (ed.)
  1993	*Women, Development and Empowerment: A Pacific Feminist Perspective* (Suva,
        Fiji: Star).

Gruber, J.
  1989	'How Women Handle Sexual Harassment', *Social Science Research* 74:1: pp.
        3–7.

Gutek, B., A. Groff and A. Tsui
  1996	'Reactions to Perceived Sex Discrimination', *Human Relations* 49:6: pp. 791–
        814.

Halapua, Winston
  2003	'Militarism and the Moral Decay in Fiji', *Fijian Studies* 1:1: pp. 105–26.

Hashi, Sohail H.
  1996	'International Society and its Islamic Malcontents', *The Fletcher Forum on
        World Affairs* (Winter/Spring): pp. 23–31.

Hau'ofa, Epeli
  1989	*A New Oceania: Rediscovering Our Seas of Islands* (Suva, Fiji: Star).

Heise, Lori, and Claudia Garcia-Moreno
  2002	'Violence by Intimate Partners' in Etienne G. Krug, Linda L. Dahlberg, James
        A. Mercy, Anthony B. Zwi and Rafael Lozano (eds.), *World Report on Violence
        and Health* (Geneva: World Health Organization), pp. 88–94.

Herr, Judy Zimmerman, and Robert Herr (eds.)
  1998	*Transforming Violence: Linking Local and Global Peacemaking* (Philadelphia:
        Pandora Press).

Hester, Marianne, Liz Kelly and Jill Radford (eds.)
  1997	*Women, Violence and Male Power* (Buckingham, UK: Open University Press).

Heyward, Carter
  1982	*The Redemption of God: A Theology of Mutual Relation* (Lanham, MD: Univer-
        sity Press of America).
  1989	*Touching Our Strength: The Erotic as Power and the Love of God* (San Francisco:
        Harper and Row).

Heyzer, Noleen
  2000 'Critical Issues Confronting Women in the New Millennium' in *Sixth Commonwealth Ministerial Women's Affairs Meeting: A Commonwealth Secretariat.* Paper 8 (New Delhi, India).

Hood, Helen
  2003 'Speaking Out and Doing Justice: It's No Longer a Secret But What Are the Churches Doing About Overcoming Violence Against Women?' *Feminist Theology* 11:2: pp. 216–25.

Houtart, François
  1997 'The Cult of Violence in the Name of Religion: A Panorama' in Wim Beuken and Karl-Josef Kusher (eds.), *Religion as a Source of Violence?* (London: SCM Press; Maryknoll, NY: Orbis Books), pp. 1–10.

Huffer, Elise, and Asofou So'o (eds.)
  2000 *Governance in Samoa* (Suva, Fiji: Institute of Pacific Studies/University of the South Pacific).

Hunt, Mary
  1992 'Waging War at Home: Christianity and Structural Violence', *Miriam's Song* V: n.p.

'Is Free Trade Really Beneficial?'
  2003 Available at: http://www.aworldconnected. org.

Jalal, Imrana P.
  1998 *Law for Pacific Women: A Legal Rights Handbook* (Brisbane: Watson Ferguson).

Janesick, Valerie
  1994 'The Dance of Qualitative Research Design: Metaphor, Methodology, and Meaning' in Norman K. Denzin and Yvonna S. Lincoln (eds.), *Handbook of Qualitative Research* (Thousand Oaks, CA: Sage Publications), pp. 209–19.

Jenson, Anne
  1996 *God's Self-Confident Daughters: Early Christianity and the Liberation of Women,* trans. O.C. Dean (Louisville, KY: Westminster/John Knox Press).

Jesudason, Usha
  2000 'Entertaining Violence', *Echoes* 17. http://www.wcc- Coe.org/wcc/what/ jpc/echoes/echoes-18-09.html.

Jewett, Paul K.
  1975 *Man as Male and Female* (Grand Rapids, MI: William B. Eerdmans Publishing Company).

Jewkes, Rachel, Purna Sen and Claudia Garcia-Moreno
  2002 'Sexual Violence' in Etienne G. Krug, Linda L. Dahlberg, James A. Mercy, Anthony B. Zwi and Rafael Lozano (eds.), *World Report on Violence and Health* (Geneva: WHO), pp. 149–65.

Johnson, Elizabeth A.
  1988 'Ephesians' in Carol A. Newsom and Sharon H. Ringe (eds.), *Women's Bible Commentary* (Louisville, KY: John Knox Press), pp. 428–32.

1995   *She Who Is: The Mystery of God in Feminist Discourse* (New York: Crossroad).

Johnson, John M.
1995   'Church Response to Domestic Violence' in Carol J. Adams and Marie M. Fortune (eds.), *Violence Against Women and Children: A Christian Theological Sourcebook*, pp. 412–21.

Johnson, Lydia
1992   'Beyond the Story: A Possible Future for Pacific Narrative Theology', *Pacific Journal of Theology* II: 7: pp. 45–48.
2003a   'Liberating Learning: Two Case Studies in Emancipatory Theological Education' in Roswith Gerloff (ed.), *Mission is Crossing Frontiers: Essays in Honour of Bongani Mazibuko* (Pietermaritzburg, SA: Cluster Publications), pp. 382–413.
2003b   ' "Weaving the Mat" of Pacific Women's Theology: A Case Study in Women's Theological Method' in Lydia Johnson and Joan A. Filemoni-Tofaeono (eds.), *Weavings: Women Doing Theology in Oceania* (Suva, Fiji: Institute of Pacific Studies/SPATS), pp. 10–22.

Johnson, Lydia, and Joan A. Filemoni-Tofaeono (eds.)
2003   *Weavings: Women Doing Theology in Oceania* (Suva, Fiji: Institute of Pacific Studies/SPATS).

Johnson, M.P., and K.J. Ferraro
2000   'Research on Domestic Violence in the 1990s: Making Distinctions', *Journal of Marriage and the Family* 62: pp. 948–63.

Jones, William Jr
1972   'Reconciliation and Liberation in Black Theology: Some Implications for Religious Education', *Religious Education* 67 (September/October): pp. 386–91.

Juergenmeyer, Mark
1996   'The Terrorist Who Longs for Peace', *The Fletcher Forum for World Affairs* (Winter/Spring): pp. 5–15.

Kanongata'a, Keiti Ann
1992   'A Pacific Women's Theology of Birthing and Liberation', *Pacific Journal of Theology* II: 7: pp. 3–11.
1994   Paper presented, EATWOT Consultation. Southern Cross Hotel, Suva, Fiji.

Kanyoro, Musimbi A.
1997   Lecture, Augustana University College, Alberta, Canada, March 1992. Cited in Gnanadason 1997: pp. 41–42.

Kanyoro, Musimbi A., and Nyambura J. Nyoroge (eds.)
1996   *Groaning in Faith: African Women in the Household of God* (Nairobi: Action Publishers).

Kaufmann, Michael (ed.)
1987   *Beyond Patriarchy: Essays by Men on Pleasure, Power and Change* (New York: Oxford University Press).

Keller, Catherine
  1986 *From a Broken Web: Separation, Sexism and Self* (Boston: Beacon Press).

Kelly, Liz, and Jill Radford
  1997 ' "Nothing Really Happened": The Invalidation of Women's Experiences of Sexual Violence' in Marianne Hester, Liz Kelly and Jill Radford (eds), 1997, pp. 17–25.
  1998 'Sexual Violence Against Women and Girls: An Approach to an International Overview' in Dobash and Dobash, *Rethinking Violence Against Women*, pp. 56–67.

Kennedy, Margaret
  2003 'Sexual Abuse of Women by Priests and Ministers to Whom They Go for Pastoral Care and Support', *Feminist Theology* 11:2: pp. 226–35.

Kessler, Diane (ed.)
  1999 *Together on the Way: Official Report of the Eighth Assembly of the World Council of Churches* (Geneva: WCC Publications).

King, Ursula (ed.)
  1992 *Feminist Theology from the Third World* (Maryknoll, NY: Orbis Books).

Kinukawa, Hisako
  1994 *Women and Jesus in Mark: A Japanese Feminist Perspective* (Maryknoll, NY: Orbis Books).

Kirk, Jerome, and Marc L. Miller
  1988 *Reliability and Validity in Qualitative Research* (Beverly Hills, CA: Sage Publications).

Kirk-Duggan, Cheryl
  2001 *Misbegotten Anguish: A Theology and Ethics of Violence* (St. Louis, MO: Chalice Press).

Koss, M.P.
  1993 'Changed Lives' in Michele Paludi (ed.), *Ivory Power* (New York: SUNY Press), pp. 73–92.

Koss, M.P., *et al.*
  1994 *No Safe Haven: Male Violence Against Women at Home, at Work, and in the Community* (Washington, DC: American Psychological Association).

Kotoisuva, Edwina
  2003 'Domestic Violence: A View from the Fiji Women's Crisis Centre', *Pacific Journal of Theology* II:30: pp. 41–45.

Kroeger, Catherine Clark
  1995 'Let's Look Again at the Biblical Concept of Submission' in Carol J. Adams and Marie M. Fortune (eds.), *Violence Against Women and Children: A Christian Theological Sourcebook*, pp. 135–40.
  1996 'God's Purpose in the Midst of Human Sin' in Catherine Clark Kroeger and James R. Beck (eds.), *Women, Abuse and the Bible: How Scripture Can be Used to Hurt or Heal*, pp. 202–15.

Kroeger, Catherine Clark, and James R. Beck (eds.)
1996   *Women, Abuse and the Bible: How Scripture Can be Used to Hurt or Heal* (Grand Rapids, MI: Baker Book House).

Krug, Etienne G. *et al.* (eds.)
2002   *World Report on Violence and Health* (Geneva: World Health Organization).

Kwok, Pui-Lan
1995   *Discovering the Bible in the Non-Biblical World* (Maryknoll, NY: Orbis Books).
2001   'Racism and Ethnocentrism in Feminist Biblical Interpretation' in Elisabeth Schüssler Fiorenza (ed.), *Searching the Scriptures: A Feminist Introduction* (New York: The Crossroad Publishing Company), pp. 101–14.
2003   *Introducing Asian Feminist Theology.* Introductions in Feminist Theology Series (Cleveland, OH: the Pilgrim Press).

Kyung, Chung Hyun
1991   'Come Holy Spirit – Renew the Whole Creation' in Michael Kinnamon (ed.), *Signs of the Spirit: Official Report, WCC Seventh Assembly* (Geneva: WCC Publications), pp. 37–47.
1993   *Struggle to be the Sun Again: Introducing Asian Women's Theology* (Maryknoll, NY: Orbis Books).

Laidlaw, Toni Ann, Cheryl Malmo, *et al.*
1990   *Healing Voices: Feminist Approaches to Therapy with Women* (San Francisco: Jossey-Bass Publishers).

LaPorte, Jean
1982   *The Role of Women in Early Christianity* (New York: Mellon Press).

Lebacqz, Karen
1991   *Professional Ethics: Power and Paradox* (Nashville, TN: Abingdon Press).

Lebacqz, Karen, and Ronald G. Barton
1991   *Sex in the Parish* (Louisville, KY: Westminster/John Knox Press).

Leibrich, J., and J. Pauline Ransom
1995   *Hitting Home: Men Speak About Domestic Abuse of Women Partners* (Wellington, NZ: New Zealand Department of Justice/AGB McNair).

LeMoncheck, Linda, and Marie Hajdin
1997   *Sexual Harassment: A Debate* (New York: Rowman and Littlefield Publishers).

Lewa, Seinimili
2002   'Men Discuss the Problems of Women', *The Fiji Times*, 15 November.

Lloyd, Genevieve
1984   *The Man of Reason: 'Male' & 'Female' in Western Philosophy* (London: Methuen and Co. Ltd.).

Loades, Ann (ed.)
1990   *Feminist Theology: A Reader* (Louisville, KY: Westminster/John Knox Press).

Loomer, Bernard
1976   'Two Conceptions of Power', *Criterion* 15: pp. 12–29.

Lora, Carmen
  2002 'Globalization and its Effects in Latin America— Especially on Women. http://mtsusidelines.com/news/2002/20/02.

MacDonald, Lesley Orr
  2000 'Violence in the Church', *Echoes* 17. http://www.wcc-coe.org/wcc/what/jpcechoes/echoes-18-02.html.

Madhu Bhusan, Unpublished document, Vimochana. Bangalore, India: n.d.

Madraiwiwi, Joni
  2003 'Domestic Violence and the Law', *Pacific Journal of Theology* II:30: pp. 46–48.

Maiava, Iosefa
  2003 Paper presented, Pacific Regional Workshop on Strengthening Partnerships for Eliminating Violence Against Women. Pacific Forum Secretariat, Suva, Fiji, 17–19 February.

Mananzan, Mary John, *et al.*, (eds.)
  1996 *Women Resisting Violence: Spirituality for Life* (Maryknoll, NY: Orbis Books).

Mandela, Nelson
  2002 'Foreword' in Etienne G. Krug *et al.*, *World Report on Violence and Health*.

May, Rollo
  1972 *Power and Innocence: A Search for the Sources of Violence* (New York: W.W. Norton).

McAllister, Pam
  1982 *Reweaving the Web of Life: Feminism and Nonviolence* (Philadelphia: New Society Publishers).

McCann, Dennis
  1986 'Conscientization' in James F. Childress and John Macquarrie (eds.), *The Westminster Dictionary of Christian Ethics* (Philadelphia: Westminster Press), pp. 120.

McCollum, H., Liz Kelly and Jill Radford
  1994 'Wars Against Women' *Trouble and Strife* 28: pp. 12–18.

McCutchen, Tanya
  2002 'Drunken Dad Kills Son With One Punch', *The Daily Post*, 14 October.

McFague, Sallie
  1982 *Metaphorical Theology: Models of God in Religious Language* (Philadelphia: Fortress Press).
  1987 *Models of God Theology for an Ecological, Nuclear Age* (Philadelphia: Fortress Press).
  2003 Guest Lecture. 'Eco-Theology of the Oceans' course, Dr. Ama'amalele Tofaeono. Vancouver School of Theology, 16 September.

McGowan, Andrew Brian
  1999 *Ascetic Eucharists: Food and Drink in Early Christian Ritual Meals* (Oxford: Clarendon Press; New York: Oxford University Press).

McMullen, Christine
    2003   'One Day I Went to a Theological Consultation on Domestic Violence', *Feminist Theology* 11:2: pp. 197–202.

McWilliams, Monica
    1998   'Violence Against Women in Societies Under Stress' in Rebecca E. Dobash and Russell P. Dobash (eds.), *Rethinking Violence Against Women*, pp. 112–38.

Meo, Ilisapeci
    1990   'Why Do Women Remain Silent in Meetings and Discussions with Men?', *Pacific Journal of Theology* II:3: pp. 45–47.
    1993   'The Role of the Church in Combating the Exploitation of Women Garment Workers in Fiji', M.Th. thesis, Pacific Theological College.
    1997   'Women's Journey Toward Empowerment Through Theological Education: A Personal Testimony', *Journal of Constructive Theology* 3:1 (July): pp. 15–33.
    2003   'Asserting Women's Dignity in a Patriarchal World' in Lydia Johnson and Joan A. Filemoni-Tofaeono (eds.), *Weavings: Women Doing Theology in Oceania*, pp. 150–60.

Meyers, Carol
    1988   *Discovering Eve: Ancient Israelite Women in Context* (New York: Oxford University Press).

Meyer-Wilmes, Hedwig
    1997   'Excessive Violence Against Women in the Name of Religion' in Wim Beuken and Karl-Josef Kuschel (eds.), *Religion As A Source of Violence?* (London: SCM Press; Maryknoll, NY: Orbis Books), pp. 55–63.

Mezirow, Jack
    1990   *Fostering Critical Reflection in Adulthood: A Guide to Transformative and Emancipatory Learning* (San Francisco: Jossey-Bass).

Miller, Jean Baker
    1986   *Toward a New Psychology of Women* (Boston: Beacon Press).

Moane, Geraldine
    1966   *Gender and Colonialism: A Psychological Analysis of Oppression and Liberation* (New York: St. Martin's Press).

Moengangongo, Mosikaka
    2003   'Tonga' in Taiamoni Tagamoa (ed.), *Pacific Women: Roles and Status of Women in the Pacific Societies* (Suva, Fiji: Institute of Pacific Studies/University of the South Pacific), pp. 61–68.

Mollenkott, Virginia Ramsey (ed.)
    1987   *Women of Faith* (New York: Crossroad).

Moltmann, Jürgen
    1974   *The Crucified God* (New York: Harper & Row).

Moran, Gabriel
    1979   *Education Toward Adulthood: Religion and Lifelong Learning* (New York: Paulist Press).

Morgan, Phoebe
    2001   'Sexual Harassment: Violence Against Women at Work' in Claire M. Renzetti, Jeffrey Edelson and Raquel K. Bergen (eds.), *Sourcebook on Violence Against Women*, pp. 208-19.

National Advisory Council on Women's Education Programs
    1980   *A Report on the Sexual Harassment of Students* (Washington, DC: US Department of Education).

Newsom, Carol A., and Sharon H. Ringe
    1998   'Introduction to the First Edition' in Carol A. Newsom and Sharon H. Ringe (eds.), *Women's Bible Commentary: Expanded Edition with Apocrypha* (Louisville, KY: Westminster/John Knox Press), pp. xix-xxiv.

Niditch, Susan
    1998   'Genesis' in Carol A. Newsom and Sharon H. Ringe (eds.), *Women's Bible Commentary: Expanded Edition with Apocrypha*, pp. 13-29.

Njorage, Nyambura
    1997   Address, Sixth Assembly of the All-Africa Conference of Churches. Harare, Zimbabwe, October 1992. Cited in Aruna Gnanadason 1997, pp. 44-45.

Oduyoye, Mercy Amba
    1995   *Daughters of Anowa: African Women and Patriarchy* (Maryknoll, NY: Orbis Books).

Oduyoye, Mercy Amba, and Musimbi R.A. Kanyoro
    1992   *The Will to Arise: Women, Tradition and the Church in Africa* (Maryknoll, NY: Orbis Books).

Omar, Rashied Imam A.
    2002   'Islam and Violence', *Current Dialogue* 39 (June). http://www.wcc-coe.org/wcc/what/interreligious/cd39-02.html.

'Overcoming Violence'
    2002   *DOV Newsletter* 2 (January). http://www.wcc-coe.org/wcc/dov/03news-e.html.

'Overview of Efforts to Eliminate Violence Against Women in the Pacific'
    2003   *Strengthening Pacific Partnerships for Eliminating Violence Against Women: A Pacific Regional Workshop Report, Suva, Fiji Islands, 17-19 February 2003*, pp. 79-85. Suva, Fiji: Commonwealth Secretariat, UN Development Program/UNIFEM, Pacific Islands Forum Secretariat, and Secretariat for the Pacific Communities.

Pacific Women's Resource Bureau
    1993   'Combating Violence Against Women: The Campaign Continues', *Women's News* 8: pp. 22-24.

Pagelow, Mildred D.
    1981   *Woman-Battering: Victims and Their Experience* (Beverly Hills, CA: Sage Publications).

Palu, Valamoto

2003   'Tapa Making in Tonga: A Metaphor for God's Care' in Lydia Johnson and Joan A. Filemoni-Tofaeono (eds.), *Weavings: Women Doing Theology in Oceania*, pp. 62–71.

Park, Andrew Sung, and Susan L. Nelson (eds.)

2001   *The Other Side of Sin: Woundedness from the Perspective of the Sinned Against* (New York: State University Press).

Pase, Mine

2003   'Gospel and Culture: Samoan Style' in Lydia Johnson and Joan A. Filemoni-Tofaeono (eds.), *Weavings: Women Doing Theology in Oceania*, pp. 72–78.

Pelletier, Yandro

2002   'Qualitative Study on Domestic and Sexual Violence Against Kanak Women in New Caledonia: Or, Violence Against Women as a Social and Cultural Symptom, Viewed from a Gender-Based Perspective' in *Report, IEDES Attachment* (Paris: University of Paris, in collaboration with the Pacific Women's Bureau of the Secretariat of the Pacific Community, Noumea, New Caledonia).

Peters, Charlotte

2002   'Sexual Offender Cops 4-year Term', *Fiji Sun*, 12 November.

Poling, James N.

1991   *The Abuse of Power: A Theological Problem* (Nashville, TN: Abingdon Press).

2002   *Render unto God: Economic Vulnerability, Family Violence and Pastoral Theology* (St Louis, MO: Chalice Press).

2003   *Understanding Male Violence: Pastoral Care Issues* (St Louis, MO: Chalice Press).

Poling, Nancy

1999   *Victim to Survivor: Women Recovering from Clergy Sexual Abuse* (Cleveland, OH: United Church Press).

Pollard, Alice

1988   'Solomon Islands' in Taiamoni Tagamoa (ed.), *Pacific Women: Roles and Status of Women in the Pacific Societies* (Suva, Fiji: Institute of Pacific Studies/ University of the South Pacific), pp. 39–46.

Prasad, Mridula

2003   Presentation, Forum on Violence Against Women and Children. Pacific Theological College, Suva, Fiji, June.

Presbyterian Church USA

1997   'Policy Statement on Sexual Harassment in the Workplace' cited in Aruna Gnanadason, *No Longer a Secret: The Church and Violence Against Women*, p. 43.

Procter-Smith, Marjorie

1997a   'Reorganizing Victimization: The Intersection Between Liturgy and Domestic Violence' in Carol J. Adams and Marie M. Fortune (eds.), *Violence Against Women and Children*, pp. 428–43.

1997b 'The Whole Loaf: Holy Communion and Survival' in Carol J. Adams and Marie M. Fortune (eds.), *Violence Against Women and Children*, pp. 464–78.

2001 'Feminist Interpretation and Liturgical Proclamation' in Elisabeth Schüssler Fiorenza (ed.), *Searching the Scriptures: A Feminist Introduction*, pp. 313–25.

Raiser, Konrad
2002 *For a Culture of Life: Transforming Globalization and Violence* (Geneva: WCC Publications).

Rambachan, Anantanand
2002 'The Co-Existence of Violence and Non-Violence in Hinduism', *Current Dialogue* 39 (June). http://www.wcc-coe.org/wcc/what/interreligious.cd39-05.html.

Razack, S.
1994 'What is to be Gained by Looking White People in the Eye? Culture, Race and Gender in Cases of Sexual Violence', *Signs: Journal of Women in Culture and Society* 19:4: pp. 24–48.

Renzetti, Claire M., Jeffrey L. Edelson and Raquel K. Bergen (eds.)
2001 *Sourcebook on Violence Against Women* (Thousand Oaks, CA: Sage Publications).

'Response to the Plenary on the Ecumenical Decade of Churches in Solidarity with Women'
1992 In Diane Kessler (ed.), *Together on the Way: Official Report of the Eighth Assembly of the World Council of Churches* (Geneva: WCC Publications), Chapter VI.

Rodgers, Jimmie
2003 Opening Address, Pacific Regional Workshop on Strengthening Partnerships for Eliminating Violence Against Women. Pacific Forum Secretariat, Suva, Fiji, 17–19 February.

Ropeti, Marie
1997 'One Gospel: Pacific Island Women's Perspective', *Pacific Journal of Theology* II:17: pp. 31–53.

Ruether, Rosemary Radford
1981 *To Change the World* (New York: Crossroad).
1983 *Sexism and God-Talk: Toward a Feminist Theology* (Boston: Beacon Press).
1985 *Women-Church: Theology and Practice* (San Francisco: Harper & Row).
1998 *Women and Redemption: A Theological History* (Minneapolis, MN: Fortress Press).
2000 *Christianity and the Making of the Modern Family: Ruling Ideologies, Diverse Realities* (Boston: Beacon Press).

Russell, Diana
1982 *Rape in Marriage* (New York: Macmillan).
1984 *Sexual Exploitation: Rape, Child Sexual Abuse and Sexual Harassment* (Beverly Hills, CA: Sage Publications).
1997 *Sexual Exploitation: Rape, Child Sexual Abuse, and Workplace Harassment* (Buckingham, UK: Open University Press).

Russell, Letty M.
  1974   *Human Liberation in a Feminist Perspective* (Philadelphia: The Westminster Press).
  1976   *Liberating Word: A Guide to Nonsexist Interpretation in the Bible* (Philadelphia: The Westminster Press).
  1979   *The Future of Partnership* (Philadelphia: The Westminster Press).
  1987   *Authority in Feminist Theology: Household of Freedom* (Philadelphia: The Westminster Press).
  1993   *Church in the Round* (Louisville, KY: Westminster/John Knox Press).
  1996   'Methodology in Liberation/Feminist Theologies: A Theological Spiral of Action Reflection'. Graphics, J.S. Clarkson. Appendix in *Women's Theology: Pacific Perspectives* (Suva, Fiji: SPATS).

Russell, Letty M. (ed.)
  1985   *Feminist Interpretation of the Bible* (Philadelphia: The Westminster Press).

Russell, Letty, and Shannon Clarkson (eds.)
  1996   *Dictionary of Feminist Theologies* (Louisville, KY: Westminster/John Knox Press).

Russell, Letty, Kwok Pui-Lan, Ada Maria Isasi-Diaz and Katie Geneva Cannon (eds.)
  1988   *Inheriting Our Mothers' Gardens: Feminist Theology in Third World Perspective* (Philadelphia: The Westminster Press).

Rutter, Peter
  1989   *Sex in the Forbidden Zone: When Men in Power – Therapists, Doctors, Clergy, Teachers and Others – Betray Women's Trust* (Los Angeles: Jeremy Tarcher).

Sanday, Peggy Reeves
  1981   *Female Power and Male Dominance: On the Origins of Sexual Inequality* (Cambridge, UK: Cambridge University Press).
  1991   'The Socio-Cultural Context of Rape: A Cross-Cultural Study', *Journal of Social Issues* 37:4: pp. 5–27.

Sanday, Peggy Reeves, and Ruth Gallagher (eds.)
  1990   *Beyond the Second Sex: New Directions in the Anthropology of Gender* (Philadelphia: University of Pennsylvania Press).

'San Jose Declaration of Latin American Women on Violence Against Women'
  1996   WCC Latin America Regional Workshop on Violence Against Women. San Jose, Puerto Rico.

Schmidt, Ruth
  1993   'After the Fact: To Speak of Rape', *Christian Century* (January): p. 14.

Schneiders, Sandra
  1990   'God is More than Two Men and a Bird', *U.S. Catholic* (May): pp. 20–27.

Schoeffel, Penelope
  1998   'The Samoan Concept of *Feagaiga* and its Transformation' in J. Huntsman (ed.), *Tonga and Samoa: Images of Gender and Polity* (Christchurch, NZ: Macmillan Brown Centre for Pacific Studies), pp. 85–105.

Scholer, David M.
1996   'The Evangelical Debate over Biblical Headship' in Catherine Clark Kroeger
       and James R. Beck (eds.), *Women, Abuse, and the Bible: How Scripture Can Be
       Used to Hurt or Heal*, pp. 28–57.

Schottroff, Louise
1995   *Lydia's Impatient Sisters: A Feminist Social History of Early Christianity* (Louisville,
       KY: Westminster/John Knox Press).

Schreiter, Robert
1997   *The New Catholicity: Theology Between the Global and the Local* (Maryknoll,
       NY: Orbis Books).
2002   *Doing Local Theology: A Guide for Artisans of a New Humanity* (Maryknoll, NY:
       Orbis Books).

Schwager, Raymund
1987   *Must There Be a Scapegoat? Violence and Redemption in the Bible*, trans. Maria
       L. Assad (San Francisco: Harper and Row).

Segundo, Juan Luis
1974   *A Theology for Artisans of a New Humanity. Vol. 4: The Sacraments Today*
       (Maryknoll, NY: Orbis Books).

Seymour, J. L., and D. E. Miller (eds.)
1990   *Theological Approaches to Christian Education* (Nashville, TN: Abingdon Press).

Shainess, Natalie
1984   *Sweet Suffering: Woman as Victim* (Indianapolis, IN: Bobbs-Merrill).

Sharma, Seema
2002   'Daughters Give Letters of Reconciliation', *The Fiji Times*, 20 November.

Siamomua, Amelia Kinahoi
2003   Address, Pacific Regional Workshop on Strengthening Partnerships for Elimi-
       nating Violence Against Women. Pacific Forum Secretariat, Suva, Fiji, 17–19
       February.

Sigimanu, Ethel
2003   Paper presented, Pacific Regional Workshop on Strengthening Partnerships
       for Eliminating Violence Against Women. Pacific Forum Secretariat, Suva,
       Fiji, 17–19 February.

Singh, Raymond
2002   'Father Rapes Crippled Daughter', *The Daily Post*, 2 October.

Slatter, Clare
1992   'Violence Against Women: The Social, Political and Economic Factors'. Paper
       presented, Consultation on Violence Against Women. Bergengren House,
       Suva, Fiji.
1996   'Women and Political/Economic Issues' in *Women's Theology: Pacific Perspec-
       tives* (Suva, Fiji: SPATS), pp. 62–66.

Sobrino, Jon
1978   *Christology at the Crossroads* (Maryknoll, NY: Orbis Books).

Soronakadavu, Meresiana
2003   'The Traditional Role of Fijian Women, with Reference to Christian Justice' in Lydia Johnson and Joan A. Filemoni-Tofaeono (eds.), *Weavings: Women Doing Theology in Oceania*, pp. 161–64.

South Pacific Association of Theological Schools
1996   *Women's Theology: Pacific Perspectives* (Suva, Fiji: SPATS).

Spence, Nancy
2003   Address, Pacific Regional Workshop on Strengthening Partnerships for Eliminating Violence Against Women. Pacific Forum Secretariat, Suva, Fiji, 17–19 February.

Stanko, Elizabeth A.
1997   'Reading Danger: Sexual Harassment, Anticipation and Self-Protection' in Marianne Hester, Liz Kelly and Jill Radford (eds.), *Women, Violence and Male Power*, pp. 48–62.

Starhawk
1987   *Truth or Dare: Encounter with Power, Authority and Mystery* (San Francisco: Harper & Row).

Stortz, Martha Ellen
1993   *PastorPower* (Nashville, TN: Abingdon Press).

Stückelberger, Christoph
2003   'Globalization: Ethical Perspectives'. Unpublished article in the authors' possession.

Tagamoa, Taiamoni (ed.)
1988   *Pacific Women: Roles and Status of Women in the Pacific Societies* (Suva, Fiji: Institute of Pacific Studies/University of the South Pacific).

Tamez, Elsa (ed.)
1988   'Women's Re-reading of the Bible' in Virginia Fabella and Mercy Amba Oduyoye (eds.), *With Passion and Compassion: Third World Women Doing Theology*, pp. 163–75.
1989   *Through Her Eyes: Women's Theology from Latin America* (Maryknoll, NY: Orbis Books).

Tandon, Yash
2000   'The Violence of Globalisation', *Echoes* 17. http://www. wcc-coe.org/wcc/jpc/echoes/echoes-18-08.html.

Tapu-Qilio, Fetaomi
2003   'Singing the Lord's Song in a Strange Land: The Theological Quest of Young Exiles of the Pacific' in Lydia Johnson and Joan A. Filemoni-Tofaeono (eds.), *Weavings: Women Doing Theology in Oceania*, pp. 175–80.

Taule'ale'ausumai, Feiloaiga
1992   'The Struggle of Pacific Women in Ministry', *Pacific Journal of Theology*, II:7: pp. 31–38.

Tenten, Maleta
2003   'The Relationship Between *Katekateka* and Women's Ordination in the Kiribati
       Protestant Church' in Lydia Johnson and Joan A. Filemoni-Tofaeono (eds.),
       Weavings: Women Doing Theology in Oceania, pp. 32–42.

Terpestra, D., and D. Baker
1988   'Outcomes of Sexual Harassment Charges', *Academy of Management Journal*
       31:1: pp. 181–90.

Tessier, L. J.
1997   *Dancing After the Whirlwind: Feminist Reflections on Sex, Denial, and Spiritual
       Transformation* (Boston: Beacon Press).

Thangaraj, M. Thomas
2002   'Thinking Together: A Narrative', *Current Dialogue* 39 (June). http://
       www.wcc-coe.org/wcc/what/interreligious/cd39-09.html.

'The National Situation: A Biblical Response from Women'
1986   *Stree Reflect Series* 1 (All India Council of Christian Women/National Council
       of Churches in India), n.p.

'Theological Education in a Global Society: Emerging Practice and Issues'
2002   Final Report, WOCATI General Assembly. Chiang Mai, Thailand, December.
       http://www.wocati.org.

'The Rape of Bosnia'
1992   Editorial, *International Herald Tribune*, 8 December.

The Tribune 46
1991   (International Women's Tribune Newsletter) (June): n.p.

Thistlethwaite, Susan Brooks
1981   'Battered Women and the Bible: From Subjection to Liberation', *Christianity
       and Crisis* 41:18 (November): pp. 308–13.
1985   'Every Two Minutes: Battered Women and Feminist Interpretation' in Letty
       Russell (ed.), *Feminist Interpretation of the Bible*, pp. 96–107.

Thorne-Finch, Ron
1992   *Ending the Silence: The Origin and Treatment of Male Violence Against Women*
       (Toronto: University of Toronto Press).

Tofaeono, Ama'amalele
2000   *Eco-Theology: Aiga – The Household of Life: A Perspective from Living Myths and
       Traditions of Samoa* (Erlangen: Erlangen Verlag).

'Tofamamao: No More Violence in Paradise—Apia Declaration'
1996   World Council of Churches Pacific Regional Workshop on Violence Against
       Women. Apia, Samoa, 12–15 March.

Torgeson, Karen
1993   *When Women Were Priests: Women's Leadership in the Early Church and the
       Scandal of their Subordination in the Rise of Christianity* (San Francisco:
       HarperSanFrancisco).

Towandong, Judy
    1996 'Papua New Guinea: Violence Against Women' in Aruna Gnanadason, Musimbi Kanyoro and Lucia Ann McSpadden (eds), *Women, Violence and Non-Violent Change* (Geneva: WCC Publications), pp. 118–21.

'Towards a Relevant Pacific Theology: The Role of the Churches in Theological Education'
    1986 Report of a Theological Consultation, Suva, Fiji, 8–12 July. Suva, Fiji: Lotu Pasefika Productions.

Trible, Phyllis
    1978 *God and the Rhetoric of Sexuality: Overtures to Biblical Theology* (Philadelphia: Fortress Press).
    1992 'Eve and Adam: Genesis 2–3 Re-read' in Carol. P. Christ and Judith Plaskow (eds.), *Womanspirit Rising: A Feminist Reader in Religion*, pp. 74–83.
    1984 *Texts of Terror: Literary-Feminist Readings of Biblical Narratives* (Philadelphia: Fortress Press).

Tuigamala, Filemoni
'Samoan Myth and Traditions', trans. Joan A. Filemoni-Tofaeono. Unpublished manuscript in Joan Filemoni-Tofaeono's possession.

Ucko, Hans
    2002 'Introduction to the "Thinking Together" Group Consultation on Religion and Violence', *Current Dialogue* 39 (June). http://www.wcc-coe.org/wcc/what/intereligious/cd39-01.html.

United Nations
    1994 *Declaration on the Elimination of Violence Against Women*. Resolution No. A/RES/48/104 (New York: United Nations).

U.S. Equal Employment Opportunity Commission
    1998 *Sexual Harassment.*
           http://www.access.gop.gov/nara/cfrwaisdx29cfrl604.html.

U.S. Merit Systems Protection Board
    1992 *Sexual Harassment in the Federal Government Workplace* (Washington, DC: U.S. Government Printing Office).
    1981 *Sexual Harassment in the Workplace: Is it a Problem?* (Washington, DC: U.S. Government Printing Office).

Van Roosmalen, E., and S. McDonald
    1998 'Sexual Harassment in Academia: A Hazard to Women's Health', *Women and Health* 28:2: pp. 33–55.

Veale, Rob
    2003 Paper presented, Pacific Regional Workshop on Strengthening Partnerships for Eliminating Violence Against Women. Pacific Forum Secretariat, Suva, Fiji, 17–19 February.

Vula, Timoci
    2002 'Suva Magistrates Court Yesterday Jailed a 66-year-old Grandfather', *The Daily Post*, 26 July.

Vuli, Alefina

2003   Presentation, Forum on Violence Against Women and Children. Pacific Theological College, Suva, Fiji, June.

Vusi, Judith

2003   'Lord of the Insignificant: A Christ for Ni-Vanuatu Women' in Lydia Johnson and Joan A. Filemoni-Tofaeono (eds.), *Weavings: Women Doing Theology in Oceania*, pp. 58–61.

Walker, Lenore

1979   *The Battered Woman* (New York: Harper and Row).

1984   *The Battered Woman Syndrome* (New York: Springer).

Wandra, Ellen

1991   'The Dialogue Which We Are.' Unpublished essay. Cited in James Poling, *The Abuse of Power: A Theological Problem* (Nashville, TN: Abingdon Press).

Weaver, Denny

2001   *A Non-Violent Atonement* (Grand Rapids, MI: William B. Eerdmans Press).

Webb, Susan L.

1994   *The Global Impact of Sexual Harassment* (New York: MasterMedia Ltd.)

Weems, Renita

1995   *Battered Love: Marriage, Sex, and Violence in the Hebrew Prophets* (Minneapolis, MN: Fortress Press).

Weissmann, Deborah

2002   'The Co-existence of Violence and Non-Violence in Judaism', *Current Dialogue* 39 (June). http://www.wcc-coe-org/wcc/what/interreligious/cd39-07.html.

Wénin, André

1996   'La Bible pour démasquer la violence', *Bulletin de Pax Christi* 19:3 (September): pp. 23–45.

Wete, Tamara

2003   'Woman as "Life-Giver": Toward a Renewed Understanding of Women's Ministry and Leadership in the Evangelical Church of New Caledonia and the Loyalty Islands'. M.Th. thesis, Pacific Theological College.

Williams, Delores

1996   Address, World Council of Churches' Central Committee, Ecclesiology and Ethics Consultation. Geneva, Switzerland.

Williams, James G.

1991   *The Bible, Violence and the Sacred: Liberation from the Myth of Sanctioned Violence* (San Francisco: HarperSanFrancisco).

'What Difference Does Religious Plurality Make?'

1994   Paper presented, Consultation on the Relationship between Religion and Violence. Ecumenical Institute/Bossey, Geneva, Switzerland.

World Council of Churches

    1991   *When Christian Solidarity is Broken: Guidelines for Use at Ecumenical Gatherings* (Geneva: WCC Publications).

    2001   'General Principles and Objectives for Churches Seeking to Overcome All Forms of Violence Against Women'. Final statement, WCC–DOV Consultation, Dundee, Scotland, 23–28 August.

    2002   *World Council of Churches Staff Rules and Regulations* (Geneva: WCC Publications).

World Health Organization

    1996   *Violence: A Public Health Priority*. Global Consultation on Violence and Health, Document WHO/EHA/SPI.POA.2. (Geneva: WHO).

    1997a   *Violence Against Women: Definition and Scope of the Problem* (Geneva: WHO).

    1997b   *Violence Against Women: Rape and Sexual Assault* (Geneva: WHO).

    2002   *Intimate Partner Violence* (Geneva: WHO). http://www.who.int/violence_injury_prevention.html. n.d.

    2003   'Putting Women First: Ethical and Safety Recommendations for Research on Domestic Violence Against Women', *Global Programme on Evidence for Health Policy, World Health Organization*. WHO/EIP/99.2 (Geneva: WHO).

Wren, Brian

    1989   *What Language Shall I Borrow? God-Talk in Worship: A Male Response to Feminist Theology* (London: SCM Press).

Yabaki, Akuila

    2003   Paper presented, Pacific Regional Workshop on Strengthening Partnerships for Eliminating Violence Against Women. Pacific Forum Secretariat, Suva, Fiji, 17–19 February.

Yates, Gayle Graham

    1975   *What Women Want: The Ideas of the Movement* (Cambridge, MA: Harvard University Press).

Printed in the United States
91679LV00001B/241-267/A